PRAISE FOR *A DREAM OF ZION*

"Bravo to Rabbi Salkin for gathering these impressive personal testimonies. They serve an urgent and vital purpose—reminding us of the nearly four-thousand-year bond between the Jewish People and Israel, and educating us on Israel's enduring meaning for American Jewry."
   —**David A. Harris,** executive director, American Jewish Committee

"A touching, emotional, funny book…. Every essay touches a nerve in every American Jew who loves Israel. I highly recommend this book as a personal joy to read and to give as a gift to those who ask, 'Why should I care about Israel?'"
                —**June Walker,** chairperson, Conference of Presidents
                        of Major American Jewish Organizations

"The shared *ahavat Yisrael* (love for the Land and the People of Israel) uniting the incredible diversity of voices in this important anthology redefines 'Pro-Israel.'"
                —**Rabbi Arik W. Ascherman,** executive director,
                                Rabbis for Human Rights

"Rabbi Salkin and Jewish Lights did it again! Thank you for this inspiring gift for Israel's 60th! A must for lovers and dreamers of Zion around the world … and a great resource for anyone who explores a contemporary engagement with Israel."
   —**Rabbi Uri Regev,** president, World Union for Progressive Judaism

"A powerful collection of personal testimonies … Christians who care about Christian-Jewish relations need to read this collection in order to understand the inescapable importance of Israel in that relationship. It also helps us understand why church statements and actions against Israel are so painful to Jewish friends."
                        —**David Blewett,** national director,
     National Christian Leadership Conference for Israel (NCLCI)

"Here are voices from all over the community, from all ages, from all kinds of Jews. Together they show us the how and the why of our profound connection to Israel. This book answers the questions, why do we care so much and why should the fate of this tiny country affect us in America so deeply? The answers are personal and communal and revealing. This is an important book for all those interested in the Jewish people and their incredible story."
             —**Anne Roiphe,** novelist, journalist and author of 13 books

"In this sixtieth year of Israel's independence, it is incumbent on American Jewry to take a step back to reflect on the meaning of Israel's existence in our own lives. Rabbi Jeffrey Salkin has done us an immense favor in bringing together such a wide spectrum of writers and thinkers to ponder this question."

—**Rabbi Robert R. Golub,** executive director, MERCAZ USA, the Zionist arm of the Conservative Movement

"As Rabbi Nachman of Breslov wrote—'wherever I travel I go to Israel.' For me and millions of other Jews—as well as Christians—Israel, both spiritually and existentially, is at the very core of our identities. Wherever we go in life, Israel is on our minds, in our hearts and shaping our ethos. *A Dream of Zion* does a wonderful job in bringing together a rich variety of paths through which we encounter and relate to Israel, her struggle for peace and security, and the meaning it has for our lives. If you love Israel—both the nation and state—and it vibrates the strings of your *neshama,* this book is a must read."

—**Rabbi Yechiel Eckstein,** president, International Fellowship of Christians and Jews

"*A Dream of Zion* is exactly that—filled with miracles and triumph, the joy of coming home, and at the same time, aspiration and hope, that Israel can become the land flowing with justice and righteousness. Sixty years of love can be found on page after page, a worthy testament to the vitality of the dream and of the reality."

—**David M. Elcott,** PhD, executive director, Israel Policy Forum

"Explores the connection to Israel from many varied perspectives that reflect on the historical, religious, and contemporary underpinnings of this special and unique relationship. You will identify with some, disagree with others, but you are certain to be stimulated to thoughtful reflection on this central aspect of Jewish life."

—**Malcolm Hoenlein,** executive vice chairman, Conference of Presidents of Major American Jewish Organizations

"In this compelling volume one hears the multiplicity of views and emotions American Jews have for Israel. It demonstrates that there is no single American Jewish perspective of Israel. At this time when there are so many misconceptions about American Jewish attitudes towards Israel this book will serve an important purpose."

—**Deborah E. Lipstadt,** PhD, Dorot Professor of Modern Jewish and Holocaust Studies, Emory University

A DREAM OF ZION

Other Jewish Lights Books
by Rabbi Jeffrey K. Salkin

*Being God's Partner: How to Find the Hidden Link
between Spirituality and Your Work*

*The Bar/Bat Mitzvah Memory Book: An Album for
Treasuring the Spiritual Celebration*

*For Kids—Putting God on Your Guest List: How to
Claim the Spiritual Meaning of Your Bar or Bat
Mitzvah*

*Putting God on the Guest List: How to Reclaim the
Spiritual Meaning of Your Child's Bar or Bat
Mitzvah*

AMERICAN JEWS REFLECT ON
WHY ISRAEL MATTERS TO THEM

A
DREAM
OF
ZION

Edited by Rabbi Jeffrey K. Salkin

JEWISH LIGHTS Publishing
Woodstock, Vermont

A Dream of Zion:
American Jews Reflect on Why Israel Matters to Them

2007 First Printing
© 2007 by Jeffrey K. Salkin

Library of Congress Cataloging-in-Publication Data
A dream of Zion : American Jews reflect on why Israel matters to them / edited by Jeffrey K. Salkin.
p. cm.
Includes index.
ISBN-13: 978-1-58023-340-8 (hardcover)
ISBN-10: 1-58023-340-6 (hardcover)
1. Israel and the diaspora. 2. Jews—United States—Identity. 3. Jews—United States—Attitudes. 4. Jews—Attitudes toward Israel. 5. Jews—Public opinion. 6. Public opinion—United States. I. Salkin, Jeffrey K., 1954–
DS132.D74 2007
956.94—dc22

2007028851

10 9 8 7 6 5 4 3 2 1

Jacket design: Jenny Buono
Jacket art: *Jerusalem Sunrise* (© 2005) was created by Michael Bogdanow, an artist, lawyer, author, and musician living in Lexington, Massachusetts. It is a contemporary "Mizrach" (Hebrew for east) and represents our looking east to Jerusalem and to Israel. The original is in the collection of Temple Ner Tamid in Bloomfield, New Jersey. The artist's contemporary, spiritual works of art inspired by Judaic texts can be seen on www.MichaelBogdanow.com.

Manufactured in the United States of America
❀ Printed on recycled paper.

Published by Jewish Lights Publishing
A Division of LongHill Partners, Inc.
Sunset Farm Offices, Route 4, P.O. Box 237
Woodstock, VT 05091
Tel: (802) 457-4000   Fax: (802) 457-4004
www.jewishlights.com

CONTENTS

PART III—FAITH & COVENANT:
A LIVING, VIBRANT PART OF MY RELIGIOUS FAITH   93

PART IV—TIKKUM OLAM: A LIGHT UNTO THE NATIONS—HOPES FOR REPAIRING THE WORLD AND DREAMS OF A BETTER WORLD   135

PART V—AN AMERICAN HISTORICAL PERSPECTIVE: THE WORDS OF THE FATHERS AND MOTHERS   205

Contents by Contributor

Publisher's Note

The purpose of this note is to provide additional insights about:

- The origin of and overall approach to *A Dream of Zion: American Jews Reflect on Why Israel Matters to Them,* the methodology used to gather the contributions for it, and the structure of it.
- What we have learned—and you might learn—from reading and using it.

In our work with Judea and Ruth Pearl on the National Jewish Book Award–winning *I Am Jewish: Personal Reflections Inspired by the Last Words of Daniel Pearl,* a project in honor of their son, Daniel, the goal was to create an inspirational book that would encourage people to reflect on Danny's words, "I am Jewish," and the meaning of these words in their own lives, in understanding their identity.

Many Jews were particularly moved by Danny's words in which he affirmed his Jewish identity. Many were inspired to think about or analyze their feelings toward their lives as Jews and to explore their own sense of identity as Jewish people.

Across the world, from Singapore to Europe and in many cities in the United States and Canada, Jewish communities have used the concept of *I Am Jewish* to create events in which people wrote and spoke of their own feelings and thoughts about being Jewish. Synagogues, federations, Jewish community centers, and other organizations developed these events that have been attended by thousands of people. Many congregations have even provided copies of *I Am Jewish* to their members prior to the High Holy Days and shaped their High Holy Day services to incorporate personal explorations of the core question of Jewish identity. Others have done the same thing at other times of the year. Rabbi Jeffrey Salkin created one of the earliest of these events in 2004 at The Temple in Atlanta. Led by Judea Pearl, Daniel's father, leaders of the Atlanta Jewish community read their own "I am Jewish" statements. Almost one thousand people attended this powerful evening. (For further information about these events, see "The *I Am Jewish* Movement" on the Jewish Lights website www.jewishlights.com).

From this experience, in 2004, Rabbi Salkin, whose life-changing books we have published for over a decade, developed later in 2004 the idea for a related book that would help people explore another aspect of their identity as Jewish people—their relationship to Israel. We at Jewish Lights were enthusiastic about the idea from the start, but we also knew, based on the experience obtaining participation from prominent people to *I Am Jewish*, that many people sadly have conflicted feelings about their Jewish identity, and some are even afraid to publicly acknowledge their positive feelings about Israel. But, we also knew that the result would be worth the effort even if it took several years. And it did.

In our founding mission statement as publishers we wrote: "Our books focus on the issue of the quest for the self, seeking meaning in life. They are books that help you to understand who you are and who you might become as a Jewish person...." As we at Jewish Lights celebrate the purchase of the two-millionth Jewish Lights book, an event that tells so many positive things about the present condition of the American Jewish community, we could not think of a better way to acknowledge the occasion than to publish a book to celebrate the sixtieth anniversary of the birth of the State of Israel; a book that would help people understand the importance of Israel in their lives and help them further explore their identity as Jews and Americans.

In the time it has taken to gather the material included in this book, some other books exploring the same topic have appeared, most notably the important book by the eminent Harvard professor of law, and courageous Israel activist, Alan M. Dershowitz, *What Israel Means to Me* (2006). While the contributions to this book necessarily cover some of the same ground as Professor Dershowitz's book, *A Dream of Zion* adds to the discussion by its categorization and analysis of the responses, and by providing a historical section showing the evolution of American Jewish attitudes toward the establishment of a Jewish state since the nineteenth century. We hope that this additional material will facilitate the kind of public discussion of what Israel means to you that has taken place, and continues to take place, in relation to Jewish identity as a result of *I Am Jewish*. And events that have taken place since 2006, including growing anti-Semitism and anti-Israel sentiment in many countries, calls for a boycott of Israel in countries such as the United States and the United Kingdom, the sad episode of former President Carter's much-disputed book, and the unending terrorism against Israel and Israelis, makes the need for developing and strengthening our understanding of our relationship to Israel all the more important.

As we wrote in the "Publisher's Note" to *I Am Jewish,* the saying "two Jews, three opinions" well reflects the Jewish community's broad range of views on any topic. This book is an attempt to capture this richness of interpretation and to further inspire Jewish people to reflect upon and take pride in their identity. We began the project with confidence that, despite the diversity, common denominators would shine through clearly and distinctly—and they did.

In order to achieve the goals that Rabbi Salkin and Jewish Lights had in mind, we decided it was important to include input from highly respected leaders in all fields throughout the American Jewish community, and to restrict participation to people from the United States. This was not intended to ignore the importance of the Jewish community in the rest of the world, but to provide a highly concentrated picture of the view from our own country whose involvement with Israel is so important to both nations. The invited contributors included top scholars, artists, entertainers, government officials, authors, media personalities, scientists, community leaders, rabbis, and others not well known, covering the entire religious, professional, and political spectrum of the United States Jewish community.

Rabbi Salkin and Jewish Lights staff began by developing, in consultation with many people, comprehensive lists of potential contributors by geographic, occupational, and religious categories. After a thoughtful analytical process, we invited several hundred people to contribute their thoughts to the book, keeping in mind that their dreams of Zion would vary widely with their backgrounds, experiences, and beliefs.

While comprehensive in its coverage, it was not our intention for this book to be a scientifically designed survey of Jewish thought and views on the subject of Israel, and we recognize that while our design was broadly inclusive, individual decisions on participation make for an idiosyncratic selection of people and of their ideas. Also, we intentionally did not invite participation from many thoughtful people who contributed to *I Am Jewish* in order to provide a further range of ideas and opinion.

Contributions range from major essays to a few paragraphs, and come from adults of all ages, including college students. They are in the form of personal feelings, statements of theology, life stories, and historical reflections. Most contributions are original. A few have been previously published in whole or in part, and all were selected to represent the contributors' thinking on the questions:

- What is the role Israel has played in your life?
- What keeps you connected to Israel?
- How does Israel fit into your sense of what it means to be Jewish and American?

As you will see, clear themes did emerge. The responses to our invitation are organized into four broad categories providing statements of what it means to the contributors when they answer these questions and "dream of Zion." The responses have been integrated to provide a thought-provoking and inspiring diversity of opinion that we hope will lead to further discussion in the Jewish community in the United States and elsewhere.

The categories in which the responses have been organized reflect the major relationships of our lives.

- **Identity and Heritage:** "My Ancestral Home Reborn Is an Essential Part of My Identity"—Our relationship to ourselves, how we define who we are in the most fundamental way; our relationship to family, community, culture, tradition, and our collective history.
- **Refuge:** "A Refuge from Anti-Semitism, a Place of Safety"—Our centuries-long experience of anti-Semitism, climaxing in the Holocaust that was able to take place in part because there was

no place of automatic shelter for Jewish people, is never far from a dream that remains a nightmare.

- **Faith and Covenant:** "A Living, Vibrant Part of My Religious Faith"—Our people's relationship to God, and our understanding of the relationship between God and the Jewish people, provides a connection to the Promised Land, for Jewish people the "Word become Land"; Israel as an essential part of Judaism's meaning as a religion and of Jewish spiritual life.
- *Tikkun Olam:* "A Light Unto the Nations—Hopes for Repairing the World and Dreams of a Better World"—Our messianic search for justice and peace in Israel's relationship to a world of a broad range of Jewish denominations, and to the world of non-Jews; what our dream of Zion means for what we do with our lives—and what we hope Israel does in the context of its struggle for survival as a Jewish state—as we and it address our responsibilities in the world.

We hope this book will motivate people throughout the Jewish community to think more about their lives as Jews and their relationship to Israel and that, in particular, it has a profound effect on the way Jewish young people shape their identity and their relationship to Israel in years to come. We also hope it will help people of other faiths to better understand the reasons for the strong bond between the American Jewish community and Israel.

Stuart M. Matlins,
Publisher and Editor in Chief
Jewish Lights Publishing

Introduction

The late Yehuda Amichai, one of Israel's greatest poets, offers these words·

> Why is Yerushalayim plural,
> One on high and one below?
> …
> I want to live in one "Yerushal"
> Because I am just "I" and not "I"s.
> —from *Patuach Sagur Patuach,* my own translation

Amichai is reflecting on one of the great grammatical conundrums in the history of Jewish geography: why is the Hebrew word for Jerusalem—*Yerushalayim*—in the plural form? Yes, there is the earthly Jerusalem and the supernal Jerusalem, and the "new city" of Jerusalem and the old walled city of Jerusalem as well. Jerusalem/Yerushalayim is little if not its raging dualities.

But this is not what the poet wants. He doesn't want to live in Yerushalayim in its plural form. He would rather live in *Yerushal—* an imaginary, singular form of Yerushalayim. After all, he concludes, he exists in the singular form, and not in the plural. He does not have "I"s. He has only one I, one self, he says—not a collection of selves.

With great admiration for Yehudah Amichai, he may be an I (yes, a Hebrew pun; *ani* means "I"), but most American Jews are not a single I. Rather, they are entire committees of Is: "I am an American," "I am a Jew," "I am a parent," "I am a child," "I am a sibling," "I am a doctor," "I am a Zionist," "I am at home in America".… A few years ago the Jewish Museum in New York exhibited a piece called *Lover's Quarrel* by the artist Dennis Kardon. It depicts a man from the back attached to his double as if they were

Siamese twins. One likeness wears a baseball cap; the other wears a yarmulke. The piece asks the question: why is there a lovers' quarrel in the Jewish soul? For, in truth, we are fully and simultaneously at home with many loyalties.

For many years I have understood the culturally amphibious nature of American Jewish life. We live within several realities, and the ongoing existence of the State of Israel makes that dramatically clear. Our physical addresses may be located in the United States of America but our soul has a second home—a home (that perhaps we never even visit) in the Land of Israel. America-centered and Israel-concerned, we bounce back and forth between those identities.

And yet, in recent years, various polls and surveys have revealed that American Jewish attitudes toward Israel are in the process of a troubling transformation. Many American Jews have lost that deep sense of connection to the State of Israel. Tourism (not to mention aliyah, immigration to Israel, which has never been American Jewry's strong suit) has diminished, financial support has lessened, and the ability of many American Jews to defend the State of Israel intellectually has become ever shakier.

Why? Who knows? To quote *Casablanca*, round up the usual suspects. The lingering effects of the intifadas; the perception that Israel is a dangerous place to live and visit; the phenomenon of Israelis leaving Israel to make their lives and livelihoods elsewhere; the various critiques of Israel based on behaviors and incidents in its struggle to find peace with its Arab citizens and neighbors that particularly affect American liberal and academic circles; the perception that there is a religious gap in Israel that disenfranchises non-Orthodox Jews—each of these has subtly and slowly chipped away at American Jewish perceptions of Israel. Add this to the mix: the majority of today's American Jews were born either shortly before or after 1948 and therefore have no memory of the Shoah and no memory of a world without Israel. We take Israel for granted.

I decided to create this book because of my awareness of this ennui and wanted to contribute my efforts to battling it. It is a tool for American Jews to use to strengthen their faith in the State of Israel, to me the greatest Jewish enterprise of modernity. This book contains short essays by almost a hundred American Jews. Some of them are famous, some are not so famous. They are a joyful mixed multitude of Jewish professionals, politicians, artists, writers, academics, educators, rabbis, thinkers, students, entertainers, and businesspeople. They are young and old; secular, observant, and everywhere else on the spectrum; liberal, conservative, and confused. They constitute a nice round sample of American Jewish opinion. And they all have something to say about Israel. Their statements are in these pages to inspire us, teach us, challenge us, and move us. My hope is that Jewish communities around the country will be motivated to hold public forums in which local people comment on their own relationship with Israel, thus furthering the conversation.

A Dream of Zion: American Jews Reflect on Why Israel Matters to Them comes into the world not just at any time, but at a particularly important time. I write these words on the precise fortieth anniversary of the Six Day War and the reunification of Jerusalem, a watershed moment in my own personal Jewish identity and in the Jewish consciousness of an entire generation of Jews. Moreover, in May 2008 the Jewish world will celebrate the sixtieth anniversary of the creation of the State of Israel. When compared to most of the nations of the world, sixty years is but a blip in time. Still, the novelty of Israel's existence and what she has already achieved, despite internal and external conflicts, is a source of awe. If it is not the redemption itself, it is surely the beginning of the redemption, *atchalta de'geulta*. We present this book to the world, therefore, as a sixtieth-birthday offering to the Jewish state. At a significant birthday, tradition mandates that we say, "May you live to be one hundred and twenty years old" (*ad meah v'esrim*)! For a state, though, certainly the Jewish state, that is far, far too little time. May Israel live beyond our ability to count the years.

A Dream of Zion came into being through the sincere efforts of many people. First of all, there are the many contributors to this book. They all participated willingly and lovingly, and they were blissfully forgiving when I cajoled, prodded, chased, and nudged them for their essays. These are all busy people; I am grateful for their contributions and efforts. I am ever indebted to my friend Stuart M. Matlins, publisher of Jewish Lights, for being my partner in this endeavor of the heart. In vaguely Herzlian tones, he urged me never to abandon hope in this project and in its power. Lauren Seidman and Emily Wichland of Jewish Lights have, as always, diligently kept me on task and true to deadline. They have been wonderful colleagues. My assistant Dianne Ratowsky went way beyond the call of duty in helping make this book a reality. She chased down e-mail and snail-mail addresses for potential authors, contacted (and recontacted and recontacted) them, and waded through the barely parted waters of the publishing world, tracking down copyrights for material written by authors who had long since gone to the World to Come. She has been a loyal colleague, which is good enough, but she has also remained unflappable, which is even better.

And finally, I am grateful to God. Of all the blessings that are in our rich liturgical and spiritual repertoire, there is one that I have always loved perhaps more than the others. It is the prayer that I utter as soon as I see the coastline of Israel from the descending plane as it prepares for landing at Ben Gurion Airport. *Baruch atah Adonai, ha-machazir shechinato l'Tziyon:* Blessed is Adonai, who restores the wandering Divine Presence to Zion. We live in a time when we might uniquely experience God's presence in the Land of Israel, for history, in its own way, is an unfolding divine voice.

Jeffrey K. Salkin

PART I—IDENTITY & HERITAGE:

MY ANCESTRAL HOME REBORN IS AN ESSENTIAL PART OF MY IDENTITY

"The Lord said to Abraham: 'Go forth from your native land and from your father's house to the land that I will show you. I will make of you a great nation, and I will bless you; I will make your name great, and you shall be a blessing.'"

Genesis 12:1

RABBI DAVID WOLPE is the rabbi of Sinai Temple in Los Angeles. He is the author of six books, most recently *Floating Takes Faith: Ancient Wisdom for a Modern World.*

"The task of this generation with regard to Israel is the task of parents with regard to children. We criticize our children, but only after we establish our love…. And when our children hear the problems Israel has had, the things it has done wrong, the cruelty and neglect that sometimes mark our land, we must ensure that first, they hear words of love."

The first time I saw the Wall, I was profoundly unimpressed.

"It's a wall," I thought. I was twelve years old.

The second time I saw the Wall, it moved me beyond words, for now I understood that its lack of grandeur was eloquence. The Jewish people did not dream of Zion because it was the land of silver spires and gold-paved streets. They dreamed of the land of their ancestors, the uneven paving of narrow streets, and the mute eloquence of stones that seem to bear the sunlight within.

The first time I saw Safed, I thought it was a lovely city.

The second time I visited Safed, I saw the graves of the kabbalists. I stood wondering what it was like to transcend this world, if only for a moment. To glimpse something greater than we are usually given to see; to have fled from the cruelties of a faraway land and end up in a place where Shabbat comes like a bride over the hills. It was now an artist colony, transmuted into a place to capture the beauty of this world. But once it had been a mystic preserve, dedicated to the beauty of another world.

My love for Israel is a love of deepening understanding, of unsheathing a heart at first closed to the subtle marvels of a complex, anguished land. Looking for the spectacle of the Bible, I was met by the bustle and wonder of the modern state. More than almost any place on earth, Israel dwells simultaneously in the past and the future, as sacred text battles it out with border crossings, and diplomacy navigates around ancient claims. What will be? What once was? To ask either question in Israel is to ask the other. And each is as tangled and uncertain as the human heart.

In 1947 a British Jewish soldier died in Israel. There was a debate about where he should be buried. No family member claimed one way or the other, and so the decision was made to bury him in a grave in Beer Sheva, where the inscription reads: "Died far away from his country, but at home." For those of us who live outside Israel, there is a longing mixed with distance. There is strangeness followed by the deeper acquaintance that leads to love. Modern Hebrew must express the flash, dazzle, and superfluities of Dizingoff, all in the idiom of Sinai's majesty. It is bewildering and beautiful.

Every land is a land of paradox. The charm of Italy is edged against the grandeur of Rome. The elegance of France belies its tumultuous history. But Israel has something more: the waves of different cultures, the establishment of a democracy by those who came from tyrannies, the software startup in the shadow of the valley where Samson slew Philistines. Modern art is built of jarring juxtapositions; all of Israel is a canvas.

The task of this generation with regard to Israel is the task of parents with regard to children. We criticize our children, but only after we establish our love. For a generation that knew a world without Israel, love was taken for granted. Today, when Israel is more often seen as a problem than a miracle, we must first declare, loudly, in full-throated song from rooftops, that we love our land. We must remind the world, again and again, that we know what fate has befallen the Jews without their land. We must remind ourselves that for thousands of years we prayed for rain not when rain would benefit the grapes of France, where we lived, or the crops of Babylonia, where we lived, but the craggy hillsides of Israel, of which we only dreamed. We kept our metaphysical watches to the time of Jerusalem.

We never forgot. And when our children hear the problems Israel has had, the things it has done wrong, the cruelty and neglect that sometimes mark our land, we must ensure that first, they hear words of love.

We who live outside the land have to be sufficiently imaginative to understand all we do not know. In Europe, a bloody battlefield for centuries, there is a monument for every 10,000 fallen soldiers. In Israel, there is a monument for every sixteen fallen soldiers. When in the Bible we read of Egypt that there was no house in which there was not dead, that has come true in Israel—in terms of friends, family, schoolmates; it is a society that lives under a pressure so far unimaginable in this spacious and generous land.

Israel does not yield its secrets at once—it is a land that requires revisiting, like a great classic book. The eternal image is the little hills called *tels* that dot the land in which layers of civilization rest one upon the other. A superficial unearthing will give you little. But keep digging and the ages yield up their treasures, the long-ago inhabitants hand their mysteries to you as a reward for your patience and your love.

"God gave all men all earth to love / But since our hearts are small / Ordained for each one spot should prove / Beloved over all." So writes Rudyard Kipling of Sussex. For Jews, having wandered across the world, and having spoken virtually every language of humanity, this one spot, the sliver of a land bridge between two colossal empires, proved beloved over all. So long as the nation of Israel lives, the Land of Israel will hold sway in the center of our hearts. It takes a lifetime to soak in its paradoxes and its mysteries, but who would wish for a love that demands less?

SYLVIA BARACK FISHMAN is professor of contemporary Jewish life in the Near Eastern and Judaic Studies Department, and codirector of the Hadassah-Brandeis Institute, both at Brandeis University. Her most recent book is *The Way Into the Varieties of Jewishness* (Jewish Lights).

> "So this is the bottom line: I love Israel because I feel at home there…. As a Jew, I am part of [a] dual vision and [a] dual responsibility. I care about people in many places and try to help in ways that I can. Still, looking after Israel is a personal privilege, because Israel is my family."

I am standing near the anti-Israel protesters' cordoned-off section at a rally supporting Israel. It's the only place left to stand. Along with four thousand other Boston Jews, I am listening to an inspiring talk by an African American clergyman. The handful of very young, pierced, and tattooed protesters shake their heads disapprovingly at Reverend Hamilton's words, especially when he points out a contingent of labor leaders among Israel's supporters.

Finally, in exasperation, one protester holding a sign that says "We are Jewish and we don't support Israel" turns to a blond, ponytailed teenager standing outside the cordon. "Why do you support Israel?" she asks. The teen is answering confidently, all animation and smiles. I drift off into my own reflections.

"Why do I support Israel?" I ask myself. All the persuasive words I've used with Israel's critics are there, of course. The events of Jewish history in the recent and not-so-recent past. The utter vulnerability of a people without a land. The wickedness of the world in its double standard toward the Jews. But really, what is Israel to me? I've tried to think this through rationally but keep running up against a sea of personal emotion.

When I was growing up in Sheboygan, Wisconsin, thoughts of Israel were part of the air we breathed. My father had served in Italy during World War II and had made his way over to Palestine where, he recalled with still evident relish, he ate fresh eggs for the first time since he entered the service. He came back with a certificate registering his infant daughter—me—in the Jewish National Fund Registry of Children. On subsequent trips, as my sisters and I grew older, he brought back sheet music for Israeli songs he had heard. We stumbled through the songs on the piano, and imagined a country that looked like the covers of Theodore Bikel record albums.

Finally I got to Israel myself during the summer of my junior year in college, working on a kibbutz (collective settlement) for room and board. It was 1963. Lizards ran across the hot rocks under fierce blue skies in the blazing Mediterranean sun. Gray-bearded men with tzitzit swinging outside their coats rode the sanitation wagons and swept Jerusalem's streets. I certainly wasn't in Kansas (or Sheboygan) anymore! Jerusalem was seamed with fences and gates, and as a Jew, I wasn't allowed to get near the Western Wall. The closest approach was an overview from the heights of Ramat Rachel.

(Later, when I visited Israel after the Six Day War, I was amazed at the throngs of Muslims who streamed around the Old City. Muslims had kept Jews out of old Jerusalem when they were in charge, but now that the tables were turned, Jews allowed Muslims access to their holy places. "Because you were strangers in the land of Egypt," I thought, and I was proud.)

In Kibbutz Yavneh I helped take care of the two-year-olds, and I learned to make an Israeli mixture of sour cream, milk, and sugar for the little ones to drink, as well as sugared tomato juice by using a grater. Fathers would drive up on their tractors to share lunch with their toddlers as we sat in a circle on the lawn. The women, in their rough boots and sandals, worked hard, but mostly in the kitchen, laundry, or children's areas; only American girls lobbied to work with the cattle or in the fields. When those women and men cleaned up for Shabbat and came to services on Friday night, their faces shone and they sang the *Kabbalat Shabbat* service like angels. Many of the people were European intellectuals—smart, warm, funny, and very appealing—but at the kibbutz meetings, members voted on which of the teenagers would be sent to college and which would not. I admired their solidarity, but I realized that I was too American to surrender my destiny to the group. Still, I felt drawn to them. In some mysterious way, this place was home.

Subsequent trips reinforced that strong sense of peoplehood. In 1984, traveling south on the last crowded bus to Beer Sheva on a Friday afternoon, we took whatever seats we could find. My two-year-old, sitting in a seat toward the front of the bus, began to cry. Uniformed soldiers sitting on the floor of the bus—traveling home for Shabbat—simply picked the little one up and passed him from person to person back to me. This would be terrifying in New York, but on that bus it seemed fine. That was a symbol of Israeli culture—if a baby cries, it's everybody's business. Israelis are often faulted for articulating opinions about everything and not giving Westerners enough personal space—just try asking one person for directions and everyone answers and someone may even walk you to your destination—but this is the interference that comes with feeling that you are part of a large family. It may be cumbersome, and often irritating, but it is the behavior of people who feel like they're home.

After their retirement, my parents frequently spent several months a year in Israel. One November afternoon, my mother and I took a walk. A sharp wind blew, presaging the coming rain. A distracted young woman passed, pushing a stroller. My mother stopped her: "The wind is blowing into your baby's ears," said my mother in English. "Zip up her hood to keep her warm." In Boston such interference would be greeted with anger or silence, but here it evoked gratitude. "You think so?" the Israeli woman answered in English, her brow creasing. "Thank you." She zipped up the hood, brushing a kiss on her daughter's cheek, and continued on her way.

Five months into the second intifada in spring 2000, everyone was on edge, but interactions retained their characteristic personalism, informality—and wit. Shopping in a fruit store on Rehov Aza in Jerusalem, I watched the vendor urging shoppers to buy the grapes. "They're sweet," she said. "They get sweeter every day." A portly *haredi* (ultra-Orthodox) gentleman popped a grape into his mouth. "You're right," he agreed, looking her straight in the eye, "they are sweet, but tomorrow they'll be even sweeter."

Down the street, an overweight woman in black capri pants smacked a little boy and shrieked at him in Hebrew. The thrill still catches me unawares—hearing Hebrew as the language of the imperfect street and its imperfect people in this imperfect country.

So this is the bottom line: I love Israel because I feel at home there. Because Hebrew is the language my people have used, in combination with others, across the planet and the centuries. Because Israeli food and music were brought by Jews from Iraq and Poland and Morocco and everywhere else Jews have lived. Because Israeli culture incorporates many Jewish values: The cherishing of children. The redeeming of an abducted community member. Using your brain when there are no other natural resources. Talking and reading and writing. Because even secular expressions of Israeli culture draw on Jewish wellsprings. Israel is often a "light unto the nations," but its first moral responsibility is to look after its own citizens and its own survival.

As a Jew, I am part of that dual vision and that dual responsibility. I care about people in many places and try to help in ways that I can. Still, looking after Israel is a personal privilege, because Israel is my family.

 **MATTHEW BROOKS** is the executive director of both the Republican Jewish Coalition, an organization dedicated to enhancing ties between the Jewish community and the Republican Party, and the Jewish Policy Center, a think tank that examines public policy from a Jewish perspective.

"We carry a responsibility to support Israel and to keep her strong. As Americans and as Jews, we are eternally connected to that tiny piece of land at the crossroads of three continents, where amid all the diversity, we find ourselves at home."

There is an old map of the world that shows the continents of Africa, Europe, and Asia spreading from a central point like the leaves of a three-leaf clover. The central point, of course, is Israel. Israel has been the meeting point of trade routes, religions, cultures, and political forces throughout human history, and it bears traces of all of those influences.

Israel is, in fact, the soul of diversity. You can find people from every corner of the globe making their home there. If you go the length of Israel from north to south, you can pass from snow-covered mountains to shimmering desert. Every cuisine is represented there, and languages abound. The wide variety of Israel's plants and animals may be surpassed only by its variety of political opinions.

Yet the first time I visited Israel, I was most surprised to find that this tiny country, land of so much diversity, felt so much like home.

First, those people from every corner of the globe are fellow Jews. Differences in looks, language, or religious observance notwithstanding, we share a profound connection.

I also found that while the U.S.–Israel alliance has much to do with shared security concerns and other national interests, its bedrock is the friendship of two democracies with the same core values. The values that have brought America freedom and prosperity and leadership in the world are integral to Israel as well.

I have had the opportunity to visit Israel several times. I have seen Israel gripped by terrorist violence and tragedy, and I have seen her celebrate life and freedom. I come back from each trip convinced anew of the necessity of Israel. It is a refuge, an economic powerhouse, a religious homeland, a bastion of democracy. We need Israel to be there, always, and so we carry a responsibility to support Israel and to keep her strong. As Americans and as Jews, we are eternally connected to that tiny piece of land at the crossroads of three continents, where amid all the diversity, we find ourselves at home.

SAMUEL BAK, born in Vilna in 1933, is an internationally renowned artist for whom Yad Vashem dedicated an extensive retrospective entitled *An Arduous Road: Sixty Years of Creativity* in 2006. He is the author of a much-acclaimed memoir, *Painted in Words*. Bak lives near Boston, Massachusetts.

"My inner Israel is still intact. A mythic, nostalgic, and almost dreamlike reality that helps me to define my identity as a Jew. Moreover, as a wandering Jew. A seasoned traveler who carries with him to all the places he goes the bundle of his transportable roots."

Be'avonotay harabim? Is it "because of my many sins" that sometimes the Zion of my dreams seems to me so unattainable...?

Magical, genetic, and cultural, the blood that flows in my veins comes to me from my two Jerusalems, my two separate birthplaces. One is *Yerushalayim de'Lita* ("the Jerusalem of Lithuania"), the city in which I was born in 1933, my ever-beloved Vilna, a world-famous center of rabbinic traditions, rational Judaism, and secular ideologies that blossomed within a community of extraordinary Jews. The Shoah destroyed it.

The other Jerusalem is the ancient capital of Israel, a city that more than a half-century ago gave birth to my own idea of who I was as a young artist, a Jew, and an Israeli, survivor, wanderer, and seeker of unanswerable questions. Oh how I loved that quiet and somnolent Jerusalem of hot days and cold nights, of blinding lights and dark shadows, of pale stone walls covered by layers of golden desert dust! How I loved the small, provincial Jerusalem where everybody knew everybody else. Its modest Knesset; its seemingly Viennese cafes frequented by the elderly *yekkes* (German Jews) in their threadbare prewar garb; its Jews with *payis* (side curls) and its Jews wearing the blue shirts of the secular left; its Hebrew University, a center of universal culture that functioned in a dispersion of shabby and provisory quarters. Sometimes I dared to explore our provisory border with the

Arab world. Streets of bombed and abandoned houses that separated us from the belligerent Jordanians and their dangerous snipers.

I made aliyah in 1948, almost against my will. A survivor, I arrived at an Israeli Haifa from a Displaced Persons camp in Bavaria. There, in Germany in my early teens, I dreamed of a brilliant artistic career in a mythical Paris. But Mother's vision was very different from mine, and utterly precise:

> We will live in a Jewish state where you shall get, for the first time in your life, proper schooling. Certainly, you will serve in the army and carry a rifle and no non-Jew will dare to tell you what you can or cannot do. And later, my child, if you decide to study in Paris, you will go to Paris with a Jewish passport. A passport displaying the proud blue and white Jewish Star of David that will have restored our broken world and wiped out any trace of the yellow one. Your sweet name shall be nicely marked down on it in beautiful Hebrew letters and you shall show around this precious document with pride and self-satisfaction!

Has my psyche conserved this feeling of "self-satisfaction"? I wonder. As an artist I consider it downright dangerous to indulge in practices that destroy a person's sense of self-criticism. But Mother's determination to make me part of the Israeli experience proved to be a wise move; it exposed me to a journey of great enrichments. Today my gratitude to her tenacity is without end. Israel has given me the command of the Hebrew language and a fair knowledge of the language's history, literature, and culture. It made me share my life with others, survivors as well as sabras, all of us invested in one collective enterprise; it taught me to sacrifice personal comfort, wear the sweat-drenched khakis of *Tzahal* (the Israel Defense Forces), and be part of my country's never-ending struggle. Moreover, Israel's wars taught me what the word "solidarity" means and what it is able to create: strong bonds of friendship with extraordinary people. Their lives were constructed from particles of personal and shared memories, very similar to mine.

Having accumulated in various epochs of my existence twenty years of life in Israel, I think that I now possess—independently of where I live—an inner Israel that dwells in my soul. It nourishes my being and shapes my identity. No, it isn't the Israel of the present day, a country of tough fighters and mythic heroes, of ever-reopening wounds that bleed and hurt, of polarized ideologies and crazy fanaticisms, of choices that are very difficult, if not impossible, to make. But it is a country that remains utterly necessary, if not indispensable.

Why can't I live there? Some twenty-five years ago I was in the midst of a crisis. Had my artistic discourse become too idiosyncratic? Were my paintings too explicitly echoing the pains of my distant past? I realized that there was something "sinful" about the way I chose to deal with my work. Did I speak too much of the Shoah and of the aftereffects of survival? Oddly enough, Israel's ongoing struggle for its own survival was paralyzing my work. My art demanded distance. In order to make it flourish, it demanded a sacrifice, a search for other, quieter shores. I moved to Italy, France, Switzerland, and finally the United States.

In spite of this, my inner Israel is still intact. A mythic, nostalgic, and almost dreamlike reality that helps me to define my identity as a Jew. Moreover, as a wandering Jew. A seasoned traveler who carries with him to all the places he goes the bundle of his transportable roots.

The past fifty years of my artistic career have equipped me with three different passports. My European one symbolizes the sum of the pictorial traditions that characterize my artistry. My American one represents the generosity of the country that is my home. And, oddly enough, the Israeli passport, the one with the beautiful Hebrew letters, speaks of my everlasting nostalgia for peace and tranquility. It is my elusive dream of an unattainable Zion. A Zion that is almost, almost within my reach.

RABBI KARYN D. KEDAR, senior rabbi of Congregation B'nai Jehoshua-Beth Elohim in Glenview, Illinois, is the author of several books on inspirational and spiritual uplift, including *The Bridge to Forgiveness: Stories and Prayers for Finding God and Restoring Wholeness* and *God Whispers: Stories of the Soul, Lessons of the Heart* (Jewish Lights Publishing).

> "I think that to be a Zionist is to be in love—passionately, irrationally, eternally. And to be in love with Israel is to hear at once the voices of a child's song, of our ancient past, and of the dangers of the present."

The phone rang. It was my daughter Talia. She has just finished her first semester studying art at Oranim, a college in Israel. That day she had submitted her portfolio to the scrutiny of her professors. They liked her work. They said that she hears the sound of color. "You hear the sound of color?" I asked. "What does that mean?"

"I don't know," she said. "That's all they basically told me." She continued to chat and the sound of her voice took me back to a memory of her as a small girl.

When Talia was a child, we lived in a Jerusalem neighborhood called Pisgat Zeev, which was surrounded by biblical history as well as dangers from the first intifada. At the entrance to the neighborhood was the town where Jeremiah the prophet once lived; in the valley below was where our Mother Rachel wept for her children; and on the mountain above was where King Saul built his palace. I felt like I belonged, grounded in Jewish history and past. However, intermingled with these sites were Arab villages, some of which were active participants in the uprising—Molotov cocktails, stone throwing, and gunfire. So every day, when I brought my daughter Talia home from preschool, I would have two thoughts: "I can't believe I live in the neighborhood of Rachel, Jeremiah, and King Saul!" and "Is Talia safer in her car seat? What if they throw a burning bottle of gasoline into the car? Will I be able to get her out quickly?"

Then one day, I was driving her home from preschool and I heard her softly singing to herself. As I strained to hear which nursery rhyme she was singing, I realized that she was chanting prayers— the morning blessings. Just as I began to rejoice in her Israeli education, Talia began to make up her own words:

"*Baruch atah Adonai*, Blessed are You O God and I should eat all my vegetables."

"*Baruch atah Adonai*, Blessed are You O God and I should be healthy."

"*Baruch ata Adonai*, Blessed are You O God and I should live and not die."

I was stunned. Silenced. Yes, she had a true Israeli education—a small child versed in Hebrew language, Jewish tradition, and present dangers.

I looked in the rearview mirror as I turned the corner and I saw that she was buckled in her car seat.

When she was thirteen we left Israel and we now have two homes, one here and one there. But Talia never lost what she seemed to know living among the prophets and sages. After graduating high school in America, she joined the Israeli army, fell in love with an Israeli boy, and now makes her home in the lovely northern village of Kiriyat Tivon where she studies art. So now, listening to her voice, I think that to be a Zionist is to be in love—passionately, irrationally, eternally. And to be in love with Israel is to hear at once the voices of a child's song, of our ancient past, and of the dangers of the present.

And also to hear the sound of color:

The color of blue crashing like the waves of the Mediterranean shouting of eternity, of belonging, of being home from a long journey. The color of red sunsets at the edge of the sea announcing majesty, brilliance, and power. The color of sandy vistas holding words of revelation and then tossing them like an echo of divinity: their sound bouncing off sharp-edged mountains and constantly riding the dust-filled wadis. Hear, my child, the color of winter rains, fresh with renewal, washing the weary earth of its stagnation. And then a rainbow of color—the wildflowers of the spring shouting a brilliant spray of joy. They are as delicate and fragile as children at play, who in their naïveté sing despite our painful history and harsh reality. And, dear

Talia, always hear the color of blue; like a sky so vivid and real, that hope can never really be lost, despite it all.

Yes. Despite it all. Color. Listen.

 **David M. Suissa** is an advertising executive who writes a weekly column for the *Jewish Journal of Greater Los Angeles*. He is also founder and editor in chief of *OLAM* magazine, and founder of Meals4Israel.com, a fundraising arm for soup kitchens in Israel.

> "But somehow, Israel's different. It tastes different, it feels different, it sounds different. Why?... In Israel, everyone talks to each other as if they're family."

"I can't explain it." I hear that over and over again when people try to describe Israel. They see modern buildings and cars and beaches and slums and cafes and malls and traffic and everything else you'll find in a Western country.

But somehow, Israel's different. It tastes different, it feels different, it sounds different. Why?

How can we explain this difference without settling for the sentimental clichés we're all so familiar with—you know, waiting and yearning for two thousand years to return to our homeland, feeling that sense of belonging and peoplehood that you can only find in Israel, and so on? Those are true, of course, but they're also general and abstract—they don't grab me in the *kishkes* (guts).

For me, there is one little observation about Israel and its people that tells me more than a hundred books. It's not their phenomenal accomplishments in science, medicine, the arts, literature, and the digital world; nor is it even their near-miraculous ability to survive in one of the world's nastiest neighborhoods; or even that Israel protects human rights like freedom of speech and freedom of religion like no other country in the Middle East—all of which I'm incredibly proud of.

No, what really gets me is the way Israelis talk to each other. In particular, the way they talk—and even argue—with someone they've never met before. Think about it. You meet a complete stranger and you're instantly comfortable enough to argue with that person.

I simply can't imagine going around my city of Los Angeles and seeing strangers talk to other strangers as if they've known each other all their lives. Personally, the thought of barking "What the hell are you talking about?" to a total stranger makes me cringe—unless, of course, I'm with my brother and sisters.

Don't get me wrong. It's not that my parents didn't teach us how to be polite. It's simply that when the *mishpacha* (family) is around, we don't agonize too much over etiquette—we're family so we're familiar, which makes us very comfortable.

It doesn't offend us if someone forgets to say "please."

Now, I know that a lot of people will look at this peculiar aspect of Israeli society and call it an absence of good manners, which can have some unfortunate side effects, especially when people passionately disagree. I can sympathize with that.

But after more than twenty visits to the Holy Land, I've also come to appreciate what's behind this Israeli tendency toward instant informality.

In Israel, everyone talks to each other as if they're family.

Considering they've waited two thousand years to attend their family reunion, I guess I can sympathize with that, too.

STEPHEN JOEL TRACHTENBERG has served as the president of The George Washington University in Washington, D.C., where he also teaches public administration. He has previously been the president of the University of Hartford (CT). His writings include *Reflections on Higher Education, Thinking Out Loud,* and *Speaking His Mind.*

"Israel has been a part of my life since before I was born."

Israel has been a part of my life since before I was born. In 1918 my grandfather came home to Odessa. He had been in the Czar's army and a German prison camp. Odessa, he figured, wasn't much better than either. So he said, "*Feh!*" and moved the family, including Shoshana, my mother, to Palestine. Had my grandfather stayed put, the family might have perished during World War II or lived under the benign rule of the Soviet Union. It was the best thing he ever did. It was a good idea even if the family lived for much of their time there in a World War I surplus tent. Unable to find steady work in Palestine, my grandfather moved to the Bronx, opened up a hand laundry, and lived behind the store. By 1928 he had enough money to bring the rest of the family to America.

Now we fast-forward a few years. In 1970 my fiancée, Francine, and I decided to get married. This should have been a simple matter. It was not. The two families, Francine's and mine, had different ideas about how the wedding should go. My father, Oscar, had been an insurance man for many years and had, by actual count, attended more than 418 weddings and bar mitzvahs. Naturally he intended to pay all those good people back by inviting them to the wedding of his son, an only child and, obviously, one of nature's noblemen, if not an outright prince with pedigree.

Francine's family had a more modest ceremony in mind. They thought the wedding should take place in Aunt Anita's backyard; in other words, a quiet, small family affair, not requiring the use of Madison Square Garden. The prospective son-in-law may have been a prince, but his parents were not Rothschilds. I realized that this was a problem that could cause a rift between the Zorns and the Trachtenbergs and was not the best way to start a marriage. So I had an idea. After millennia of saying, "Next year in Jerusalem," it was now quite possible for Jews of the Diaspora like us to go to Israel, and Jerusalem in particular, to get married. That was the trump card I played.

My mother went along with the idea, but with mixed emotions, I think. Francine's mother, Selma, was not trumped. Her mother, Francine's grandma, would love to see her granddaughter get married, but she was not well enough to take the trip to Jerusalem. She said this and then asked me to come up with another idea. I made a counter offer. I said that instead of negotiating like a couple of backroom politicians, why don't we ask Francine to go to Grandma and get her opinion: we'd let that guide us. So Francine went to her grandmother, and here is the transcript of the conversation:

Francine: Grandma, I want to get married, but our parents disagree about where.

Grandma: You love this boy?

Francine: Yes.

Grandma: He loves you?

Francine: Yes.

Grandma: He's Jewish?

Francine: Yes.

Grandma: He wants to marry you?

Francine: Yes.

Grandma: He makes a living?

Francine: Yes.

Grandma: Any place he says!

Grandma, as you can see, was a woman of few but powerful words.

So we were going to be married in Jerusalem and I had a plan. But were the authorities going to let us get married? Not so fast. First, we had to prove that we were Jewish. Second, we had to prove we had no previous marriages. Third, we had to prove that Francine knew the duties and obligations of a Jewish wife. And we could only do this by bringing to a *bet din* (a rabbinical court) in Jerusalem affidavits signed by three pious people of faith who knew us in Boston where we were living. As luck would have it, there were three rabbis in Boston to whom we could explain, one after the other, why we wanted to get married in Jerusalem. They provided us with the letters assuring all that we were worthy, true Jews, and the real McCoy. Fine.

On with the wedding—almost. I wanted to get married at the Western Wall, but I was told that there were regulations forbidding weddings there. I asked to see the regulations. There were none, but there was a tradition that no one should get married at the Western Wall. I decided at that point that getting affidavits and fighting a regulation were possible, but fighting a Jewish tradition, especially one concerning the Wall, was a losing proposition.

With the assistance of my best man, Alan Dershowitz, I arranged to get married on the roof of a building about a hundred yards from the Wall. We got a rabbi, we got a *huppah,* and best of all we got a telephone with a live hook-up that hung above the *huppah* so that Francine's grandma could hear the wedding take place. There we were, on the roof, with a view of the Western Wall and the hills of Judea, Francine looking terrific in a Lily Pulitzer caftan she had bought at Filene's; me in a blue suit and a beard looking like a *rebbe* (a Hasidic rabbi)—and many people on neighboring rooftops watching the wedding. Believe me, we have no shortage of witnesses to our marriage. And Grandma heard every word.

Since so much of my connection with Israel is also part of my connection with Francine, I should point out that she was the president of the Solomon Schechter School in Hartford, Connecticut, where our boys went to school, and she is now president of the District of Columbia Jewish Community Center.

So I can conclude that my connection with Israel began before I was born and made for a happy marriage and, therefore, a happy life. I will also no doubt spend eternity in a Jewish cemetery that, if not exactly in Israel, will have virtual access to the land of Zion. They tell me it's a local call.

PENINNAH SCHRAM, internationally known storyteller, teacher, author, and recording artist, is associate professor of speech and drama at Stern College of Yeshiva University. She is the author of nine books of Jewish folktales, including *Jewish Stories One Generation Tells Another* and *Stories Within Stories: From the Jewish Oral Tradition.*

"There are countries that have more beautiful museums than Israel. There are countries that have older universities than Israel. There are countries that have much more magnificent architecture and art than Israel. But Israel is like your mother."

When I completed graduate school in the spring of 1958, I made plans to travel to Europe with a college friend. We wanted to spend nine weeks during the summer touring Western Europe, especially England, France, Switzerland, and Italy. However, since I didn't have the funds to pay for the trip, I had to ask my parents for their permission and the monies.

When I spoke to my father, he said, "Listen, Peninnah, better to go to Israel."

"But, Pa," I replied, "I don't want to go to Israel. I want to go to England and France and Italy. I want to see Buckingham Palace, the Louvre Museum, and all the places and artists that I've been studying about for years in English, History, and Art History classes." I reasoned with him, hoping it was in a convincing tone.

I knew that my father, who was a cantor from Lithuania and an ardent Zionist from childhood, had always hoped that he could live in Israel but it never came to be. My mother, who had come from Russia, loved America with every fiber! So instead, from 1935 until 1949, my father went to Israel three times.

Hearing my argument about going to Europe, my father listened but was not convinced. Instead he looked at me and said, "Peninnah, Israel is like your mother. There are mothers who are more fashionably dressed than your mother. There are mothers who are better educated than your mother. There are mothers who speak without an accent like your mother does. But your mama is your mama. So, too, there are countries that have more beautiful museums than Israel. There are countries that have older universities than Israel. There are countries that have much more magnificent architecture and art than Israel. But Israel is like your mother."

I sat there and I listened to my father.

But after another conversation with my parents, I went to Europe that summer with my friend, after all.

I didn't go to Israel until 1961. At the time, my husband and I were living in Paris for two years. Just before the High Holy Days we decided to travel to Israel on the cruise ship *Herzl* of the Zim lines. To get to the ship, we first went by train from Paris to Marseille and from there took the boat to Haifa. We actually celebrated Rosh Hashanah on board ship. Being on the Mediterranean Sea was a beautiful experience, but the moment I remember most is when, early one morning, we went out on deck and saw the outlines of Haifa rising through the morning fog. We saw the glittering golden dome of the Bahai Temple.

When we glimpsed Israel for the first time, it was a breathtaking moment. Suddenly everyone began to sing "Hatikvah" (Israel's national anthem).

Only when I saw Israel, walked on the land, smelled the fragrant jasmine, and touched its soil did I truly understand what my father had meant when he said, "Better to go to Israel."

Since that time I have been to Israel dozens of times, going at least once a year for the past twenty-five years. You see, my daughter attended the Hebrew University for her junior year abroad and never returned to America because she fell in love with Israel. She met a wonderful Moroccan Israeli and they fell in love. Since my daughter graduated from the Hebrew University, she and her husband live in Israel. I have three grandchildren, all sabras.

Whenever I complain that she is too far away, my daughter reminds me that my father always wanted to live in Israel. When I ask, "But what about my mother's dream of coming to America and thanking God that she could live in the land of freedom and opportunity?" my daughter replies, "You can fulfill your mother's dream, but I am fulfilling your father's dream." So what can I say to that?

DAVID SILVERSTEIN is a senior at Vanderbilt University and a former officer of NFTY (North American Federation of Temple Youth).

"I have always struggled with the term 'American Jew.' Which identity comes first? Are they interconnected or separate entities?... With my trip [through birthright israel], my Jewish identity became complete. I understood what I was praying for and where I came from. By being able to understand Israel more, I have been able to understand my position as an American Jew."

I have always struggled with the term "American Jew." Which identity comes first? Are they interconnected or separate entities? Outside of New York, being Jewish in America isn't always the easiest thing. I live most of the year in Nashville, Tennessee, and after brushing knuckles a few times with anti-Semitism, I can tell you that "Shalom y'all" won't always get you very far. You have to seek out Judaism and I've become very comfortable with that reality. Before my trip to Israel, it was hard for me to treat the two identities even in the same sentence. That trip would bring my two identities—American and Jewish—together.

When I was growing up, my household was filled with a fantastic Jewish atmosphere complete with everything from Shabbat on Friday nights to observance of the major holidays and attendance at synagogue functions. Curiously, Israel was nearly absent from all family conversation. It just wasn't an issue that was emphasized. I had to take this journey into my own hands and, for a time, be blindly proactive about finding a way to go.

For me the problem was getting to the Middle East. In the back of my mind I counted the days until I would be eligible for the birthright israel program. I had grown up in the Reform Jewish youth community and support for Israel was prevalent, but moreover, as a teenager I was surrounded by others my age who would throw around weighty words like "Zionism" and "Eretz Yisrael" and mean it. I didn't identify with them. I wanted to be able to form my own opinions through my own experience.

In May 2004, I went with the Vanderbilt University Hillel (my home university) on a Taglit birthright trip to Israel. I was fortunate to spend nearly three weeks in Israel, and then I extended my trip and met my father for another week of travel. When I think back on the opportunities birthright gives to thousands of young people, it's brilliantly absurd that a program like it actually exists. While some may say that "the program" changed their life, I say differently. Birthright is not necessarily magical, but it successfully tackles a big issue that faces young Jews in America today—the "getting there factor." Birthright israel brought me there; Israel did the rest. I would argue that the same goes for thousands of others like me.

My perspective on Israel was actually shaped by something that happened after the program ended. When my father arrived we decided together that we would take a trip to see the cave of Machpelah, the burial grounds of the Jewish patriarchs and matriarchs. I did not fully understand the weight of the day's destination. I knew the cave was located in Hebron and that getting there would mean crossing borders and experiencing security screenings by the IDF. We arrived in a Jewish settlement and stopped in a rabbi's house for a rest. I looked around and realized that there were bullet holes dotting the walls and cabinets in his kitchen. I was overwhelmed with emotions and was so confused that I blurted out to the rabbi, "Why do you live here?" He looked at me aghast and replied immediately, "If my family cannot live near the site of our forefathers, where can we live?"

Since that day, my Jewish and American identities have been very much interwoven. I wasn't just an eighteen-year-old who had come home showing photographs of the sunrise at Masada. Rather, I felt that I was coming home. I now understood that, in addition to my "real" home, I had an additional home somewhere else.

When I speak or think about Israel, I try to handle it with care. I treat it like the greatest gift I have ever received. With my trip, my Jewish identity became complete. I understood what I was praying for and where I came from. By being able to understand Israel more, I have been able to understand my position as an American Jew. I look at it as a passion play of two cultures trying to work together instead of against each other. It enabled me to finally be proud to be both.

RABBI GORDON TUCKER is the senior rabbi of Temple Israel Center in White Plains, New York, and adjunct assistant professor of Jewish philosophy at The Jewish Theological Seminary. He is also honorary chairman of the Masorti Foundation for Conservative Judaism in Israel and has just completed twenty-five years of service on the Rabbinical Assembly's Committee on Jewish Law and Standards.

"Greatness does not reside solely in antiquity, and miraculous achievements have their modern embodiments as well.... In the Jewish homeland, even secularism produces its own rich moments of transcendence."

I have visited Israel approximately fifty times. As is the case with most American Jews, Jerusalem tends to be the center of virtually every visit, and no one could possibly gainsay the magic of the ancient capital of the Jewish people, nor its natural beauty. But when I spent four months on a sabbatical from my congregation in 2003, I chose to spend those months in Tel Aviv, a city I knew only as most tourists know it (which is to say, barely at all). People often talk about how in Jerusalem, you can feel and hear the footsteps and voices of great Jewish figures. They mean David and Solomon, Isaiah and Jeremiah, Ezra and Judah Maccabee, Yohanan ben Zakkai, and so on. True.

But I learned that greatness does not reside solely in antiquity, and miraculous achievements have their modern embodiments as well. Over the period of four months, I learned that it is an indescribable privilege to be able to walk every day in the footsteps of people like Hayyim Nahman Bialik and Shmuel Yosef Agnon, Yosef Chaim Brenner and Arthur Ruppin, Abraham Isaac Kook and Meir Dizengoff, all of whom graced Tel Aviv, the first city in the world since the Babylonian exile to have been built by and for Jews, and to be inhabited by self-governing Jews. Because of that, it has its own sacred aura to it.

I felt it when I walked down Rothschild Boulevard, near the very intersection at which Tel Aviv was started as "Ahuzat Bayit" in 1909, and saw a storefront that houses an office design firm. On the outside wall is a plaque bearing the emblem of the Irgun (Zionist National Military Organization operating in then-Palestine from 1931 to 1948) from 1947. Surrounding the emblem are these words: *Ha-el she-yatzar barzel lo ratzah ba-avadim.* "The God who created iron did not want humans to be slaves." This means that the iron weapons that were used to carve out a free Jewish state in the face of many implacable opponents and a mostly uncomprehending world were understood to be not only tools of independence, but as serving some transcendent purpose in the world. You don't need to be an Irgun-nik to appreciate that message, which draws on our deepest collective memories of Egyptian bondage and liberation.

Along the beach just a bit north is a memorial for the *Altalena*. It was off the Tel Aviv sands in June 1948 that the first Jewish government since 63 BCE made a fateful and still controversial decision to impose military discipline by firing on an Irgun armaments ship. And just a bit south along the water, another memorial—for the twenty-one teenagers who were killed in a suicide bombing at the Dolphinarium nightclub in June 2001. These young people were primarily Russian-speaking immigrants, and the memorial has two inscriptions—one each in Hebrew and Russian. The Hebrew inscription translates as "We shall not stop dancing." And the Russian inscription gives the reason: "This is our home." These and so many more pieces of the sacred history of our people's reentry into history pulsate in the streets of Tel Aviv.

Tel Aviv has its elites. Among the joys I found there was the ability to walk to the opera, the ballet, and an impressive array of dance and theater companies. But in preparing to leave at sabbatical's end, I felt that I had to say goodbye to a whole different set of people. The waitresses at the local cafes and wine bars. The attendants at the lot where I parked my car. The members of Masorti synagogue Kehillat Sinai, where I was a "civilian" member for four months. The trainers at the health club next door. The taxi drivers I saw every day outside my building. They are among the unidentified "extras" and chorus members without whom the play called Zionism has no stage presence at all. And whenever I return to Israel, I am careful to spend quality time in this unique city, because it taught me that in the

Jewish homeland, even secularism produces its own rich moments of transcendence.

SHIRA DICKER is a writer and publicist living in Manhattan.

> "At first it didn't have a name, this intimate connection to a place, this sense of homecoming. It is reflexive, like breathing, the most organic thing I have ever experienced."

At first it didn't have a name, this intimate connection to a place, this sense of homecoming.

It is reflexive, like breathing, the most organic thing I have ever experienced.

Because I came upon it as a young child, it has stayed with me always.

To me, it is no dream, but not because I have merely willed it so, to paraphrase Theodor Herzl.

It is not a dream because it is based in the remembrance of a perfect homecoming, first experienced in that heady time immediately after the Six Day War.

Like many American rabbis, my father jumped at the opportunity to take his young family to Israel in 1968 for his sabbatical year. A Conservative rabbi with a pulpit in Queens, New York, my father joined scores of his colleagues who were giddy with idealism in the face of Israel's miraculous military victory against all odds.

Within a twenty-four-hour period, my life took on an authenticity I didn't realize had been missing in my life as a second-grader living in Douglaston, where the New York City line meets Nassau County in Long Island.

Fruit, vegetables, and bread came equipped with new dimensions of flavor and texture. The air was always scented—with orange blossoms, with honeysuckle, with falafel, with goat, with human sweat, with optimism. Faces looked open and alive, refreshingly unadorned. The color palette was closer to hues found in nature; the garish colors of American culture in the sixties faded from my vision. Legs and arms were bared and browned. The sound of Hebrew—guttural and melodic—enveloped me. Outside, the vistas seemed endless, but inside, spaces were smaller. Bodies pressed closer. Gestures were larger. Children were free.

My first impression of Israel was the pervasive heat of Holon on a summer night, an arid room with no air conditioner—or even a fan—being allowed to sleep only in my underpants, watching a lizard make its way up a rough, unpainted wall. Next, a dark but air-conditioned apartment in Tel Aviv, being plunked into the midst of a group of kinetic Israeli kids at a day camp on the Tel Aviv beach. The camp was called Biduron. I was the only American kid in my age group.

Within a week my skin turned dark brown and with my black hair and dark eyes, I looked more Israeli than any of the other campers. Being on the shores of the Mediterranean, my Sephardic blood asserted itself. In New York I was an awkward, adopted child, introspective, too tall, ethnic without being exotic, painfully aware of my otherness, yet forced to pretend that nothing was different about me in an era that claimed that nurture was everything.

And yet in Israel, where no one could deny my outsider status as an American, my intrinsic, painful otherness faded away.

Running on the Tel Aviv beach, my muscles lengthened and strengthened. My hair, always chopped unattractively short in the "pixie" style of the time, grew longer. I loved the smell of the ocean, the sun on my skin, the residue of the salty water. The Mediterranean had an amniotic effect on me. The language of the water took root within me. Hebrew began spilling out of my lips.

And then, a miracle.

My strange name—Shira—mispronounced by nearly everyone at home, was finally at home. My foreign name (misconstrued as Sheila or Shirley or Sherry or Sharon, fine names all, just not my name), the bane of my existence in New York, was suddenly a thing of beauty. It made Israelis smile. Shira.

With an accent, it became *Shee-rrra*.

A song. A poem. The name of a famous novel by S. Y. Agnon.

The summer in Tel Aviv gave way to the school year in Jerusalem, in the apartment of the philosopher and writer Pinchas

Peli, 9 Brenner St. in the Rehavia section. That block is still there, unchanged. I attended third grade in Jerusalem at Evelina d'Rotschild. The school is still there. There is so much to say about my experiences living in Jerusalem during that time, a year that has shaped my entire existence.

There is so much to say about my innumerable return trips, which include two other year-long visits. About a close call with a terrorist attack in September 1997. About friends and family who live there now. About the fantasy of dividing my life between the Upper West Side of Manhattan and Jerusalem.

Yet, when I consider my personal dream of Zion, I find myself on the beach in Tel Aviv in the summer of 1968, a seven-year-old child running on the sand, communing with the waves, rocked in the amniotic fluids of the maternal Mediterranean, touching my past and my eternity, feeling a sense of perfect homecoming.

RABBI DAVID ELLENSON is president of Hebrew Union College–Jewish Institute of Religion and holds the I. H. and Anna Grancell Chair in Jewish Religious Thought.

"I believe deeply in Jewish peoplehood, and I pray that every student who graduates from Hebrew Union College and assumes a position of leadership among the Jewish people will internalize a notion of connection to and responsibility for Jews everywhere. Such feelings cannot be acquired without a firsthand encounter with the State of Israel."

I was raised in a home in Virginia where the State of Israel was placed at the very center of my consciousness. My mother often told tales of how her cousin had fought for Israeli independence in 1948 through his service in the Haganah, and the story of how *Medinat Yisrael* had fulfilled the millennia-old dreams of the Jewish people through the efforts of the *halutzim* and in the aftermath of the Shoah filled our home. Her own unceasing participation in Hadassah testified to her commitment to the Jewish state. While she felt a sense of deep satisfaction in all the programs Hadassah initiated, she took special pride in Hadassah Hospital and the efforts of their doctors and nurses to bring first-rate medical care to all inhabitants—Jewish and Arab—of Jerusalem. Her own Zionism was supplemented by the deep religious commitment of my father to Eretz Yisrael—though it would be wrong to regard his vision as akin to post-1967 messianic visions of *Eretz Yisrael Hashleimah* (the greater Land of Israel). David Ben-Gurion and Abba Eban—no less than George Washington and Thomas Jefferson—were the greatest of heroes in my household, and my sense of self was forged by narratives in which these Israeli, as well as American, statesmen were placed at the center of my life. My dual relationship to Israel and the United States are surely reflective of the "double consciousness" that W.E.B. Du Bois once remarked characterized the modern situation.

I took my first trip to Israel in the summer of 1965 when I was a teenager. I played on a Jewish Welfare Board basketball team, and I remember, more than anything else, standing on King David Street in Jerusalem—not far from where the Hebrew Union College now stands—and gazing over at the walls of the Old City where I was forbidden entry because Arab restrictions would not allow me, as a Jew, to enter and see the Western Wall and the other sites attached to the ancestral capital of my people. I have often been astounded that, in the aftermath of the Six Day War and the reunification of Jerusalem, those who call for the internationalization of Jerusalem or speak of the need for a single-state solution to the Israeli–Palestinian conflict seem to have forgotten the unjust and exclusionary treatment accorded Jews during these years. Their lapse of memory has made me suspicious of solutions to current problems that would leave Jewish presence in Jerusalem and in the country as a whole dependent upon the goodwill of others, and I acknowledge that the power of this teenage memory is more decisive than any other factor in accounting for my own belief that Jewish sovereignty in the Jewish state is necessary even as I recognize that a "two-state solution" to this "land of two peoples" is required if coexistence will ever come to the region.

As a young adult in 1972 I lived for a year on Kibbutz Mishmar HaEmek in the Jezreel Valley, and there I lived the life of a kibbutznik. I worked in the fields of the kibbutz and toured all parts of the Land. The next year, I entered Hebrew Union College–Jewish Institute of Religion in Jerusalem, attracted to the Reform seminary in large measure because of its Year-in-Israel program. My oldest daughter, Ruth, was born that year at Hadassah Hospital. I will never forget my mother coming to visit us after her birth, and the joy she felt that her own granddaughter had not only been born in Jerusalem, but in the very hospital to which she had devoted so much of her life.

Throughout my career as an academic, I have had the privilege of teaching and lecturing at various Israeli universities. In 1997 to 1998 I was a fellow for a year at the Institute for Advanced Studies as well as a Lady Davis Visiting Professor of the Humanities in the Department of Jewish Thought at the Hebrew University. In addition, I have been blessed to teach not only at HUC in Jerusalem but also at Machon Pardes and the Shalom Hartman Institute in Jerusalem every summer for over a decade. On all these occasions, my family has accompanied me and all of us have ties of friendship and memory that inextricably link each of us to the people and State of Israel. Indeed, my wife, Jackie, is now chair of the Hadassah Foundation and I can only imagine the great satisfaction and joy my mother would feel knowing that her daughter-in-law is so deeply involved in providing needed financial assistance to a variety of worthy projects in Israel. My ties and those of my family—including my brother, whose wife is an Israeli of Yemenite descent—to Israel are visceral and my attachments run deep.

Of course, it is in my role as president of Hebrew Union College–Jewish Institute of Religion that my link to Israel is now most deeply maintained. I am very proud that HUC–JIR, even during the darkest days of the recent intifada, maintained its requirement that every rabbinic, cantorial, and education student at the College–Institute study for at least one year in Israel. I believe deeply in Jewish peoplehood, and I pray that every student who graduates from Hebrew Union College and assumes a position of leadership among the Jewish people will internalize a notion of connection to and responsibility for Jews everywhere. Such feelings cannot be acquired without a firsthand encounter with the State of Israel.

Our students' year-long sojourn in Israel bespeaks a spiritual–religious commitment that the late Brandeis Professor Simon Rawidowicz captured in his famed work *Babylon and Jerusalem*. In that book Professor Rawidowicz employed the two sites contained in his title as emblematic of the unity of Jewish existence in both the Diaspora and the Land of Israel, and he employed the metaphor of an ellipsis to capture the integral connectedness that binds Jews everywhere into one people. It is an image that captures the educational policy that informs the Hebrew Union College–Jewish Institute of Religion. It is an ideal that animates and informs my own attachment to the State of Israel as well, even as I dwell primarily in America.

GEORGE S. BLUMENTHAL has been involved in founding companies that provide cable services in Europe and cellular phone services worldwide for more than twenty years. Over five years ago he realized that high-speed Internet access could revolutionize the teaching of Jewish history as well as the field of medical record-keeping. He then set out to bring the story of the Jewish people to anyone, anywhere, at anytime.

"My life is about the continuity beyond myself. It is about the continuity of the Jewish people that extends back beyond the lives of my parents and forward beyond the lives of my children."

I have finally found a measure of peace.

Four years ago, I had an epiphany that would alter who I am as a Jew. Suddenly, I realized how I could put my deep passion for Israel and the Jewish people into action. I immediately understood how I, a Jew with a strong commitment but little formal Jewish training, could contribute to the continuity of my people and the State of Israel.

I was in the house of Shlomo Mousaieff, the biblical antiquities collector, whom I had met just two months earlier. Having decided to make a film about Mousaieff and his vast collection, I was working with the film crew when I became acquainted with Ardon Bar Hama, a gifted Israeli photographer. On the second day of our shoot, Ardon introduced me to digital photography. All of a sudden, I saw it! I could take this new medium and photograph all the artifacts (such as those at The Jewish Museum of New York—JewishMuseum.org) and rare documents (such as The Dead Sea Scrolls—DeadSeaScrolls.tv) that tell the history of the Jewish people. Then, using another new technology, high-speed delivery of information over the Internet (wired or wireless), I could present all this material to anyone, anywhere, at any time in the world. It would be a way to educate young Jews no matter what their background, and let others know who we were.

This revelation came to me late in life. I was already in my sixties. I had always desired to honor my Jewish heritage and my exceptional parents, who narrowly escaped Nazi Europe and raised me to be a passionate Zionist. Growing up as the only Jewish child in my neighborhood on the west side of Cleveland, I also experienced anti-Semitism firsthand. However, I was raised with little formal Jewish education, and as an adult I pursued other interests.

I became an early pioneer in the field of communication technologies. In 1981, I chaired Cellular Communications Inc., which was one of the original applicants for the first cellular telephone licenses. In 1993, a spinoff of CCI was one of the first in the world to offer telephone and cable access simultaneously. When high-speed Internet became available, that company, now renamed Virgin Media, became the first company in the world to offer telephone, cable, and high-speed access (called Triple Play).

I have wonderful children, great friends, my business experiences have been gratifying, and I have had a lot of other extraordinary experiences in my life, yet there remained a void inside me. This being said, I did not believe that I could contribute to the continuity of my heritage and to the perpetuation of Israel, a place that I had visited over fifty times since childhood.

After meeting Bar Hama, this changed. I began traveling with him to various institutions in Israel, the United States, and Europe (including the Vatican) and offering to create free digital photography for archival purposes and free websites for this material without retaining any rights to it. Little by little, the project gained momentum. In 2003, I launched a pilot website (JewishHistory.com) that is dedicated to illuminating aspects of the Jewish Bible through archaeology and the works of Rembrandt, month-in and month-out; the average visitor spends at least thirty minutes per visit on the site. In 2004, in cooperation with a group of well-known scholars, the Center for Online Judaic Studies (cojs.org) was born; and in 2007 we launched Passoversite.org, in conjunction with The Jewish Theological Seminary and VisionsVoices.org, which is dedicated to women and prayer. Both of these sites have been viewed in more than fifty countries worldwide. By the end of 2007, we will launch a web-based archaeological dig for children with Jerusalem of the biblical period at the center of the site. All in all, we have supplied digital photography for more than thirty institutions around the world and have created or conceptualized more than ten websites. I never would have envisioned that my expertise in communications would one day lead me back, full circle, to my Judaism.

Recently, I bought my first real estate in Israel: eight gravesites for myself and my family. Many see death and birth as the frame through which to understand a life. But for me, being buried in Israel is not the culmination of my life as a Jew. My life is about the continuity beyond myself. It is about the continuity of the Jewish people that extends back beyond the lives of my parents and forward beyond the lives of my children. With the Center for Online Judaic Studies, I hope to contribute to this continuity, bringing to life the past of the Jewish people and helping to ensure its future.

 **SUSAN WEIDMAN SCHNEIDER** is one of the founding mothers of *Lilith* magazine (www.Lilith.org) and has served as its editor in chief since 1976. A popular speaker on gender issues and a widely-published author, her books include *Jewish & Female: Choices and Changes in Our Lives Today* and *Intermarriage: The Challenge of Living with Differences between Christians and Jews.*

"It's an enormously powerful reflexive attachment that I feel, independent of any formal Zionist principles, independent of modern Israel's politics or governments, independent of the widespread prejudices directed at Eretz, separate from warm feelings for Israeli friends and relatives."

In my family of origin, Zion was no dream.

I was really stumped when, in 1950, my grandfather, Mordecai Weidman, gave me a key chain with an emblem commemorating the founding of the State of Israel. Wasn't Israel always there? In nursery school in Winnipeg I sang "Hatikva" before I learned "God Save the Queen" or "O, Canada."

Israel—*Eretz* (the Land), as it was casually referred to in my childhood home—was spoken of as a kind of family outpost, though when I was a child Mordecai was the only one I knew personally who'd touched the soil there. Here's the story. In 1882, facing increasing anti-Semitic violence, my paternal great-grandparents fled the village of Orli (near Bialystock) with Mordecai and two other sons. With the help of Baron de Hirsch funds, they landed in Winnipeg. Hard labor building the railroad, bitter cold winter in an unheated shed, three frustrating years trying to farm the frozen prairie, then settling in town to forge a Jewish community. And then, and then … in 1904, for reasons no one alive now can entirely parse out, the great-grandparents made aliyah, *spurred,* so it goes, by my great-grandmother's desire. They lived in Jerusalem, near Mea Shearim. (One family rumor is that my great-grandfather built their stone house himself. The house is still there; photos of my grandfather and my great-uncle still hang in one of the rooms. My cousins, my children, and I pay homage to the house and the ancestors in person whenever we can.) And I remember hearing stories of how the family in Winnipeg sealed money into tin cans, and butter (separate cans, I always hoped), and shipped them to Eretz, where there was terrible privation even early in the twentieth century.

Neither of these great-grandparents survived World War I, so in 1923 Mordecai and his brother Haim Leib ("HL" to the family) set sail to visit their parents' graves. Literate men, they kept a diary. After travels through Europe and a return to Orli (and a visit to their old yeshiva in Bialystock where, they report, "the system now used is *Ivrit b' Ivrit*"—Hebrew taught in Hebrew), they visited Egypt and thence to Eretz Israel. Their first stop was to say kaddish at the graves of their parents, and then they toured the country. They met with the chief rabbi, Rav Abraham Isaac Kook, and decided to give the stone house for a maternity hospital (now used by a charity providing food and other assistance to needy pregnant women and to mothers of young children). The "Brothers Weidman," as they are called in news reports of the time, recorded their enchantment with Israel in their joint diary, which on their return to Winnipeg they printed up as a little pamphlet in a dual-language edition: English and Yiddish. The theme, beautifully enunciated, I usually paraphrase as, "We went to Egypt and we saw dead monuments. Then we went to Israel where we saw living monuments." Of Degania, the first kibbutz, they wrote that the members may not be *frum* (religiously observant), "but their work is kosher." The Yiddish version of the diary tells how the hard work on the kibbutz was breathing "new breath" or "new spirit" into the Jewish people.

My great-grandparents are buried on the Mount of Olives, and now in my address file I keep track of just where under "G," for "graves." Until my first visit, I'd never learned my great-grandmother's given name. We'd just had a daughter and named her Rachel, not as a precise namesake but in memory of my husband's aunt, whose role had been as family matriarch. So you can imagine how moved I was when, after clambering from row to row, grave to grave, I brushed away sand from the headstone on the ground and saw from the roughly etched Hebrew letters that the woman buried there had been

"Rakhel Weidman mi Vinnipeg," daughter of Reb Nachman haLevy. Rachel!

Leaving Orli, she had fled. But leaving Canada for Eretz was a free choice. Why did she go, in 1904? And what was her life like there, with both Orli and Winnipeg in her memories? I try often to imagine. I think about her and write about her. And now that I can find them pretty easily, I've gone several times to greet my ancestors on that hillside. Once I even carried a pot of paint and a brush and my children re-inked the hollows of their ancestors' names. It's an enormously powerful reflexive attachment that I feel, independent of any formal Zionist principles, independent of modern Israel's politics or governments, independent of the widespread prejudices directed at Eretz, separate from warm feelings for Israeli friends and relatives. Rakhel and Dov Ber pull me back.

 **HOWARD SCHWARTZ** is professor of English at the University of Missouri-St. Louis. His most recent book, *Tree of Souls: The Mythology of Judaism*, won the 2005 National Jewish Book Award in the category of Reference.

"One day, God decided to transform a bare and deserted land into a holy land."

In June 1977, I went to Israel for a year-long sabbatical. I was editing an anthology of modern Jewish poets. I had a good selection, but I wanted to include an Ethiopian poet. Everyone said, "Ask Dov Noy. He'll know." I phoned Professor Noy and asked to meet with him. He said to come to his home in Rechavia at 9 p.m. on Monday night. When I arrived, his small apartment was completely full, with at least fifty people. It turned out that he had told everyone to meet him at the same time.

He had us squeeze into his living room and introduce ourselves. I met artists, writers, musicians, folklorists, scholars, and very interesting visitors from many lands. When I was able to speak to Noy for a moment, I told him about my quest for an Ethopian poet, and he promised me that such a poet would be there next week. And he was. By then I was hooked on these unpredictable Monday night gatherings, and for the rest of my year in Israel I came as often as I could. At first I barely managed to catch Noy as he chatted with each of his guests. But after a while he invited me to come over during the day, when no one else but his wife, Tamar, was there.

During these visits Noy told me about how he had studied under Stith Thompson, father of the modern study of folklore, at Indiana University, and then established the study of folklore in Israel. After great resistance, he succeeded in creating a department of folklore at the Hebrew University. And he told me with relish about his greatest accomplishment—founding the Israel Folktale Archives (IFA), housed in Haifa, that to date has collected over 23,000 stories from every ethnic group in Israel. The IFA is an amazing treasure house of every kind of folktale—fairy tales, fables, supernatural tales, mystical legends, even myths. In my view it will eventually be counted, along with the YIVO archives in New York, as a worthy addition to the essential texts of Jewish literature that include the Bible, the pseudepigrapha, rabbinic legends, medieval Jewish folklore, and kabbalistic and Hasidic texts.

To my way of thinking, Dov Noy seduced me into the field of Jewish folklore. He invited me to explore the archives, and I found an abundance of wonderful tales. One of the stories I came across was called "Elijah's Violin," told by Flora Cohen of Egypt. I thought, "What a wonderful title for a book of Jewish fairy tales!" I decided to edit such a book, and in 1983 *Elijah's Violin & Other Jewish Fairy Tales* was published, the first of four volumes of Jewish folktales that I collected. When he saw *Elijah's Violin,* Noy told me that I was the first to include the IFA stories side by side with traditional Jewish texts. More recently I edited *Tree of Souls: The Mythology of Judaism,* and I was able to identify more than fifty of the IFA tales as myths.

Needless to say, meeting Dov Noy in Jerusalem was a major turning point in my life, almost as important as meeting my wife, Tsila, during the same year in Israel. He has remained my mentor and inspiration. In my view, his contribution to Jewish studies is as immense as that of Gershom Scholem in Kabbalah or Martin Buber in Hasidism. He certainly deserves the Israel Prize he received for his work in 2004. He saved thousands of precious Jewish tales that would have undoubtedly been lost if not for his timely intervention, tales from the Jews of eastern Europe and the Middle East—and everywhere else—who made their way to Israel, bringing their stories with them.

In 2005 I met Dov Noy for dinner in Jerusalem and read him one of the IFA tales I had identified as a myth and included in *Tree of Souls* (IFA 593, told by Efraim Tzoref of Poland). Noy beamed as he heard it, and he agreed that it was indeed a myth of origin, explaining how a desolate land was transformed into a beautiful, holy one. It also served as an origin myth of the Kinneret (Sea of Galilee) and the Sea of Eilat, in which bits of God's ring fly to earth like comets and create them.

How the Holy Land Became Holy

God wears an exquisite ring on His finger. It contains precious gems of every kind: amethysts, emeralds, and sapphires, among them. Each of those gems lights the firmament with holy sparks, twinkling like a million stars.

One day, God decided to transform a bare and deserted land into a holy land. Until that time, there had been nothing more than a desolate range of mountains. Then God turned the ring on His finger, and sparks flew over the Galilee and the Jordan valley. They landed in the desert, as far as the Dead Sea, and all at once the mountains were transformed, covered with a bluish gleam, and luminous circles surrounded the Jordan valley.

God saw that it was good and turned His ring again, and fiery sparks covered the mountains like a glimmering tallit. God raised His hand, and a bit of a precious stone flew over the Negev and landed with such force that it melted and became the Sea of Eilat. It sparkles and shines day and night, never forgetting its origin in God's ring.

God's gaze turned to the north, and He turned His ring once more and the most beautiful of God's sapphires fell to earth and became the Sea of Galilee.

 **Alan Mittleman** is professor of philosophy and head of the Department of Jewish Philosophy at The Jewish Theological Seminary. The author of several books on modern Jewish thought, he serves as director of the Louis Finkelstein Institute for Religious and Social Studies.

"We need to recall what the world looked like when it was new. This is no less true for Jews in the matter of Israel…. Somehow, the living reality of Israel, all of its dreadful problems notwithstanding, encourages and strengthens me. I never quite return to that early heady love affair. Rather, the comfort of a mature relationship is reaffirmed. Better solidity than rapture and transport."

During a semester in which I was a visiting professor at Princeton, I overheard a cell phone conversation on the train (how can you not?). A young student was loudly complaining to a friend about how awful her room assignments had been during her Princeton career. She seemed embittered. The Princeton housing office had just not done right by her, she believed. As a newcomer to Princeton, I found her litany of complaints annoying. How could she possibly gripe about a four-year opportunity to study at one of the great universities of the world on a campus that is so astonishingly beautiful? Even if you had to live in a Quonset hut, it would still be a privilege to study there. Why are people who are so lucky so opaque?

It's easy for outsiders to see things with fresh eyes, to surmount the myopia of the everyday. We need them. We need to hear from people who bring, in their innocence, a virginal perspective. Failing that, we need now and then to become outsiders to our own perspective. We need to recall what the world looked like when it was new. This is no less true for Jews in the matter of Israel.

When I went to Israel for the first time as a college sophomore in 1974, I had an indescribably moving, orienting experience. (On the basis of my own experience decades ago, I can well understand what birthright trips do for young Jews today.) It changed the course of my life. I became, for the first time, deeply fascinated with being Jewish. My subsequent education, career, manner of life—everything—was shaped by that first exposure. I was not able to return to Israel until 1987. The country had changed (Jerusalem streets that were sleepy in 1974 were busy thoroughfares in 1987) and I had changed. Professionally engaged in Jewish life as a staffer at the American Jewish Committee, I was only too aware of the problems, the hardships, and the hard work of explaining and defending Israel. Israel had become more a task than a joy. It was wonderful to go again, but I could no longer see it with young, amazed eyes.

I have returned to Israel dozens of times since then. Each time is special. The oppressive complex of doubts and fears about the future of the country, nurtured by the omnipresent media and weighing on my Diaspora Jewish soul, is alleviated when I set foot on the ground. Somehow, the living reality of Israel, all of its dreadful problems notwithstanding, encourages and strengthens me. I never quite return to that early heady love affair. Rather, the comfort of a mature relationship is reaffirmed. Better solidity than rapture and transport.

Like that anonymous Princeton student, the Jewish people have the immense privilege to persevere in the immensely hard work of sustaining a state. It is so easy in the midst of the infinity of attendant hardships to lose sight of how extraordinary this is. We need frequently to remind and so to renew ourselves.

LISA D. GRANT is associate professor of Jewish Education at the Hebrew Union College–Jewish Institute of Religion, New York. Her research interests include adult Jewish learning, professional development of Jewish educators, and the role Israel plays in American Jewish life.

> "That is the essence of why Israel matters— because as Jews, we share so much in common no matter on what side of the ocean we choose to make our home."

Israel is integral to how I define myself and live my life as a Jew. It connects to all aspects of my being—the personal and the collective, the past and the present, the symbolic and the real, the immediate and the transcendent, the heartbreak and the hope. For over thirty-five years I have lived in two worlds, one foot here, one foot there, as Arik Einstein sings in his song "Sitting on the Fence." In 1971 my parents fulfilled their intense commitment to Israel by making aliyah. I was sixteen at the time and a reluctant participant in this adventure. I stayed in Israel through high school and then came rushing back to the States. I spent my college years in periodic angst about my decision, but only when I would go to Israel for the summer. The rest of the time I was fully absorbed in American life.

When I left Israel, I left organized Jewish life for over ten years. If I was going to live in America, I would be American. Israel and Judaism became totally private matters. I rarely spoke about Israel with my friends. I *never* set foot in a synagogue. But when it came time to choose between two boyfriends, I chose the Jewish one. And after the birth of our children, I began a slow and cautious return to Judaism. The more thickly engaged in Jewish life I became, the more significant Israel became for me as well. Not just as a place to visit the grandparents, but also as a place where I needed to be on a regular basis to foster personal and professional relationships, to grapple with social realities, to fully experience Jewish time and space, and to feel a sense of shalom—in the sense of wholeness, if not yet peace.

My experiences of and in Israel touch me in profound ways—emotionally, intellectually, socially, and spiritually. I am connected to Israel through sacred text and modern Hebrew literature, through landscape and history, through people and stories, through conversations and actions. Israel leaves me angry and charmed, frustrated and joyful, cursed and blessed. At times I feel utterly overwhelmed by the weight of history, the multiple claims on and visions for this punished land. Other times I feel overwhelmed by a memory or a moment when even the mundane can be remarkable just because the ordinary is so extraordinary.

Certainly my experience of and relationship to Israel are far from the normative American Jewish experience. But I believe that there are two interrelated aspects about why Israel matters to me, which I hope can provide meaning to others as well. First, I acknowledge and even embrace the weighty complexities inherent in an Israel that is multilayered with historical, religious, political, cultural, social, and existential significance. Just as with any relationship worth preserving, sustaining this relationship takes hard work. It's the difference between falling in love, a whirlwind of emotion when everything besides the love is inconsequential, and preserving the love that takes day-to-day effort, constant communication, give and take, and forgiveness. It is a partnership, a *brit l'olam*, a covenant for all time.

The second and related aspect is that I acknowledge and even embrace the formative tensions between the opposing forces that shape what it means to be a Jew. Indeed, the tensions among and between these forces are an inherent part of the Jewish soul, as Hayyim Nahman Bialik said long ago. Just as we navigate between the many other dualisms that are part of Jewish existence—the tensions between universal and particular values, religion and peoplehood, the individual and community, the sacred and the profane, tradition and change—so, too, can we navigate the dualisms inherent in Israel in all of its manifestations, symbolic and real.

Recently I was asked to give the closing benediction at a ceremony whose theme was Jewish unity. The immediate and obvious choice was to begin with Psalm 122, one of the fifteen "Songs of Ascent" that were part of the processionals in ancient days during the three pilgrimage festivals. The psalm speaks about the power of Jerusalem in bringing us together. A key verse reads: "Our feet stood inside your gates, O Jerusalem, Jerusalem built up, a city knit together, to which tribes would make pilgrimage." Rabbinic commentators make much of this line—both for the fact that Jerusalem is repeated twice and for the phrase "a city knit together," perfect for our theme that day. In a beautiful midrash on this psalm, God says, "I will not enter into heavenly Jerusalem until I can enter the earthly Jerusalem, for it is said, Until the holy one is built in your midst, I will not enter the city" (Hosea 11:9). That message compels us to think about the work we need to do to make the earthly Jerusalem a city worthy of God's presence. The midrash closes with the statement that "Jerusalem is a city which makes all Israel into a fellowship." And that is the essence of why Israel matters—because as Jews, we share so much in common no matter on what side of the ocean we choose to make our home.

ARTHUR KURZWEIL is a writer, teacher, editor, and publisher. Best known for his classic best seller *From Generation to Generation: How to Trace Your Jewish Genealogy and Family History,* his most recent books are *On the Road with Rabbi Steinsaltz* and *Kabbalah for Dummies.* His website is www.arthurkurzweil.com.

"I don't know why, having never lived in Israel, I consider Israel my home. But of one thing I am certain, and this is no secret: without Israel, life for Jews throughout the world would surely be, spiritually and physically, entirely different."

I learned a secret about the Holy Land from my teacher.

In Rabbi Adin Steinsaltz's masterpiece *The Thirteen Petalled Rose,* he writes: "The holiness of the Holy Land has nothing to do with who the inhabitants are or what they do; it is a choice from on high, beyond human comprehension."

When I read that, I asked, "What does 'holiness' mean? What is holiness?"

In the same book, Rabbi Steinsaltz answers me: "The holy is that which is out of bounds, untouchable, and altogether beyond grasp; it cannot be understood or even defined, being so totally unlike anything else."

So why is the Holy Land holy? We don't know. It is beyond our comprehension.

And what is holiness? We don't know. It is altogether beyond our grasp.

Israel is always a mystery to me.

I don't know why, at the age of nineteen, I bought a one-way ticket to Israel.

I don't know why, when the airplane landed, I exited and immediately bent down to touch the ground.

I don't know why Israel aggravates me so much.

I don't know why I consider every Jew in Israel a member of my family.

I don't know why, during my most recent trip to Israel, I spent most of my time visiting the graves of the most awe-inspiring personalities of Jewish history, including the graves of my favorite Talmudic rabbis, Rabbi Akiva and Nachum ish Gamzu, as well as the greatest kabbalist who ever lived, the Ari (Rabbi Isaac Luria, Safed, sixteenth century).

I don't know why I love to pray facing Jerusalem.

I don't know why, having never lived in Israel, I consider Israel my home.

But of one thing I am certain, and this is no secret: without Israel, life for Jews throughout the world would surely be, spiritually and physically, entirely different.

 **DEBBIE FRIEDMAN** is a prominent composer and singer of contemporary Jewish music. In the course of a career that spans more than three decades, she has recorded numerous albums and performed in countless venues. Many of her songs have become standards within the Jewish world.

"I became friends with all of the kitchen women. They were all Holocaust survivors (no wonder they were crazy). Eventually I almost moved to the kibbutz. It became like my home."

My first visit to Israel was after I graduated from high school. I went with the sole intention of learning Hebrew. I was horrified when I found myself on a kibbutz surrounded by English-speaking people.

I neither spoke nor understood Hebrew. My repertoire of Hebrew songs was rather extensive, so I was able to make connections to Hebrew words that had echoes in the prayers I knew. Sometimes in the more contemporary songs, the songs of the pioneers (which had been sung by the members of my kibbutz some thirty years prior to my arrival and not again until the Americans arrived), we were also able to make connections.

The Americans were known for their work habits, which were basically nonexistent. They much preferred taking breaks to working. Our group of volunteers was assigned to the apple orchard. We climbed up on ladders every day and plucked the ripe apples from the trees. Sometimes we were in the orange groves and we plucked the orange trees as well. Sometimes the fruit would fight back because it was not ready to be picked, and when it did the ladders would wobble back and forth.

I have always preferred the ground to heights, even when I am in planes. I always wish we could taxi to wherever we were going. I would be much happier.

This was my situation: Everyone in our group spoke English and I hated the ladders and the trees and the fuzz in my nose. I loved the orchard, from a distance. I didn't like being outside, and most of all, getting dirty has never pleased me. I asked to be transferred to a place where no one spoke English and I was on the ground floor.

And so it came to pass that I was sent to the kitchen. They sent me to work with Devorah, whose reputation preceded her. She was a wild woman in the worst sense of the word.

There were five women who worked in the kitchen and who did not know that I was an experienced institutional cook. I couldn't tell them because they spoke no English and I spoke no Hebrew, but from seventh grade until I graduated from high school, I had worked weekends and after school in the food service at a college.

First they brought an entire flatbed of green onions for me to clean. After I had cleaned four or five onions, my eyes were so filled with tears that I could not see. I went to one of the women and said in my most fluent Hebrew: "*Lo, lo!*" (no, no!).

The next thing I knew, another woman who was another lover of the American volunteers (the kitchen was full of them) wheeled a cart full of dead chickens, unshorn of their feathers. On the cart there was also a big tub of boiling water. The woman who would show me how to clean the chickens actually walked and talked like a chicken. She grabbed the chicken by its feet, dunked it in the water, held it there for a few seconds, pulled it out, and, with a shriek like a chicken, said: "*Kacha*" ("Like this!"). She pulled a handful of feathers and *kacha*, she pulled some more feathers out and they were flying all over the place. She continued until the chicken was free of feathers. She pointed to me and signaled for me to do the same.

The five women stepped away. I am sure they were thinking: "We got this one."

There were ten very dead *shechted* (slaughtered) chickens. When I finished with their plumage, I sat each one up on the back ledge of the kitchen shelf and posed them. Some were sitting arm in arm. A couple had their wings around each other. Some rested their heads on each other's shoulders.

I told the women I was finished and they came over to check my work and started to scream in laughter. They asked me my name and invited me to their homes for coffee.

Within three months I was fluent in Hebrew. I became friends with all of the kitchen women. They were all Holocaust survivors (no wonder they were crazy). Eventually I almost moved to the kibbutz. It became like my home.

I think of that day and those chickens *every* time I see a chicken. That image of them sitting on the counter, and the shock and laughter of those women who had been so stern, have never left me. Their harshness disappeared and they became warm and inviting. Those chickens enhanced my life. They opened the kibbutz world of Hebrew and friendship and family to me, offering all I needed to understand kibbutz life. I had sufficient experience to know my work was here in America and that I would always have a home on my kibbutz.

RABBI ALAN SILVERSTEIN is the rabbi of Congregation Agudath Israel in Caldwell, New Jersey. He is a past president of the Rabbinical Assembly and of the World Council of Conservative Synagogues.

"During an extremely brief trip in the summer of 2006, I felt for the first time as though I truly had penetrated the soul of the Jewish state. I learned the truth of the adage, 'One does not fully comprehend Israel until he or she is present at the funeral of a fallen soldier'.... Israelis told us time and again, 'The Arabs have twenty-three Arab states and fifty Muslim states on their side. All we have is you, the Jews of the Diaspora'."

Over the past thirty-five years I have been privileged to spend dozens of occasions in Israel: for spiritual nourishment, for personal study, in celebration of life-cycle ceremonies, visiting my relatives, pursuing projects on behalf of Masorti/Conservative Judaism, to show solidarity with Israeli under siege, as part of Jewish identity-raising "missions," and much more. During an extremely brief trip in the summer of 2006, I felt for the first time as though I truly had penetrated the soul of the Jewish state. I learned the truth of the adage, "One does not fully comprehend Israel until he or she is present at the funeral of a fallen soldier."

On Wednesday, August 1, Michael Levin, age twenty-two, the son of my family's closest friends, was fatally wounded by Hezbollah sniper fire in southern Lebanon. Michael was an American *oleh* (new immigrant), one of 2,300 *chayalim bodedim* (lone soldiers) whose families had remained in the Diaspora. He had risen in the ranks to become an officer in an elite paratrooper unit, a sharpshooter, and a courageous warrior. My wife, my daughter, and I accompanied Michael's loving parents, his two sisters, and one other household of intimates to Israel for the burial at Mt. Herzl Military Cemetery in Jerusalem. Amid our boundless grief we witnessed a profound out-pouring of love.

The image of Israeli military and governmental toughness melted before our eyes. Starting with the moment of personally noti-fying Michael's loved ones of his passing, at no time was the Levin family left without advocates. The Israeli Consul General in Philadelphia, El Al personnel, and the military's bereavement unit made it clear: "Rabbi, please encourage Michael's family not to have even a moment's hesitation in asking for any special consideration. Nothing is either too large or too small. We are here to give as much comfort as is humanly possible."

We feared that Michael's funeral would be a poorly attended, stark military service. At the Levin family's request, I prepared a eulogy. We waited for the other details to unfold. To our amaze-ment, on Tisha B'Av (the commemoration of the destruction of the First and Second Temples in Jerusalem) 5766, two to three thousand people attended. It was a sea of Am Yisrael: religious and secular, old and young, *olim* (immigrants to Israel) and sabras (native Israelis). It was an outpouring of Jewish unity by people who had loved Michael and by many more who had never even met him. Theirs was a collective expression of the message the Levins received throughout the trip: "The entire State of Israel is with you in your grief. Michael is our family member, too."

My stereotypic view of the Israeli army also was changed forever. The IDF is deservedly known for its toughness, not its compassion. Yet the soldiers in Michael's elite paratrooper unit exhibited profound love and admiration for him. Their raw emotions and genuine grief bonded them powerfully to the Levin family. "We will forever regard Michael as one of us." *Shiva* (condolence) visits by the unit commander and by military brass affirmed that Michael's sacrifice would be remembered. Future Israeli soldiers will learn about his life and courage and be inspired by his example.

In the midst of war on the home front, Israeli society briefly came to a stop to pay deference. Israelis told us time and again, "The Arabs have twenty-three Arab states and fifty Muslim states on their side. All we have is you, the Jews of the Diaspora." Loneliness forged Israel's bond with Michael, a "lone soldier." Press and television hungered for contact with the grieving Levin family. Israelis from all walks of life came to our hotel to touch and be touched by Michael's courage. A retired commander of Michael's unit walked ten miles on Shabbat to pray with us at our hotel. The El Al staff came into the cabin to embrace their bereaved passengers. And Israel's President Moshe Katzav conveyed personally to Mark and Harriet Levin, "I express deep consolation to you and to all of your relatives on behalf of the entire citizenry of the State.... Our hearts are with you."

As we boarded the airplane, forty-eight hours after our arrival, to return to the *shiva* (mourning period) in Bucks County, Pennsylvania, we had been transformed by a cleansing experience. All of us felt a powerful sense of true *nehama* (comfort). We painfully realized that nothing can ever reverse Michael's death or replace his remarkable *neshama* (soul). However, our connection to the depths of soul of Am Yisrael affirmed the validity of Michael's sacrifice and made clear that his legacy shall remain as a source of blessing.

DR. BETHAMIE HOROWITZ is a socio-psychologist and independent scholar who studies major issues facing the Jewish world. She writes the regular "Trend Spotting" column in the *Forward* about noteworthy developments affecting American Jewry.

"I've set up my adult life to include some regular commuting between New York and Israel.... It's an experience that keeps me steadily connected to both places and for me that is essential. I go back and forth between the East and the West, with parts of my heart both here and there."

My personal relationship with Israel was set in motion even before I was born, not least of all because my family roots there stretch back to the eighteenth century. My grandmother was the sixth generation of her family born in Safed, where she also married and bore the first two of her four children. Around 1912 she left Palestine for Vienna, the home of her husband's family, and lately I have come to the conclusion that in her own way she was on the vanguard of Israel's *yeridah* (emigration).

On top of that, my father was raised as so ardent a Hebraist that he could recite the "Song of Hiawatha" in Hebrew! With such aristocratic ancestry, Israel figured strongly in our family lore. There were vivid stories about growing up in the Galilee, riding a donkey to Beirut through the cedars of Lebanon that I imagined to be like the lush forests of the Pocono Mountains where I went to summer camp and learned Hebrew.

Then there's my name, *bat-ami*, meaning "daughter of my people," a phrase that can either beckon or challenge, depending on the circumstances. Thankfully my parents were mindful of the American context and chose Bethamie in English, thinking that any name with the sound of *bat* in it would quickly become a liability in a land of baseball and bats out of hell. On the other hand, *bat-ami* has quite a ring to the Hebrew ear, signaling a Jewish cultural sophistication atypical among American Jews.

When I arrived in Israel for the first time in 1971 as part of a high school exchange program, my Hebrew was nearly fluent, and with Israel already a cornerstone of my own emerging sense of self, I bounded eagerly into the world around me. But there was a surprising rub. Whatever Zionist dreams I had imbibed, it was all the more shocking to realize during those months at the Hebrew Gymnasium, despite my great efforts to shed my accent, that I was really an American Jew.

This was hard to take, as it placed me lower down in the pecking order than the sabras [native-born Israelis] who by virtue of their active building of the Jewish state lived on an elevated plane, while we went back to our cushy lives in America's suburbs and the specter of an ever-thinning Jewishness.

Decades have passed, and Israel no longer stands in the same place. There is a sense of decline that comes from the falling away of archetypes. This is a big change to which we American Jews continue to adjust. We're filled with nostalgia as we look back on the old black-and-white photographs in the collective family album. The shadows were giant, the bodies muscular, and the hair still dark. But it's not where we are today.

The old model of aliyah and ascent placed Israel on center stage high up above the rest of world Jewry, while we were just waiting in the wings. It may be liturgically correct, but it fails to describe my own experience, filled as it is with regular forays to and from Israel. For me at least, the relationship has flattened out and become more equalized.

I've set up my adult life to include some regular commuting between New York and Israel—along with the Israeli dot-commers, the Jewish educators and philanthropists, the Hasidim and the young people on their post-army treks. It's an experience that keeps me steadily connected to both places and for me that is essential. I go back and forth between the East and the West, with parts of my heart both here and there.

WAYNE L. FIRESTONE is the president and CEO of Hillel: The Foundation for Jewish Campus Life. He traces his first Zionist act to the sale of his comic book collection at a synagogue fundraiser following the 1973 Yom Kippur War.

"I now suspect that the most telling measure of the rise or decline of our civilization—indeed, of any civilization—may lie in its ability to perpetually create and not merely survive. For me, this is one of the most endearing legacies of Zion. No mere dream, it continues to inspire passion, learning, and possibility."

I was utterly smitten on my inaugural trip to Israel in 1982. I awakened as a teenager to the provocative notion that I was connected to something purposeful and larger than myself. Like many of the travelers before and after me, I started to excavate shards from multi-civilizations and discovered one repetitive artifact in our text, metaphor, and memory—creation.

Several years later I returned to Ben Gurion Airport, a sheepish *oleh chadash* (new immigrant), accompanied by my less naïve Hebrew-speaking wife and our mixed-breed dog, Negev. During an initial absorption period on a kibbutz, I feared that I was woefully handicapped—linguistically, culturally, and professionally. My first few Hebrew assignments quickly confirmed my suspicions.

My most informative guide emerged in the form of a similarly constrained Russian immigrant who shared with me a hand-me-down recipe utilizing *Ha-shaar*, a beginner's newspaper, replete with helpful vowels. He recommended a disciplined routine of repetitive oral recitation of the daily headlines, news, and often macabre humor.

For more than two thousand years of *galut* (exile), Hebrew connected the scattered tribe in prayer and thought and sustained an enchantment—if not unification—that connected a land, faith, and people. Now physically reunited in this ancient land, a revitalized language incubates expressions for new technologies and wonderments.

Organically more than defiantly, Israelis explore, imagine, and create in fields, ranging from orchestral composition and nanotechnology to light wave harmonics and the Hebrew prophets. This innovative spirit is not confined to those researching doctoral dissertations or working in sterile laboratories. For example, secular and religious students at Jerusalem's Hebrew University mix ancient texts and modern melodies to generate original contemporary music. Even more recent source material—bumper stickers and graffiti—are magically converted into lyrics for a popular hip-hop band considered "hip" on today's American college campus radio stations.

These oft-maligned Israeli scientists, artists, philosophers, and educators may contribute more to humanity (not to mention world Jewry) than any other nation per capita. Far too often, it seems the best of these folk are concealed beneath the headlines of the worst stories. Conversely, our history also suggests that many of our best stories are buried by the hands of the worst characters.

I now suspect that the most telling measure of the rise or decline of our civilization—indeed, of any civilization—may lie in its ability to perpetually create and not merely survive. For me, this is one of the most endearing legacies of Zion. No mere dream, it continues to inspire passion, learning, and possibility.

Barbara B. Balser of Atlanta, Georgia, was the first woman and the first Southerner to serve as National Chair of the Anti-Defamation League.

"The mitzvah and obligation of aiding and contributing to a safe, growing, and healthy homeland for the Jewish people became a part of our family's expectations and way of life—and ultimately, my way of life. Those values accompanied me into adulthood."

Expressing my passion for Israel is challenging, because on many levels my feelings regarding Israel are so deep and emotional. But, here goes …

I grew up in Richmond, Virginia, during the 1940s and 1950s. In those days Jews, particularly in the South, were neither as secure nor as accepted as they are today. We Jews were few in number and, by and large, we socialized among ourselves. From a certain perspective, it could be said that we, too, were segregated from the greater society; however, our segregation was far less severe than that of our black brothers and sisters.

The hope and dream of a Jewish state, a homeland for the remnant that survived the Nazi terror and also a haven for Jews everywhere, were topics of constant discussion—not only in our household but also throughout the Jewish community. I remember quite clearly the joy and pandemonium when the United Nations granted the partition of Palestine and, later, when President Truman officially recognized Israel as a state.

My parents, Vivian and Ellis Bernstein, were involved in many Zionist efforts, and I, like so many others, recall our family's little blue boxes (the Jewish National Fund canisters for collecting money for Israel), planting trees and buying Israel Bonds, and the importance of learning everything we could about modern Israel. Our teachers at Temple Beth El focused on trying to teach us how to speak contemporary Hebrew. We proudly learned the latest Israeli folk songs and dances, which we could only imagine were being created and enjoyed by sabras (native Israelis) living in the new world of kibbutzim. What exciting and romantic notions of Israel we young people shared—regarding the purity and wonder of building a new country with new rules, a safe harbor for Jews, in the very heart of the Middle East on that very land that G-d had reserved for us!

The mitzvah and obligation of aiding and contributing to a safe, growing, and healthy homeland for the Jewish people became a part of our family's expectations and way of life—and ultimately, my way of life. Those values accompanied me into adulthood.

My parents are gone now, but each time I respond to concerns about Israel; each time I visit there and feel the love of Israelis for their country and their land; each time I visit with Israeli leaders and listen to their strong and principled commitments to their future and their desires for peace, I know how proud and happy

Mother and Dad would be to know how long-lasting and deeply their dreams and aspirations for a Jewish homeland have permeated my life.

Several years ago on one of our Anti-Defamation League missions to Israel, I was introduced to Tzipi Livni, a minister in Prime Minister Ariel Sharon's cabinet. I could not and cannot help but be immediately impressed with Tzipi's strength, intelligence, and determination. She tells it like it is—a quality I admire in anyone and particularly appreciate in other women.

Tzipi is a sabra, one of those resilient forces of nature about whom I romanticized as a child. She is a dreamer, a visionary, and a realist. As Tzipi recently told Steven Erlanger of the *New York Times*, she understands "the need to preserve Israel as a homeland for the Jewish people and to [preserve] our democratic values." In that article, she described her mother's expectations of her—that it was Tzipi's "duty to do what is right for generations to come." Finally, she observed: "The Jewish question was resolved by the establishment of Israel … Jews, including refugees from the Holocaust, could find a home there."

Sixty years later, this determined cabinet minister—a sabra, a woman totally committed to the safety and future of her country, our Jewish homeland, our safety net in this world that sometimes seems so overrun with bigotry and hatred—was reflecting on the very same values, lessons, and concerns my parents taught me so many years ago.

L'dor va-dor, "from generation to generation," our commitment to the past, present, and future is a constant and encompassing theme of our people. It was the inspiration of my parents, it was the fire in the belly of Arik Sharon and other leaders, founders, and fighters for the State of Israel, and it is the wind beneath the wings of Tzipi Livni and others who must guide Israel in the days and months and years ahead. May G-d grant them wisdom, strength, good health, and long lives to complete their work of securing safety and peace for the people of Israel and for the Jews of the world.

JAMES J. KATZ is currently a sophomore at the University of Pennsylvania and is planning on double majoring in Cognitive Science and PPE (Philosophy, Politics and Economics.)

"In Israel, my Jewishness was not tolerated or even encouraged, but simply taken for granted.... I think of Israel, not as a place to live when I'm old, or to be buried after I die. I think of Israel as a place to raise my children."

One of my earliest memorable trips to Israel, one summer with my family, I related the following observation to my mother.

"Ma, there are so many young Jews here."

I suppose I have to explain myself: I grew up in sunny Miami, Florida, where (as one of my high school friends liked to point out) "old Jews come to die." So my surprise at seeing so many young Jews is hardly surprising. Paradoxically, one could say that Israel is where dead Jews go to be buried, given the large number of coffins arriving at Ben Gurion International Airport every year.

However, when I think of what Israel means to me, I tend not to think of the coffins, or that my parents, currently residing in Miami, have, as my father likes to say, "invested in real estate," in the ancient Mount of Olives cemetery in Jerusalem.

When I think of Israel, I think of the year that I spent there, when I took time off in between high school and college. During that time, I studied at Yeshivat Har Etzion, an Orthodox yeshiva, and roomed with Israelis just out of high school. They were the same age as I was and were preparing to enter the Israeli army. I, on the other hand, was already accepted to the University of Pennsylvania and had every intention of going back to earn a bachelor's degree. Although at first there was somewhat of a language barrier between us (Hebrew not being my native tongue), we found we had a lot in common and became close friends.

I spent Shabbat at my Israeli friends' houses in different cities and communities all over Israel. I found home in Tel Aviv (which reminded me of my native Miami), Hoshaya (a small town in the Galilee,) Rechavia (a neighborhood in Jerusalem,) and several other places in Israel. I suppose it was then that I first seriously considered living in Israel long term. No matter where I was in Israel, I felt at ease.

The entire country was set up for my preferences of religious worship, my day of rest, and my holidays. During my stay in Israel, there was never a time when I could not participate in an activity, or had to make a special excuse for doing something Jewish, or simply felt awkward for "religious reasons." In Israel, my Jewishness was not tolerated or even encouraged, but simply taken for granted.

But that wasn't the only reason I seriously considered living there.

Every single one of my friend's families shared a dream. It was our people's millennia-old vision of a strong, peaceful, and proud Israel, offering its culture, its science, and its positive moral example to the world.

Unfortunately, certain parts of the dream had yet to be fulfilled. Although there was no shortage of proud Israelis, peace in the region remained elusive. This was the very reason that my Israeli friends had to serve in the army. The fact that they were there giving up some of the best years of their lives, taking practical steps to make our nation's dream a reality, made me decide to apply whatever talents and skills *I* possessed to making a positive difference in our people's national destiny. I didn't want to watch the History Channel's special on the Six Day War, feel proud, write a check to a worthy cause in Israel, and then go about my business. I wanted to be working for the cause that people donated to.

And where better to make a positive difference for the Jewish nation than in the Jewish state? I would be able to take part in every aspect of Israeli life. I would, like my Israeli friends, take practical steps to bring our utopian dream a little bit closer. Additionally, by merely living and working there, I would automatically make a contribution to the nation's gross domestic product.

Today, as I write this from my off-campus apartment in Philadelphia, I think of Israel. Just last week I sat in on a lecture that was given during Shavuot, and I naturally could not take notes in accordance with the rest-inducing restrictions of the holiday. I want my children to be able to feel completely at home and unburdened in their surroundings. I think of Israel, not as a place to live when I'm old, or to be buried after I die. I think of Israel as a place to raise my children.

 MICHAEL BOGDANOW is an artist, lawyer, author, and musician. His contemporary spiritual works of art (including the cover of this book) are often inspired by Judaic texts and can be seen on www.MichaelBogdanow.com.

"Israel is the birthplace of both the Jewish people and the Jewish soul…. Our collective memory of Israel, and our connection to it has never ended."

My paintings are often inspired by the color, feel, history, and meaning of Israel. From *Lech Lecha* to *Jerusalem Sunrise* shown on the cover of this book, I have used art to express what I cannot fully put into words.

The importance of Israel to me began in Houston, Texas, in the mid-1950s. It wasn't the center of the Jewish Diaspora, but it was a cool place in which to grow up Jewish. My family combined Reform Judaism and Zionism when the two were at odds and attended Temple Emanuel, a pro-Israel breakaway from the more classical Reform congregation. My own Judaism maintained these roots, and incorporated a large dose of Martin Buber.

In July 1968 I informed my single-parent mother that I wanted to make aliyah at the ripe old age of almost fourteen. She told me to give it a try and, if I lasted a year, she'd join me. A few months and immigration schools later, tail between my legs, I returned home. Fortunately I had experienced Israel at a relatively peaceful time, with the nation exuding the self-confidence that followed the Six Day War.

In 1971 I returned for a year to attend the Institute for Youth Leaders from Abroad as a representative of Young Judea. Israel was still between wars, and there was an amazing calm. Rapport with

Israeli Arabs, ventures to East Jerusalem and to all four quarters of the Old City, and hitchhiking were the norm. It was a wonderful time to experience the magic of Jerusalem, the mystery of Safed, the beauty of Ein Gedi, and the translucent waters of Eilat and Sharm el Sheikh.

Israel is the birthplace of both the Jewish people and the Jewish soul throughout our three thousand years of travels to, in, and from it. We have been evicted from countries—never to return—and have risen, as in the Golden Age of Spain, only to fall, as during the Inquisition. But our collective memory of Israel and our connection to it has never ended.

You can be upset with a loved one. I am often annoyed by the resort to military solutions rather than mediated ones and the inability to resolve the difficult issues of Gaza and the West Bank. Being upset with a loved one doesn't diminish the love, and that is true for my love of Israel.

As for Israel's future, my dream is a time of peace with its neighbors so that everyone can enjoy the splendor of this small, historic piece of land at the crossway from Asia to Africa, and from the Middle East to Europe, a land that gave birth to religions and watched as its inhabitants abolished slavery and idolatry. My dream meets with the harsh reality of politics, war, blood feuds, and memories of loved ones lost in the conflict, but the world's greatest achievements are born of dreams.

PART II—REFUGE:

A REFUGE FROM ANTI-SEMITISM, A PLACE OF SAFETY

"Thus said King Cyrus of Persia: 'The Lord God has given me all the kingdoms of the earth, and has charged me with building Him a House in Jerusalem, which is in Judah. Any one of you of all His people, the Lord his God be with him and let him go up.'"

II Chronicles 36:23

 SHULAMIT REINHARZ is the Jacob Potofsky Chair of Sociology at Brandeis University, where she is also the head of the Hadassah-Brandeis Institute. The author of many books, including *The JGirl's Guide: The Young Jewish Woman's Handbook for Coming of Age* (with Penina Adelman and Ali Feldman, published by Jewish Lights), she is also a weekly columnist for the *Jewish Advocate* in Boston.

"I remain a vocal defender of much more than Israel's right to exist. Instead I argue for the necessity of its existence given the assault on Jews throughout history."

Because I have spent so much time this year on a book tour for *American Jewish Women and the Zionist Enterprise,* a volume I co-edited with Mark Raider, Israel has been on my mind even more than ever. In city after city, I have been talking about the particular role of American Jewish women in calling out to fellow Jews to understand the need for Zionism. I have discussed Emma Lazarus's insight that America could potentially not be the haven for the Jewish people in the same way it was a haven for others. How right she was, seen from a post-Holocaust vantage point. I have tried to explain that Hadassah, as created by Henrietta Szold, was more than a fund-raising organization. Rather, it began as an educational movement, encouraging American Jewish women to study their own history and to see that history as a mandate to serve the Yishuv. I have tried to describe the passionate and eccentric Irma Lindheim, who threw away her wealth to become a kibbutz member, and in so doing, carved out a concept of *hagshama atzmit* (self-realization). And then there's the next book I also talk about. This one represents a partnership with my husband and an Israeli colleague and offers an analysis of the writings of Manya Wilbushewitz Shohat, my heroine, a woman of the Second Aliyah who helped build the State.

These projects bring back a memory of when I was ten years old and asked to write a page about anything (unbeknownst to me, my teacher was submitting the page to a penmanship contest). Not knowing what to write, I walked over to the encyclopedia in my sixth grade classroom and copied a page about Israel. Proudly, my mother repeated the story to everyone.

I think it is fair to say that I was raised to "love" Israel. My parents moved there with me shortly after the Holocaust for a brief period and "loved" it. My attachment to Israel feels like a strand of DNA—deep, immutable, fundamental. I traveled there with my mother and brother as a twelve-year-old and fell in love with it again. I met a boy in the United States when I was fifteen years old and fell in love with him in part simply because he was an Israeli. I stayed in Israel during the Yom Kippur War, which felt like sharing the fate of the nation at its most difficult hour, itself an act of love. Later, when our daughters were born, we gave them Hebrew names and took them to Israel countless times. They now go to Israel on their own, as often as they can.

As an academic, however, I have tasks other than speaking about my own research. I also review the work of professors, including Israeli professors being evaluated for promotion. When I read some of these materials in the fields of history, sociology, or literature, I am taken aback. Reading an academic dossier recently of a literary critic at a prominent Israeli university, I winced when she wrote with conviction of the "disillusion with Israeli omnipotence after the bungling of the Yom Kippur War, the overturning of the national self-image from that of defenders to aggressors (in the Lebanon war of 1982) and the intifada in the occupied territories of the later 1980s...." The commitment that I feel and try to inculcate in my own audiences for the significance of the State of Israel is frequently undermined by the work of Israelis themselves. Some of these people make me feel naïve, as if I'm stuck in a time warp of Zionist enthusiasm. I feel threatened by their post-Zionism as much as I do by the anti-Zionism I see all over the world. I wince at the nonstop anti-Israeli sentiment I hear and see all over the world. It was painful to be in Madrid, for example, on the day of the Seder bombing in Netanya and not see any signs of sympathy for the Israelis. But it was also painful to hear from a Cuban official in Havana that Jews leave Cuba ostensibly for aliyah to Israel, but they actually only go there as a stopover on their way to immigration to the United States.

At one and the same time I feel pride in the freedom of speech and expression in Israel, and fear, bewilderment, and disorientation at the things being said. I feel grateful that after the collapse of the Soviet Union, Jews have more freedom of movement than before, but I feel annoyed at their use of Israel as a tool rather than a destination.

So where does this leave me? I remain a vocal defender of much more than Israel's right to exist. Instead I argue for the necessity of its existence given the assault on Jews throughout history. I remain intrigued by the question of whether a Jewish Diaspora should exist to give Jews options and to provide Israel with support from the outside. I remain fascinated by the possibility of peace between Israel and the Palestinians, a hard-to-fathom peace that will alter both societies in marvelous ways. And I remain devoted to having an open mind, visiting Israel as often as possible, and helping in the best ways I know how. Ultimately I feel privileged to be a Jewish woman alive during this most unusual time in history when there is actually a Jewish state. I want to make the most of that privilege.

ABRAHAM H. FOXMAN has been the national director of the Anti-Defamation League since 1987 and is world-renowned as a leader in the fight against anti-Semitism, bigotry, and discrimination and a staunch advocate for the State of Israel.

"For me, as a Holocaust survivor, as a committed Jew, as a fighter against anti-Semitism and for a better world, Israel remains a hope and a shining light."

For me the question of why Israel matters has two simple answers. I can't imagine Jewish life without it. And, I attribute, at least partially, almost all the positive gains in Jewish life over six decades to the existence of the Jewish state.

If we talk about Jewish security in a dangerous world, Israel is the living lesson of "Never Again!" Jews cannot afford to be powerless, and Israel represents many things, including Jewish power, in a cruel world.

If we talk about Jewish self-confidence and maturity in the United States, it is the pride and knowledge that Jews have in a democratic, successful, and strong country that plays a significant role in that self-perception.

If we talk about the survival of the Jewish people, it is not only the fact that there is a Jewish state that persuades me, but also the interaction between a strong Israel and a strong Jewish Diaspora that gives me optimism. I mean this not only in terms of security but also because of the dynamic interplay between Israel and Diaspora Jews on the cultural, educational, social, economic, and religious levels, which undoubtedly will generate new, creative Jewish values, ideas, and expressions.

For me, as a Holocaust survivor, as a committed Jew, as a fighter against anti-Semitism and for a better world, Israel remains a hope and a shining light. I am fully aware of the criticism of Israel from within and without, some of which is merited. But those criticisms pale in comparison to my attachment and belief in the Jewish state.

The hope I have for the future of humanity, for the future of my grandchildren, is intimately tied to my belief and faith in the future of the State of Israel. That is why I have taken my children to Israel time and again to reinforce their Jewish education and identity. I am now taking my grandchildren to Israel for the very same reason.

 **REPRESENTATIVE HENRY A. WAXMAN** is a congressman from California. In 2007 Representative Waxman became chairman of the Committee on Oversight and Government Reform, the principal investigative committee in the House. From 1997 to 2006 he served as ranking member of the committee, conducting investigations into a wide range of topics from the high cost of prescription drugs to waste, fraud, and abuse in government contracting.

"As a congressman, I am proud to have played a role in many of the events that impacted Israel in the last thirty years…. Israel has a right to exist as a Jewish state. As Americans and as Jews, it is important that we honor its origins and defend its future."

My connection to Israel began as a child. I remember the exuberance of my parents and relatives that a Jewish country had been born. The blue Jewish National Fund *pushke* (canister) became a permanent feature in our home, collecting coins to plant trees and build infrastructure in the budding state.

My ties grew even stronger when my daughter moved there to raise her family. When my granddaughter was nine, she wrote me a Father's Day note: "Dear Grandpa, Happy Father's Day. You are a wonderful Grandpa and a wonderful Congressman. You show the whole world that you love Israel so much and are trying to help and that means a lot to us and also to Israel."

As a congressman, I am proud to have played a role in many of the events that impacted Israel in the last thirty years. In 1977 my wife, Janet, and I sat in amazement listening to President Anwar

Sadat's speech before the Knesset extending his hand in peace. I attended the White House ceremonies for the Camp David Accords; the signing of the ill-fated Oslo Agreement; and the dinner in honor of diplomatic relations between Israel and Jordan with the late Prime Minister Yitzhak Rabin and King Hussein bin Talal. We were in Israel for the difficult disengagement from Gaza and again last summer as Hezbollah rockets rained down on Israeli cities.

I am especially proud of my efforts to help win the freedom of Jewish refugees seeking a haven in the Jewish state. Janet and I fought for the freedom of Soviet Jews, visited refuseniks, pressured Soviet leaders to allow them to leave, and celebrated the first flights to Ben Gurion. Janet was instrumental in the effort to help Syrian Jews emigrate. We were in Israel as the airlifts of Ethiopians arrived in Operation Solomon. It is astounding to see how modern Israeli society is truly a reflection of the varied traditions and trajectories of Jewish history.

The fact is that Israelis have taken many risks to build a peaceful future and fulfill the mandate of a Jewish homeland. Despite a backdrop of wars, boycotts, and constant regional turmoil, Israel has managed to generate a vigorous economy, a vibrant democracy, and a robust military and has made pioneering advances in technology and science. The majority of Americans value our strategic partnership with Israel because they appreciate these sacrifices. They recognize the need for allies and expertise in the face of Islamic terrorism, Iran's nuclear ambitions, and a distorted United Nations system that uniformly criticizes Israel while ignoring pressing international threats.

Unfortunately it took almost twenty years for the United Nations to abandon the canard that Zionism is a form of racism. Let's hope it won't take as long for the international community to acknowledge that anti-Zionism is patently anti-Semitic.

Israel has a right to exist as a Jewish state. As Americans and as Jews, it is important that we honor its origins and defend its future.

 **THANE ROSENBAUM** is the prize-winning author of *The Golems of Gotham, Second Hand Smoke,* and the novel-in-stories *Elijah Visible.* He is the John Whelan Distinguished Lecturer in Law at Fordham Law School, where he teaches courses in human rights, legal humanities, and law and literature, and also directs the Forum on Law, Culture & Society. His forthcoming book is an anthology entitled *Law Lit, from Atticus Finch to "The Practice": A Collection of Great Writing about the Law.*

"Israel is not just a nation. It is, even more so, a state of mind.... You don't have to ever board El Al to be obsessed with Israel's existence, to love it or hate it, to feel its gravitational weight as a magnet for both revulsion and romance, to know that without it, the world would be a very different place, a planet even more tilted and adrift than it is right now."

Israel is probably the only nation in the world where so many people who have never been there and might never visit also derive so much visceral and spiritual pleasure from knowing that it exists. It is a refuge for Jews when host countries become unstable and unsafe for a people already conditioned to recognize the signs of an exodus waiting to happen.

But bizarrely, the reverse is also true: Israel is probably the only nation in the world where so many people who have no intention to ever visit are animated by such intense animus over its very existence. What other nation has so many deniers and detractors who refuse to recognize its right to exist? How many other countries are so casually threatened to be wiped off the map and have their citizens driven into the Red Sea? It is so fashionable to speak of Israel as merely an experiment in statehood—a nation on probation, still incomplete and under review, awaiting final global approval that will never come.

And there are yet other people who fall in between—evangelical Christians who are not Jewish but who believe that the Promised

Land holds a place of special significance for both Christians and Jews. While they may never make a trip to Israel, they feel better knowing that the geographic hot spots and holy sites of the Old and New Testament remain under the watchful eyes of Jews. After all, whether it is Jesus or the Messiah who one day might return to resolve all theological doubts and set everything right, one thing is for certain: the portal of entry is more likely to be closer to Tel Aviv than Toledo.

The point is: for a nation that small, surrounded by so many warring, hostile neighbors for the entire sixty years of its existence, a strategic ally for some and a geographic nuisance for most others, Israel inspires little in the way of neutral feelings. Passions run wild and way out of proportion to its relative size, natural resources, and position on the planet. If an alien traveled to earth and was shown a map of the world and was asked to guess the one country where human emotion and public opinion were most heated and volatile, Israel wouldn't stand out as an obvious choice. It looks more like an afterthought than the center of the universe, which in so many ways it is.

Israel is not just a nation. It is, even more so, a state of mind. That's the bedrock of its geography, the map that it monopolizes, the mental space and energy it consumes like a burning bush. You don't have to ever board El Al to be obsessed with Israel's existence, to love it or hate it, to feel its gravitational weight as a magnet for both revulsion and romance, to know that without it, the world would be a very different place, a planet even more tilted and adrift than it is right now.

Rabbi Nina Beth Cardin is a writer and teacher whose books include *The Tapestry of Jewish Time: A Spiritual Guide to Holidays and Life-cycle Events* and *Tears of Sorrow, Seeds of Hope: A Jewish Spiritual Companion for Infertility and Pregnancy Loss* (Jewish Lights Publishing).

> "With all of my being at home in America, and America being at home in me, I know that one day I may be forced to leave. We can say 'It won't happen here'.... Truth be told, I sleep better at night knowing there is not just the Land of Israel, but the sovereign State of Israel, the national homeland of the Jewish people."

"There never was an is without a where." (*Writing for an Endangered World*, Lawrence Buell.)

I have two worlds, two homes, two "wheres" that hold and form and animate my "is." One is America, the other is Israel. They are the fertile fields that support my life, the places where I meet my pasts' history and myths, the places where I harvest the lands' ideals, visions, and beliefs, and use them to build the structure of my world.

My world is an interlacing of these two cultures, these two ways of being. In their individual fullness, in their distinctiveness, and in their commonality, they enliven each other. Knowing and living in the one allows me to better know and live in the other. I am both perpetual native and perpetual traveler, and see with the knowing and naïve eyes of both.

A funny thing about place is that while at first you live in it, eventually it lives in you. Location becomes portable. Wherever I go, then, America and Israel go with me.

That makes sense when it comes to America. I was born here and have lived here all my life. But I first set foot in Israel when I was fifteen years old. That didn't matter. For I first "lived in Israel" through the stories of my people and my family. My grandparents met in Israel and my mother was born there. It is, in a real way, my family's homestead. But even if it weren't, it would still feel like home.

It is, after all, the place where my people took root; the hot, dry land of the patriarchs, and the verdant land flowing with milk and honey. It is the place of my dreams and memories, the place I spent my childhood, millennia before I was born.

But there is more, beyond the way Israel forms my identity; beyond the way its ideals live inside me. There is another way I relate to Israel that is less dreamy, less spiritual.

With all of my being at home in America, and America being at home in me, I know that one day I may be forced to leave. We can say "It won't happen here"; we can say we are a nation of immigrants and that Jews belong here as much as anyone else. I can sing "The Star Spangled Banner" at the top of my lungs, pay my property taxes, and vote in every election, even in the off years. But Christmas is still a national holiday and the Senate still uses public dollars to hire a chaplain as its collective pastor, and the will of America sometimes bends.

So, truth be told, I sleep better at night knowing there is not just the Land of Israel, but the sovereign State of Israel, the national homeland of the Jewish people, my constant, comforting "where" for my ephemeral, fragile "is."

SENATOR RUSS FEINGOLD is a U.S. senator from Wisconsin.

"Israel is an oasis of faith for Jews in every corner of the world, and each of us finds it in our own way."

Israel is an oasis of faith for Jews in every corner of the world, and each of us finds it in our own way. Some of us are fortunate enough to be able to travel there, while others go in our minds and hearts. As a U.S. senator and member of the Senate's Foreign Relations Committee, I have taken a deep interest in Israel and the Middle East and how we can achieve a lasting peace in the region.

Much of this interest stems from my family's connection to Israel, including many close family members who have made Israel their permanent home. When I was nineteen years old, I first visited Israel with my father and the trip had an enormously powerful impact on me. I vividly remember our visit to the Western Wall, when I brushed up against a soldier carrying a machine gun under his jacket. At that moment, I felt for the first time, through the cold steel of a weapon, what it was like to exist in a society where a constant threat of violence exists. At that time I vowed I would not return to Israel until there was peace in the region—not realizing an unforeseen event would bring me back before then. I broke that vow one time, and one time only, for the sad occasion of Yitzhak Rabin's funeral in November 1995. The first time I visited Israel I was a young man. This time I returned much changed—I had become a senator and a father—but I still felt awe and the powerful presence of faith and hope, violence and conflict that continue to characterize the Jewish state.

Israel is a testament to the will of a people who believed in Theodor Herzl's words: "If you will it, it is not a dream." Under his leadership, the participants of the First Zionist Congress proved those words true. Although this would not be attained until fifty-one years after Herzl expressed his dream, Holocaust survivors and other persecuted Jews from around the world would finally have a homeland where they could seek refuge and build lives. Jews from around the world built the dream of Israel together, and now, no matter where they live, every Jew can still draw strength from Israel today.

HAROLD GRINSPOON is a real estate entrepreneur and the founder and principal partner of Aspen Square Management. He established the Harold Grinspoon Foundation (HGF) to promote Jewish life among young people, adults, and families in western Massachusetts. He is also a board member of the American Jewish Joint Distribution Committee and the birthright israel Foundation.

"Although anti-Semitism still exists, it is not nearly as virulent as it has historically been. There is no question in my mind that the creation of the State of Israel has played a vital role in changing that reality—not only in America but everywhere in the world. The creation of the State of Israel undoubtedly gives Jews greater dignity."

When I was a boy growing up in the Boston area, anti-Semitism was as common as penny candy. Neighborhood children would often pelt me with epithets like "kike," "Jew boy," and "Christ killer." Many of those kids were forbidden to play with me. Being Jewish was an act of defiance and fortitude.

Although anti-Semitism still exists, it is not nearly as virulent as it has historically been. There is no question in my mind that the creation of the State of Israel has played a vital role in changing that reality—not only in America but everywhere in the world. The creation of the State of Israel undoubtedly gives Jews greater dignity. Israel is critical to assuring that an event as disastrous as the Holocaust—that horrifying mix of stupendous cruelty and an indifferent world—never again befalls our people.

As the homeland of the Jewish people, Israel has absorbed wave after wave of immigrants: European refugees in its earliest days, followed by large numbers of Jews from the Arab world in the 1950s, Russian immigrants, and in recent years, Ethiopian Jews. I stand in awe of the success Israel has achieved in this ingathering of Jews— whether they are educated or illiterate, young or old, healthy or infirm. At the same time, I am aware of the enormous challenge of absorbing generation after generation of immigrants, of the work that still desperately needs to be done to assure that all Israelis be afforded the opportunity to attain a high level of education, gainful employment, and full participation in nation-building and people-building.

I travel to Israel at least twice a year, and I constantly encounter the variety and richness of life there. I cannot think of another country where people with such widely different experiences live in such proximity and intensity with each other. A yeshiva student from Brooklyn, a Falas Mora immigrant from Ethiopia, a Russian-born engineer, a German-born Holocaust pensioner, a teacher born in Libya, an Israeli-born soldier—all are likely to share a *sherut* (group taxi or jitney) together, squashed in elbow to elbow. Even more amazing: they are likely to start a conversation—about anything from politics, to God, to the weather. Each comes from a world unfathomable to the others, yet they communicate with each other. They are sure to disagree and to argue their respective points passionately. But above all, they believe that they share a common destiny and future. To me, that is the miracle of Israel.

But there is also a magic to Israel. I feel it particularly when I am in Jerusalem, that inimitable city of old walls and young people. I feel simultaneously steeped in both past and future. More deeply than anywhere else, I sense the continuity of the Jewish people—my people—through time. I am both humbled and emboldened by the years of Jewish spirit, mind, and heart that are inextricably linked with this city. I feel very much attached to it, very much in tune with it, and very committed to being part of that rich continuum.

I also love to visit the Galilee region, where I have had a chance to develop close relationships with outstanding people who have a sense of pioneering mission and dedication to nation-building. Through my philanthropy, I have had the privilege of getting to know local mayors, the head of the local hospital, and the president of a local college. These people dedicate themselves to making Israel a better place. I love meeting farmers from the moshavim and kibbutzim, as well as people starting small businesses. And then there are the kids—full of dreams and enthusiasm, anxious to learn and to make something of themselves, full of contagious energy.

I feel privileged to be able to participate in a small way in nation-building and people-building in Israel, mostly through the Harold Grinspoon Foundation, which I created in 1993 to enrich Jewish life in my own region of western Massachusetts and beyond. Through the foundation, we sponsor programs that promote educational excellence and entrepreneurship in a section of the Galilee. Our philanthropy in Israel has deepened my experience and exposure to Israeli society, and that has been both gratifying and stimulating. It is my way of paying my debt to the Jewish state for having shouldered the burden of responsibility for the Jewish people, and a way of participating in that responsibility.

I am also a major supporter of birthright israel because I believe that it is an important program that enriches young Jews by giving them the opportunity to visit Israel for free. It allows our younger generation to explore their Jewish identity and relationship to the Jewish state. Jews are not only safer because of the existence of the Jewish state, but, as thousands of birthright israel participants can attest, we are also incalculably enriched by its vitality.

At the same time, I feel tremendously fortunate to be an American, to be part of a society where I have had the opportunity to flourish as an entrepreneur and participate as a citizen in this great country that I so deeply love. America has allowed me to use my talents and creativity, and to enjoy its wealth. I take an active philanthropic part in helping those who are struggling in my local community. I do this by supporting projects that promote literacy in the inner city, encourage underprivileged kids to attend college, and help young people start their own businesses. I feel deeply privileged as a successful entrepreneur to be able to give back to both my country—America—and to my people, the Jewish people.

ALVIN H. ROSENFELD, professor of English and Jewish studies and the director of the Institute for Jewish Culture and the Arts at Indiana University, has written widely on Holocaust literature, contemporary anti-Semitism, and American Jewish writers. He is the editor of *The Writer Uprooted: Contemporary Jewish Exile Literature in America.*

"As a Jew devoted to Israel's welfare and keenly aware of the importance of the Jewish state to the Jewish people as a whole, I ask myself what I can do to contribute to the country's future.... So, while speaking out may entail a degree of risk, we must speak, both to counter those who are bent on defaming Israel and to convey to the increasingly maligned Israelis that they have friends abroad who respect and admire them and who stand by them."

My first visit to Israel, in 1965, followed on the heels of my first visit to Germany. I was a young graduate student at the time, searching to discover his place between two of the defining moments of the mid-twentieth century: the Nazi destruction of European Jewry and the reestablishment of Jewish political sovereignty in the ancestral homeland. I had book knowledge of both and firsthand experience of neither. A semester's teaching stint at the University of Kiel introduced me to Germany and revealed the complexities of a country whose destructive history I felt I needed to probe deeply. A semester's immersion in Hebrew language study in Jerusalem opened both my heart and my mind to a country that instantly filled me with wonder and, forever after, with interest and love.

I have been back to Israel many times over the years. The wonder has not diminished nor has my feeling of being privileged to live as a Jew at the time of the modern Jewish state's founding and flourishing. I remain awed by its people in all of their diversity and accomplishments but also troubled by the country's vulnerability and its still-embattled, increasingly threatened state. I also worry about a weakening from within, most especially the erosion of a sense of national purpose and direction, without which the way ahead becomes harder to envision and secure.

As a Jew devoted to Israel's welfare and keenly aware of the importance of the Jewish state to the Jewish people as a whole, I ask myself what I can do to contribute to the country's future. A number of answers present themselves—one of which carries a special urgency. We are once again facing a resurgent anti-Semitism, much of which manifests itself as a fierce anti-Zionism. At a time when Israel is regularly denounced by its enemies as being guilty of "racism" and "ethnic cleansing" and demonized through comparisons to Nazi Germany and apartheid South Africa; when numerous intellectuals commonly lend credence to this vilification through their own subversions of Israel's legitimacy and right to continued existence; when teachers' and journalists' unions in Great Britain and other trade unions elsewhere in Europe call for boycotts of Israeli scholars and goods; when church groups initiate divestment campaigns from companies that have business dealings with Israel; when the president of Iran convenes an international conference that calls into question the reality of the Holocaust and openly declares his will to enact a second Holocaust by wiping the Jewish state off the map with nuclear weapons—it becomes imperative to expose these threats and obscenities for what they are and argue vigorously against them. These days the stakes are high, and silence is simply not an option. So, while speaking out may entail a degree of risk, we must speak, both to counter those who are bent on defaming Israel and to convey to the increasingly maligned Israelis that they have friends abroad who respect and admire them and who stand by them.

Six decades after the founding of their state, the Jews of Israel should not have to argue for the legitimacy of their national existence. They are at home in their land by a long-established right, and they can take justifiable pride in their country's history and achievements. To join them in affirming as much in the face of an escalating torrent of publicly expressed ill will is the least that an *ohev Yisrael* (a lover of Israel), or any decent person, can do.

NAT HENTOFF writes for the *Village Voice, Washington Times*, and United Media Newspaper Syndicate. His books include *Boston Boy* and *The War on the Bill of Rights and the Gathering Resistance.*

"When I am asked to identify my religion, I answer: 'The Constitution of the United States.' I do not believe in a god, but I do believe I am a Jew—and therefore, what happens to Israel, happens to me."

One of my earliest boyhood memories is walking up the street where I lived in Boston, carrying a blue-and-white tin box collecting money for trees in (what was then Jewish) Palestine. At the time during the "Great" Depression, Boston was arguably the most anti-Semitic city in the country. Father Charles E. Coughlin's Sunday radio talks echoed *The Protocols of the Elders of Zion*. They were so popular that sporting events were arranged so as not to conflict with them. A Jewish boy who walked the streets, including his own "ghetto" at night, did so at his peril.

Listening on the radio to the beginnings of the Holocaust—William Shirer reporting from Berlin—I knew that the trees I'd been collecting money for meant more than trees.

In Israel, during the 1980s, I interviewed, as a reporter, several of the Army colonels who had started the Peace Now movement (all had fought in Israel's previous wars)—and I began to hope that maybe there could be a two-state solution.

However, after the *intifadas* and the suicide bombers, it was clear to me that Abba Eban was right: "The Palestinians never miss an opportunity to miss an opportunity," and I finally became a strong supporter of Ariel Sharon. (If only he were to wake up now!)

When I am asked to identify my religion, I answer: "The Constitution of the United States." I do not believe in a god, but I do believe I am a Jew—and therefore, what happens to Israel happens to me.

 **Assemblyman Dov Hikind** has served the 48th Assembly District in New York since 1982. He has earned a reputation for being an outspoken advocate for his constituency, battling discrimination, anti-Semitism, Holocaust denial, and human rights violations.

"Israel stands as a bulwark against the inconceivable—the systematic annihilation of Jews. Israel is where Jews will always be welcomed, where the value of every Jewish life is immutable."

When I am in Israel I am whole; elsewhere my soul is fractured. I breathe differently, I think differently, I exist differently. Yet I also love the United States, country of my birth, and the grace it has extended to our people and to all people of the world.

At some moments, I am humbled by how extraordinary the United States is, how a first-generation American, the son of Holocaust survivors, came to sit in the State Legislature of New York for the last twenty-five years. When my mother, Frieda, at sixteen, stood before Dr. Mengele at the *Selektion* in Auschwitz, while her sister and mother were directed to the left and the line of death, could she have believed that she would bear a child who would stand proudly as a Jew in the corridors of law and justice? I've shown senators, congressman, and even a First Lady the numbers my mother has tattooed on her arm. The numbers are one in a series of millions who were marked for death in a world where law and order reigned—a law and order contrived by one of the most advanced and cultured nations in history and the most maniacal.

Israel stands as a bulwark against the inconceivable—the systematic annihilation of Jews. Israel is where Jews will always be welcomed, where the value of every Jewish life is immutable. Our grandparents hoped that that place of welcome would be Europe. It wasn't. We, as grandparents, hope the United States will be a true *medina shel chesed* (a place of lovingkindness). We can only hope.

Israel is the dwelling of our forefathers. It remained their passion and their sacrifice, a reflection of God's divinity on earth. It is our passion and our sacrifice, as well; our eternal link to the past and the future. Israel's well-being is the well-being of every Jew around the world, the only true sanctuary we will ever have in a world torn asunder by evil and hatred. The embers of anti-Semitism have been reignited in Europe where, once again, it can be unsafe for a Jew to venture into the streets of France, England, Belgium, and Germany.

I live by what happens in Israel, bearing her pain and disappointments as my own. I am intimately involved in her security and survival. I have been to Israel more than one hundred times—north, south, east, and west, from one end of the country to the other.

I was there on the eve of disengagement in Gaza, in northern Israeli cities as katyushas fell, delivering food to residents huddled in bunkers, and for the funerals of terror victims—to comfort parents, husbands, wives, children, grandparents. It is almost too much to bear, but then it is not, because of those numbers on my mother's arm—just one in a series. It is almost too much to bear, but then it is not, because Israel is no less a part of me than my arm, which only by the grace of God will never be tattooed in a series.

STEPHEN M. FLATOW lives in New Jersey and has been involved in Jewish communal affairs for many years.

"We, Jews from the Diaspora and Israelis, were in the same cultural and religious boat."

I believe I have always been connected to Israel. I was born a few months after its creation and I have vivid memories of the blue Jewish National Fund *pushke* (canister) in my mother's kitchen. Although Israel's victory in the 1967 war unleashed waves of pride, it was not until my oldest daughter, Alisa, began to attend day school that I began to intellectually understand what Israel meant to the Jewish people and me.

Alisa was the first in my immediate family to travel to Israel—beating her parents by three years. She was eleven years old, and she came back from a two-week trip excited about Israel and asking, "When can I go again?"

My first trip in 1987 followed much of the same itinerary as any traveler—the *Kotel* (Western Wall), Tiberias, Safed, Hebron, and so on. I came away from that trip with an understanding that we, Jews from the Diaspora and Israelis, were in the same cultural and religious boat.

Each of our five children made successive trips to Israel. I have noticed that children and young adults who spend time in Israel come back not just as better Jews because of the intensity of their experience, but as better people as well. Something happens to them in Israel that puts the world in perspective. I don't know if it is the size of the country (much like New Jersey where I live) or that life in Israel, which always seems to be precarious, causes a Diaspora Jew to stop and think about what is important.

That became even more important to me when Arab terrorists murdered Alisa while she was on her sixth trip to Israel in April 1995. Alisa had taken a leave of absence from Brandeis University to study Torah at an educational institution called Nishmat in Jerusalem. Unlike her sisters and many of her friends who went to Israel to study immediately after high school, Alisa wanted to study on her own terms. She wanted to live in an apartment, walk the streets, shop in the *shuk* (the Arab bazaar), and study the subjects that interested her.

Deciding to take a short vacation before Passover, she was on her way to a resort in Gush Katif when her bus was bombed outside the settlement of Kfar Darom. Seven others died as a result of that attack.

Many people are surprised that we do not blame Israeli policies of the time for Alisa's death. Terrorists murdered her for one reason— she was a Jew. That morning, Alisa was doing nothing more than riding in a bus full of Israelis. She was asleep, possibly dreaming about what it would be like to have a few days in the sunshine before Passover.

Flying to Israel to be with her, I arrived at her bedside just one hour before the doctors determined that she was brain dead. We decided to donate Alisa's organs for transplant—an act that created an uproar in Israel because of the widespread belief that Jews cannot donate organs—and we started a scholarship fund to assist other Diaspora students to study in Israel.

We have been called brave and heroic, but I believe that our actions after Alisa's death were a form of payback to the people of Israel who would invite our daughter for a Shabbat meal and who send their children into military service on Israel's borders. It was also a "thank you" to the taxi and bus drivers who wished her a *Shabbat shalom* or *chag sameach* (happy holiday) and to the people who demonstrate on a daily basis that the Jewish nation and faith are alive and vibrant after four thousand years of history.

SAMUEL HEILMAN holds the Harold Proshansky Chair in Jewish Studies at the Graduate Center and is Distinguished Professor of Sociology at Queens College of the City University of New York.

"I found myself in a Jewish state and in its capital, I discovered that what made me feel at home was finding a place where being called a Jew was not something that made me stand out, but rather something that made me feel included and an insider."

Like many Jews of my generation, the anxieties that preceded the outbreak of the 1967 war and the feelings of awe that followed it moved Israel into the center of my consciousness. I took my first trip there in 1968 with my then-fiancée, and I marveled at how the Hebrew I had learned in school came alive in the streets and how the places that were in Bible stories were not just names in a book or part of some remote past, but locations in which I could place myself. Those were days when the entire country was enchanted with the Bible, as it explored the Old City of Jerusalem, Hebron, and the many sites that were part of what soon came to be called Judea and Samaria. Yet more than all of this, in Israel I sensed a feeling that here I was in a place that I had never been before, but that felt uncannily familiar—populated by people who felt closer to me than many of those who inhabited the Boston suburb in which I had grown up. To be sure, as an immigrant child of Holocaust survivors and an Orthodox Jew, I had always felt like a bit of an outsider in Irish Catholic Boston, but in Israel that alien feeling was diminished.

Nevertheless I did not return to Israel for more than eleven years. Like so many others who have visited once, I considered Israel important but had made my life elsewhere. Then in 1979, on my first sabbatical, I brought my wife and our three children at the time back for a year. That encounter changed my relationship to the land, which since then we have visited more times than I can count. It is a place where today my children, who went to school there, have come to call home. Several have served in the Israeli army; two have married Israelis; and I have no doubt that in addition to the two who live there now, the other two will, in time, find their ways to live there as well. For my children, Israel is an inextricable part of their identity and background. For my wife and me, it is a second home.

It is hard to think of a single moment when all this came together for me, but one in particular stands out. It happened during that first sabbatical. We had sent our belongings by boat from the United States and it was delayed in arriving in Jerusalem, where we were spending the year while I worked on a book. I went into the shipping office downtown to check on its progress. While I was sitting at his desk, the clerk picked up a phone to call the port to find out when the boat was due. I listened as he inquired of the voice at the other end of the line: "There's a Jew here who wants to know where his boxes are," he began in Hebrew, and then went into the details.

I thought about that. This man used the word "Jew" to describe me. Had a shipping clerk said this in the United States. I would have run to the Anti-Defamation League to complain about the implied prejudice in his inquiry. But here in Israel, he used "Jew" as a synonym for "fellow."

That was the dream of Zionism fulfilled: a country where the term "Jew" was a synonym for "fellow," where its use was not an expression of scorn. That was what I had been looking for, and I had never known it. But now that I found myself in a Jewish state and in its capital, I discovered that what made me feel at home was finding a place where being called a Jew was not something that made me stand out, but rather something that made me feel included and an insider.

For the Jewish people, it works the same way: as a people, having a Jewish state makes us feel that we are fully included in the nations of the world, and it reclaims our national identity for us and makes it whole. Jews are no longer outsiders, sojourners, a wandering people always in the minority; in Israel we are home and full-fledged citizens of the world order.

 **REPRESENTATIVE DEBBIE WASSERMAN SCHULTZ** is the first Jewish woman to represent Florida in the U.S. Congress. She serves on the House Committee on Appropriations (where she chairs the Legislative Branch Subcommittee), on the Committee on the Judiciary, and as a Chief Deputy Whip.

"I have learned much as a public servant about Israel's strategic importance to America, but as a Jew, I now realize how important Israel is to our continuity as a people."

I grew up in a secular Jewish household. The importance of being Jewish and our cultural traditions were always stressed, but the religious aspects of Judaism were not a regular part of my life. I viewed Israel growing up as a place for religious people. I knew it was an important and vital place for Jews, but I hadn't experienced personally why this was the case. That perception changed during my first trip to Israel as a participant in a young leaders program sponsored by the American Jewish Committee in 1995, when I was a Member of the Florida House of Representatives. Since then, I have traveled to Israel two more times, once as a participant in the International Conference of Jewish Ministers and Members of Parliament and another as a panel speaker for the American Jewish Congress. I have learned much as a public servant about Israel's strategic importance to America, but as a Jew, I now realize how important Israel is to our continuity as a people.

The first time I walked alone down a city street in Jerusalem, I was enveloped by a slow realization: for the first time in my life, despite growing up in, and living as an adult in, two communities with large Jewish populations, I was in the majority. The bus drivers were Jewish; the taxi drivers were Jewish; the store clerks were Jewish—the majority of people around me on the street were all Jewish. This revelation was important for me, not because I felt discomfort in the minority, but because although it had been verbalized to me many times in my life, the reality of our homeland hit me square in the face. Jews have a homeland in Israel. My heart filled with the realization that if, G-d forbid, there was any threat to our safety as Jews, anywhere in the world, we had a place to go. I took great comfort in that knowledge.

Some Jews in the Diaspora have the ability to practice our religion freely, participate culturally as Jews, and educate ourselves and raise our children in our traditions. But thousands of Jews across the globe do not share that freedom. Israel's existence makes it possible for all Jews to have a place where all things are possible for us. That knowledge, whether it is in the back of our minds as citizens of free nations or knowledge needed at a moment's notice for a Jew in a more restrictive environment, is crucial to our continuity and our existence through the generations.

 **DANNY MASENG** is one of the most popular composers of contemporary Jewish liturgical music. He is an actor, singer, songwriter, teacher, and scholar based in New York City and he travels around the world performing and teaching Judaism and the love of Israel.

"I cannot imagine my life without Israel and I would not count on the survival of the Jewish people—spiritually, psychologically, or physically—without Israel."

Born and raised in Israel, I spent the first twenty-five years of my life there. My family has been intimately connected to the Land of Israel since 1917, when my great-grandfather Sh'muel Bloom, an ardent Zionist dreamer, began purchasing land in Palestine. My grandfather, Rabbi Harry S. Davidowitz, a graduate of The Jewish Theological Seminary, made aliyah in 1934 and was deeply involved in writing the first draft of Israel's Declaration of Independence. Unable to practice as a rabbi in his ancestral homeland, he was the first to translate the complete works of Shakespeare into Hebrew and received the Tchernichovsky Award. My grandmother, Ida Davidowitz, was the first theater critic of the *Jerusalem Post* and Henrietta Szold's assistant at Youth Aliyah. My father, a righteous gentile, was recruited for Israel's War of Independence, served in its nascent Air Force as a squadron commander, and later converted to Judaism. He married my mother in Tel Aviv, the city of my birth.

I learned the value of loss and the quality of sacrifice in Israel. I learned the intoxicating taste of the earth and the price needed to extract its goodness in Kibbutz Sarid, where my first child was born. In Tel Aviv I smelled the sea and fell asleep to its crashing waves; I awoke each morning to the cooing of the turtle doves on my grandmother's windowsill. I drank Hayyim Nahman Bialik, Shaul Tchernichovsky, Natan Alterman, and Avraham Shlonsky together with Leah Goldberg and Rachel's poetry, from all of whom I learned the beauty and the terseness of the Hebrew language. My father walked me over David's bones, through Solomon's mines, to Saul's final battlefield; my mother showed me Rachel's tomb and our lost family plot through blurry old binoculars; my grandparents showed me the orphaned mosque of Hassan Ali and the Church of the Ascension and spoke of the Nashashibis and other Palestinian families they knew and loved before the land was torn apart and history deposited fragmented souls on opposite sides of the ever-widening chasm.

I have lived through four of Israel's many wars and participated actively in two of them. All that I know about my art I learned in Israel from a host of brilliant performers, directors, and musicians, all generous to a fault with their time and wisdom. Amos Oz is still my moral compass, Yehuda Amichai still the poet of my soul's landscape, and Sasha Argov still the composer of the music I dream to write. The Bible is the ground upon which I walk, and the Sea of Galilee still leaves me speechless each time my pilgrimage brings me to its shores.

I cannot imagine my life without Israel and I would not count on the survival of the Jewish people—spiritually, psychologically, or physically—without Israel. In the fullness of time I would love to find myself as committed to Israel and as inextricably entwined with her destiny as my teachers Sister Magdalit and Reverend Petra Held, Chayim and Rachel Paz from Kibbutz Degania Aleph, and my friends Ehud Manor and Natan Yonatan, who have already returned their God-given clay to God's earth.

Michael Walzer is professor of social science at the Institute for Advanced Study in Princeton, New Jersey, and co-editor of *Dissent*. His books include *Just and Unjust Wars*, *Spheres of Justice*, *On Toleration*, and *Arguing About War*.

"I understood very clearly what these people [religious Sephardic Egyptian Jews and secular Polish Jews] had in common. They shared the hope for a place where they could live in safety and feel at home, as Jews who prayed and as Jews who didn't pray. And for them there was no other place."

In June 1957 I made my first visit to Israel. A young man, newly married, with my wife and two friends, I undertook what became in time (one version of) an American Jewish tour. We were students without much money; we drove across Europe in an old car, staying in youth hostels and cheap hotels, stopping to visit the site of the Dachau death camp (and hurrying away), wandering more easily through ancient ruins in Athens, and then sailing from Piraeus to Haifa. Seen from a sufficiently distant perspective, it was an ordinary journey, and certainly it has been made often enough since the 1950s. For me, though, it was extraordinarily moving—and not only for the expected reasons.

The ship on which we had booked passage months earlier turned out to be a refugee ship that had started its voyage from Genoa. We were the only Piraeus additions and the only paying passengers. The others were Egyptian Jews, fleeing (via Italy) in the aftermath of the Suez war, and Polish Jews, fleeing (also via Italy) in the aftermath of the "Polish October" and the reforms of Wladyslaw Gomulka. The two groups made an odd combination, hardly exhausting the range of Diaspora differences, but standing near its opposing poles. The Egyptians were good bourgeois—petty bourgeois by American material standards, but cosmopolitan in the style of Alexandrian Jewry; they all spoke French; they wore suits and dresses every day. They were also, mostly, religious the way Sephardic Jews are religious, easy-going rather than rigidly orthodox, but pious nonetheless, the men regularly assembling for morning prayer in a makeshift synagogue on board. The Poles, by contrast, were entirely secular and mostly communist, professional people rather than merchants, always casually dressed. Appalled when Gomulka allowed priests and Catholic prayer back into the state schools, and sensing that Polish anti-Semitism was also coming back, they had first pulled their children out of the schools and then negotiated their way out of the country.

Among the Poles was a man in his middle thirties who had made his living translating English books for the state publishing company. He had recently translated Jerome K. Jerome's *Three Men in a Boat*, a lovely comic novel of Edwardian vintage (political books were not permitted) that my wife and I had read and enjoyed. I have long ago forgotten his name, but he became our friend and interpreter for the duration of the voyage, and he told us a story that is etched forever in my memory. One morning his son, six or seven years old, wandering about the ship, had come upon the Egyptians praying. He watched them and went back the next morning to watch them again. Then he came to his father with a worried look on his face. "What are they doing?" he asked. "I thought that Jews were people who didn't pray."

The father never told us how he had responded. The point of the story was the thought with which it ended. Indeed, Polish communist Jews were people who didn't pray, and the boy had been taken out of school, separated from his classmates, so that he would not be forced to recite Catholic prayers (Jewish prayers would have been equally alien to his parents). But Egyptian Jews were people who did pray, and who set themselves apart from their Muslim and Coptic neighbors by the prayers they recited. What did these two groups have in common?

Also on board the ship were a couple of representatives of the Jewish Agency, sent to help the Egyptians and Poles prepare themselves for life in Israel—a life, after all, that they had neither expected nor sought. These refugees were not Zionist militants. The Poles would have been taught an anti-Zionist ideology; the Egyptians were without any ideology at all; they had simply been comfortable in their Diaspora home. The Agency people paid no attention to us, and probably felt a little contemptuous of touring American students. They talked to the refugees about where they would be taken once they arrived, about what kinds of assistance they would receive, about how important it was to learn Hebrew, and about the jobs that were likely to be available to them. And they tried to stir a little feeling for the land and State of Israel. They taught the children the songs and dances of the Israeli youth movements; they taught the Poles to sing "Hatikvah"—the Egyptians already knew it, for the song had escaped the movement and entered the synagogue decades earlier. There were a few low-key lectures, talks really, in French and Polish, on Israeli history and politics. The refugees seemed anxious and self-absorbed; the Agency people wisely didn't push too hard.

We were all on deck when Mt. Carmel, just south of Haifa harbor, came into view—our first glimpse of what the Egyptians, but not the Poles, knew as the "Promised Land." But it was one of the Poles who began, softly and hesitantly, to sing "Hatikvah." And then all of us were singing, and most of us weeping, and I understood very clearly what these people had in common. They shared the hope for a place where they could live in safety and feel at home, as Jews who prayed and as Jews who didn't pray. And for them there was no other place.

For my wife and myself, there was another place, even another promised land, America, *die goldene medineh* (the golden land) of our parents and grandparents, and we would go back there after a few months in Israel. So what did we have in common with the Egyptians and the Poles? Of course I had an intellectual answer to that question. I wouldn't have been on the ship if I hadn't already been in some sense a Zionist. I believed in the unity of the Jewish people and in the right of the Jews to national liberation and in the urgent importance, after the Holocaust, of Jewish statehood. What I came to understand between Piraeus and Haifa was the emotional correlate of those beliefs. My feeling of kinship with the people on board was so strong that even today I have no words to express it—nor, after forty-five years of writing, do I feel any need for words. Ever since that time, I have been a Zionist not only for all the other reasons but also because of that boy, who was so suddenly unsure about what it means to be a Jew and so suddenly caught up in the Jewish experience.

I have higher hopes for Israel than for it to be a place where children like him can grow up safely and figure out who they are. But that is the first thing that it has to be. Whenever my hopes lead me to criticize this or that Israeli government or policy, which happens often, I remember the Egyptians and the Poles on that ship in 1957. I suppose they have made a home in Israel and because they have, because they could, their Israel is mine too.

PART III—
FAITH & COVENANT:

A LIVING, VIBRANT PART
OF MY RELIGIOUS FAITH

"If I forget you, O Jerusalem, let my right hand
wither; let my tongue stick to my palate if I cease
to think of you, if I do not keep Jerusalem in
memory even at my happiest hour."

Psalm 137:5-6

 LYNN SCHUSTERMAN is the president of the Charles and Lynn Schusterman Family Foundation, which is dedicated to helping Jewish people flourish by supporting programs throughout the world that spread the joy of Jewish living, giving, and learning. She is also president of STAR (Synagogues: Transformation and Renewal), president of the B'nai B'rith Youth Organization, and co-chair of the International Board of Governors of Hillel: The Foundation for Jewish Campus Life.

"That first trip awoke in me a deep sense of belonging to the Jewish people. For the first time, the Jewishness that had only been a source of ethnic identification became a source of spiritual fulfillment. Charlie and I recognized a need to make a major change in our lives: we could no longer "go through the motions" of maintaining a Jewish identity. We had to do more. Much more."

The first overseas trip my husband, Charlie, and I ever took with our children was to Israel in 1977. Our decision to visit the Jewish state before any other country was not made lightly or without great discussion. The call of the great European cities and the exotic Far East would have to wait until after our family made its initial pilgrimage to the homeland of our people.

We flew from Tulsa to New York, and then we waited several hours for our flight to Tel Aviv. Rather than seemingly lasting forever, our layover at Kennedy Airport with three small children only heightened our anticipation. The minutes flew by as I anticipated what it would be like finally to board a blue and white El Al airplane emblazoned with a Star of David and flown by Jewish pilots all the way to Israel.

As our plane touched the ground and the entire cabin burst into "Hatikvah," Charlie and I were overwhelmed by emotion. In fact, we fell in love. Israel still felt like a new country then, one infused with the sabra spirit and in which the Jewish dream of self-sufficiency was intoxicating. My Jewish pilots gave way to Jewish cab drivers. Jewish car mechanics. Jewish tour guides. Jewish street sweepers. Everywhere, we saw the dream of Theodor Herzl, the dream of Jews for centuries, alive and in the flesh.

That first trip awoke in me a deep sense of belonging to the Jewish people. For the first time, the Jewishness that had only been a source of ethnic identification became a source of spiritual fulfillment. Charlie and I recognized a need to make a major change in our lives: we could no longer "go through the motions" of maintaining a Jewish identity. We had to do more. Much more.

We returned to the United States committed to new goals, to new challenges, and with a deep sense of responsibility. Instead of sending an obligatory check to a few Jewish causes, we sought to create Jewish programming that was fresh, diverse, and vibrant. Instead of taking for granted Israel's continued existence, we devoted ourselves to causes vital to its protection and security. Instead of accepting as a historical tragedy the Shoah, we vowed to do everything in our power never again to let the world stand by as our people faced danger or death.

And, as often as possible, we returned to Israel, again and again. The relationship deepened, and strengthened. Every trip to Israel yielded new discoveries, new friends, and new opportunities to assist.

Over time a much more nuanced and complex understanding of Israel began to emerge. As our experiences broadened, our commitment deepened even as we began to see the reality of life in our homeland.

This young nation, just struggling to make do from week to week, focused most of its modest resources and energy on mere survival. The attention demanded by defense and security left little time or money to address the issues all too familiar to other nation-states: poverty, neglect, failing schools, and failing families.

Perhaps we were naïve to think Israel would be immune to these challenges. We soon came to realize that building a safe and civil society was part of the dream of Zion, and we were determined to play our part in the effort.

So we bought an apartment in Jerusalem and decided to make it our second home. Like anyone moving to a new place, we immersed ourselves in our new community and searched for ways to help make it better. We tried to look for areas in which we could make the greatest difference in the shortest possible time for those in most desperate need of assistance.

Steadfast believers in the power of education, we helped to create the Israel Arts and Science Academy (IASA), a three-year residential high school in Jerusalem for the brightest high school students from throughout the Land of Israel. Later, after Charlie passed away, I became part of an effort to build Meitarim schools, which bring together in the same classrooms Israeli children of different backgrounds—religious and secular.

Providing safe and secure environments for the victims of child abuse and neglect was another area of interest for us. For more than ten years, our foundation has supported Succat Shalom, a shelter and treatment center for abused children and their families in Jerusalem, and we are currently developing a network of interdisciplinary centers for the intake and treatment of the youngest of those who suffer from abuse or neglect.

These efforts were focused on helping Israel address its social needs. It is easy to marvel at Israel's military exploits, its amazing ability to persevere against virulent enemies bent on its total destruction. That it has managed to exist against these odds is no small miracle.

But Charlie and I did not want Israel's miracle to end with military success. We wanted it to be a nation as cultured as its people, so we have helped the Israel Museum, the Jerusalem Cinematheque, the Israel Philharmonic, and Mercaz Shimshon-Beit Shmuel. We wanted to help Israelis—especially those around Jerusalem—enjoy more than a secure existence. We wanted them to enjoy a life blessed by beauty and culture.

As our relationship with Israel grew, we realized that Israel was not just there for us to help—it was there to help us. We recognized that America's Jews needed Israel every bit as much as Israel needed America's Jews.

We saw in America's young Jews a troubling lack of understanding of what Israel meant to them personally. They were unaware of one of the greatest blessings of our lifetimes—and a potential source of spiritual strength and emotional renewal. They saw Israel as a given, a fact of life, and just a place on a map.

But Israel is far more than that. It is a place to which all Jews have a spiritual claim. The architectural ruins of Meggido and the modern cities of the Sharon are all part of the same story—a story that begins with a promise to Abraham, a birthright that belongs to us all.

We felt a responsibility, as Jews who came to know Israel later in our lives, to help people much younger than us understand that birthright—and initiate a lifelong relationship with Israel.

We went looking for solutions—and we found them in a variety of programs aimed at helping students develop close, personal, and meaningful relationships with Israel. We created the Israel on Campus Coalition to promote Israel education and advocacy on North American campuses. We sponsor major academic programs for the study of Israel at Brandeis and Emory universities, and we are bringing over Israeli academics to teach at universities across the United States. Through our support for Hillel, the American International Education Foundation (AIEF), B'nai B'rith Youth Organization (BBYO), and other organizations, we have sought to imbue our young people with a deep understanding and love for Israel, and to train them to be effective advocates for Israel and the U.S.–Israel alliance.

Another of our efforts was initiated by a group of philanthropists who share our love for Israel—and we happily played a role in building Taglit-birthright israel. It began as a five-year project to enable thousands of young Jewish adults to visit Israel, at no cost. It is now going into its sixth year and soon will have exposed more than 100,000 Jewish young adults from around the world to the country they now loudly and proudly call their own.

With all of our programs, we tried to capture the feeling Charlie and I had on our first visit. We wanted America's young Jews to see a nation far more complex and special than they imagined—a nation where the majority was Jewish, where Hebrew was the language not only of the synagogue but also of the street. We wanted them to understand Israel's strategic challenges, learn its history, and see its ancient sites. But most of all, we wanted them to fall in love with the idea of Israel—a nation like any other, a nation like no other.

If anything, the response has been more satisfying than our own first visit to Israel. I have met thousands of Jewish students in Israel and in America. They have developed an appreciation for Israel's history and its special role in the life of Jews worldwide. They understand its fragile borders, its strategic challenges, and the aims of its enemies. They have made lifelong friendships with both Americans and Israelis.

And in their eyes I see something familiar: the wonder of a visitor, fresh off a long plane ride, at what it feels like finally to come home.

ARI SPUNGEN BILDNER is an undergraduate at Yale University. He plans to return to Israel soon, possibly to study abroad for a semester.

"Visiting ... we could never shed that feeling of an outsider. Yet birthright rendered the opposite effect: ironically, standing at the fringes of Israel in the Golan directly fused me to the country's spiritual soul. To borrow the hippy term, I was one with Israel."

Standing on a hilltop in the Golan Heights this past January, with both Syria and the Hula Valley in Israel visible, I was palpably shivering—not only because of the oppressively frigid winter air but also because of an epiphany. At the northern terminus of the Jewish state, the differences between the Arab nation, with thousands of years of history and culture but whose citizens lived in an authoritarian, undeveloped nation, and fifty-nine-year-old Israel, a modern, thriving democracy, were manifest. As I experienced this enlightenment of sorts, I could barely pay attention to the Taglit-birthright guide's account for the sparse agriculture and lack of infrastructure on the Syrian side, in contrast to the flourishing Israeli kibbutzim on the other. In Jerusalem and other areas of Israel's interior, these differences aren't nearly as apparent, and it's easy to take for granted how successfully *Medinat Yisrael* has realized the Zionist dream of Theodor Herzl in a political, social, and most importantly, spiritual sense. But as I stood up there, feelings of both privilege and elated disbelief at Israeli progress overwhelmed me.

Maybe it's trite to proclaim this now, but my birthright experience radically transformed my connection with Israel. While my parents had raised me to identify with Israel as a Jewish homeland, I believed, especially when I was younger, that Diaspora Jews were supposed to assume the part of the eternal admirer of its story, and ultimately we would accept, and even embrace, a natural detachment from its existence and preservation. As grateful as I am for their educational value, the trips with my parents to Israel had inadvertently served to reinforce this ethos. Visiting the major religious and tourism sites around the country, we could never shed that feeling of an outsider. Yet birthright rendered the opposite effect: ironically, standing at the fringes of Israel in the Golan directly fused me to the country's spiritual soul. To borrow the hippy term, I was one with Israel.

Israel, with its triumphs and faults, must be central to the Jewish identity. It is every Jew's duty to transcend spiritual observation to spiritual participation in the Zionist dream.

RABBI BRADLEY HIRSCHFIELD is the president of CLAL—The National Jewish Center for Learning and Leadership. Co-host of the popular weekly radio show *Hirschfield and Kula* on KXL in Portland, Oregon, he is the author of the forthcoming book *You Don't Have to Be Wrong for Me to Be Right: Finding Faith Without Fanaticism.*

"Now I see Israel as the place that inspires us to live in the present, to live life with all of its uncertainties and complexities, as fully and richly as possible, worrying less about the past and the future and relishing all that the present moment in Jewish life affords us."

Israel has meant many things to me over the years. It started with my first visit at the age of nine—when I spent the summer crisscrossing the country with my parents and three siblings, feeling like the kid in the Disneyland commercial who finally comes face to face with Mickey, declaring, "I've been waiting my whole life to see you." Later, when I was in my late teens and early twenties, it was a place of starry-eyed messianic expectations as I studied, built, and protected the land.

Now I see Israel as the place that inspires us to live in the present, to live life with all of its uncertainties and complexities, as fully and richly as possible, worrying less about the past and the future and relishing all that the present moment in Jewish life affords us.

Nowhere was this clearer than on a just-before-Pesach flight that I took to Israel from Ethiopia, traveling with a group of fifty-three Falas Mora [Ethiopian Jews who, over time, either converted to other faiths or assimilated to a point where they no longer considered themselves Jewish] who were leaving Africa for new homes and new lives in Israel.

Meeting them at midnight in a compound across from the Israeli embassy in Addis Ababa before boarding the buses that would take us to the airport, I was asked to say a few words in the dark courtyard in which we all stood.

I reminded all of us that night that we had a chance to say a blessing that had not been uttered for two thousand years. When the rabbis debate how to bless the moment in which we recall the Exodus, they are divided between those who would thank God for redemptions in the past and those who want to use the moment to pray for the redemption that they hope would yet come. But that night we recited the blessing not in the past tense, or in the future tense, but in the present tense, acknowledging the redemption that occurs right now—a redemption that could not take place without the State of Israel and the partnership of a strong Diaspora.

I see Israel as a place that offers the possibility of overcoming the rift embodied by that Talmudic debate—our people's longstanding tradition of being torn between nostalgia for a glorious mythic past and the longing for a redeemed and perfected future. Israel is the reality that finds a place for both of those, but never at the expense of the real questions of creating a successful society in which there is a place for everybody who wants one, and through which our endless ideological debates about the past and future are properly contextualized with real human needs for the present.

Israel has been many things for me in the past and will probably mean still others in the future. All of that is possible because each of those moments is, at some time, the present. For me, there is no "what Israel has always meant" or "what Israel must be"; there is only the wonderful opportunity to guarantee that as many people are as free as possible to participate in building the place in which that conversation can continue forever.

 ARYEH LEV STOLLMAN'S first novel, *The Far Euphrates* (1997), was a *Los Angeles Times Book Review* Recommended Book of the Year, an American Library Association Notable Book, and winner of a Wilbur Award and a Lambda Literary Award. His second novel, *The Illuminated Soul*, was a winner of *Hadassah Magazine's* 2003 Harold U. Ribalow Prize for Fiction. He is also the author of the story collection *The Dialogues of Time and Entropy*. Dr. Stollman is a neuroradiologist at Mount Sinai Hospital in Manhattan.

"Israel still represents two overlapping realities for me, a transcendent place that hovers before me…. Both realities tend to merge, and are, after all, part and parcel of the accumulated stories, commandments, and dreams that any bar mitzvah boy or bat mitzvah girl might happen to read in any *parasha* of any given week of the year."

In June 1967 I began learning my bar mitzvah *parasha* (Torah portion) after long school days, which included a nearly one-hour commute each way across an international border from my house in Windsor, Ontario, to the Yeshiva Beth Yehudah Day School in Detroit, Michigan. My *parasha*, *Shoftim* (Judges) from Deuteronomy, was scheduled for the end of the summer. I began practicing to read, or rather sing, the entire *parasha* from a proper Torah scroll, a textual version that does not contain vowels or cantillation marks. I was nervous because I knew that any tiny mistake would be corrected with a loud shout by members of the congregation. I was terrified about being humiliated in public. My teacher and guide for the enormous undertaking was my father, a rabbi and head of the local Orthodox congregation. My father was as patient as could be expected with a very impatient and distracted boy, but he was strict about avoiding mistakes. Since I have always been somewhat selectively dyslexic in Hebrew, I would have to be careful not to confuse those two almost mirror-image letters in written script, the zayin with the gimmel. And one of my *rabbe'im* (rabbis) said, "Aryeh, you're a smart boy, but your *dikduk* [grammar, by which he also meant my pronunciation] is atrocious." As I prepared for my big day, I would have to repeat my mispronunciations and missed notes over and over until I got them right.

The portion of *Shoftim* that I learned so well that spring and summer, and that still comes to me in long fragments at the most unexpected times, describes for us an ideal situation: a society living in the Land of Israel based on justice and the rights and duties of both leaders and people. These rights and duties are clearly spelled out perhaps most concisely in that elegant and intense phrase *Tzedek tzedek tirdof*, "Justice justice shall you pursue" (Deuteronomy 16:20).

Even before the preparation for my bar mitzvah, I had been learning the *Tanach* in its original Hebrew with all the stories of the forefathers, foremothers, and the wanderings in the wilderness. The Children of Israel and the Land of Israel that they entered and where they established their society and monarchies were a reality to me. I was always moved by the stories, the miracles, and the land. But until that June my concept of Israel was actually a virtual reality long before the term was coined. I cannot quite remember now what images my mind held for the Land of Israel that came from the ancient stories, but it was something reconstructed in my imagination from the rich, dense narrative and perhaps a few pictures I had seen here and there of my father on one of his trips to Israel in the 1950s or of my grandmother traveling to Palestine in the 1920s to see her sisters and brothers.

My childhood, pre-June 1967 Israel, was not a real place in real time but a transcendent idea and imagining outside of time. Everything that had happened there in the time of the Bible was still happening and stood suspended before my mind's eye; Rebecca going to the well, David catching a glimpse of Bathsheba bathing on her roof. The sages rightly say, "There is no before or after in the Torah."

Suddenly a new reality anchored to the present broke into my twelve-year-old consciousness. There was going to be a war in the Middle East. Every night when I got home from school there were new images on television. One evening I remember my father giving an impassioned speech at the Jewish Community Center to raise money for the beleaguered nation of Israel. Whatever some later historians may have said about Israel's secret intentions for this war, there was great fear in every Jewish community about the likely enormous casualties, about the possibility of yet another Holocaust. The people in our city—like Jews everywhere—opened their hearts and bank accounts and gave more money in that one night than they ever gave before for any cause. Everyone prayed. The war was won and the media were flooded with new visions for those of us who had been nourished on a textual imagination. The next summer my parents took us all to Israel and for the first time I saw the land and its people in all its glory with my very own eyes.

After nearly forty years of travel back and forth, Israel still represents two overlapping realities for me, a transcendent place that hovers before me, a dream-like hologram suspended in the millennia of its existence and textual outpourings, and a real, physical place with hills and valleys, deserts and lakes, and people who, on first encounter, seemed so unlike all the Jews I knew in my hometown. In the end, though, both realities tend to merge and are, after all, part and parcel of the accumulated stories, commandments, and dreams that any bar mitzvah boy or bat mitzvah girl might happen to read in any *parasha* of any given week of the year.

REBBETZIN ESTHER JUNGREIS is founder and president of Hineni, as well as an author, lecturer, and columnist for the *Jewish Press*.

"We came to realize that the return of our people to Israel would have to be complemented by a return of our people to our heritage."

The nights in Bergen Belsen were very long. I would close my eyes and try to escape by recalling stories from the Bible, stories of our sages, and stories of Jerusalem.

"This too shall pass," I would tell myself. We would yet come to Jerusalem, where the sun always shone, where no one ever went hungry, where, my mother assured me, candy bars actually grew on trees and birds sang the psalms of King David. Lying on wooden slats, the very idea that we, the dead bones, would come to life even as Ezekiel prophesied, was more than I could have hoped for.

There had been no precedent in the annals of mankind for our hopes. Never had a people risen from the grave. Never had a nation returned to its land after two thousand years, and we saw it with our very eyes. It was not a dream. Israel emerged from the ancient past into the twentieth century. The ancient prophecy was fulfilled.

As we were liberated, Israel became the focus of our existence, and more than anything else, we were determined to go there. But a cruel British quota system barred us from reaching her shores. We waited patiently in Switzerland for visas. But as the weeks became months and the months became years (1945–1947), we were forced to decide to immigrate to the United States.

But our hearts were still linked to Jerusalem. Three times a day, when we prayed, we recalled Jerusalem. At the conclusion of each meal, in the midst of every celebration, as well as in moments of grief, we recalled Jerusalem. We swore that our tongues would cleave to our palates and our right hands whither before we ever forgot Jerusalem (Psalm 137:5–6).

In 1948, as the new State of Israel was officially declared, a sense of urgency gripped me. There was work to be done—meetings, rallies, and fund-raisers. Even with a heavy accent, I spoke out on behalf of Israel, and I made a silent pledge to find my way there as soon as I finished high school.

In 1953 I finally boarded an Israeli ship bound for Haifa. When I first glimpsed Eretz Yisrael, tears flowed from my eyes and I felt as if my heart would burst. I looked forward to the sacrifice that I knew life in Israel demanded.

I could never have expected cynicism and open hostility toward religion. If we had survived the centuries, it was only because there was a greater law that dictated our existence, and that law came from G-d himself. But Israeli agnostics repudiated these eternal laws. They believed that the establishment of the State rendered the Torah obsolete; that merely by living in the land, they could fulfill their Jewishness and discard our timeless heritage. They scoffed at the idea that the return to the land was made possible only so that we might fulfill our prophetic destiny: "For out of Zion shall go forth Torah and the word of G-d from Jerusalem" (Isaiah 2:3).

Soon I became gravely ill and was hospitalized in Jerusalem. At my parents' insistence, I returned to the United States to recuperate. Not too long after my return, I married my fifth cousin, Rabbi Meshulem HaLevi Jungreis, of blessed memory, who was also a Holocaust survivor and who had come to the United States in 1947. Together, we labored on behalf of our people and Israel. We came to realize that the return of our people to Israel would have to be complemented by a return of our people to our heritage.

All our efforts in reclaiming our people culminated in June 1967, when Jerusalem was reunited with her children. Lines formed in front of every Israeli embassy; thousands of volunteers offered their resources, their strength, and their very lives. In the midst of the Six Day War, this divided and fragmented nation became one. Our love for Jerusalem overrode all jealousies and politics. In every synagogue, our people gathered to pray. It was not the Orthodox, the Conservative, or the Reform who went to Washington to plead on behalf of the Holy City, but all of us, as one.

My husband and I knew that we had to be there, and so we took our four small children and traveled to Jerusalem. It was Friday— *erev Shabbat*—when we arrived. The Sabbath Queen was quickly approaching and the entire city was preparing for the arrival of the royal guest. Everywhere, stores were closing and public transportation was coming to a halt. As the siren was sounded, stillness descended on the Holy City.

Suddenly, scores of people spilled into the streets. They came from every direction: young and old, men and women, Israelis and tourists, students and soldiers, pious Hasidim in long black coats and Westernized Jews in business suits. They came from the four corners of the world; they spoke in many tongues and espoused many ideas. Wondrously, they all merged into one—all were rushing, running to the same place, to the Western Wall.

We stood as if in a trance—my husband, my children, and I. We could not speak; there were only tears. For two thousand years we had waited for this moment.

I came close to the Wall and poured out my soul. A gentle breeze was in the air and a wonderful serenity descended upon me. I looked up at the foliage sprouting from the crevices. Strange how these little flowers grow without being watered. But then I saw the people around me, and I understood from whence these flowers received their nourishment. They were watered by the tears of a nation that had been waiting for two thousand years.

But that, too, was preordained, for Jerusalem's reunification with her children was the prelude to that seventh day. And for a very brief moment, it appeared as if our people might just understand and be prepared to respond to this awesome challenge. But all too soon, the magic of the moment evaporated.

Never before in the annals of mankind did a war last six days. The Six Day War was an open manifestation of the miracles of the Almighty, but alas, the return of our people to Jerusalem took us unawares. The moment came and the moment passed.

It is midnight at the Wall. The winds of Jerusalem are blowing. G-d still waits for you and me to usher in the Seventh Day.

What has happened to us? Why have we lost sight of the vision?

RABBI JEFFREY K. SALKIN, the editor of this volume, is a prolific teacher and writer on Jewish themes. He is best known for his best-selling books on the spirituality of bar and bat mitzvah, all published by Jewish Lights.

"Israel is at the center of my own personal spirituality. It reminds me that the spirit *is* flesh; that the spirit is land, though surely not only land and surely not all of the Land; that a people can become resurrected from its ashes."

I trace my Zionist awakening to a moment exactly forty years ago. It was during the first week of June 1967, when the combined armies of hostile Arab states threatened to, in the words of their demonic rhetoric, drive the State of Israel into the sea.

It's not that the concept of Israel had been absent from my life before that; quite the contrary. Ari Ben Canaan, the heroic Paul Newman character in the movie *Exodus*, was a welcome visitor in our home as we watched and re-watched that film whenever it appeared on the old television show *Saturday Night at the Movies*, of blessed memory.

So, too, I grew up with the reality of the Holocaust and of anti-Semitism. I recall watching a documentary on modern Jewish history with my parents in which there were ghastly scenes of Jewish skeletons in mass graves in Europe, almost immediately followed by images of Israelis dancing in the streets in May 1948 as the State was proclaimed. Hampered by a child's warped sense of time and space, I somehow thought that the skeletons had become magically transformed into the dancing crowds. My childlike sense of reality perhaps was not that far off, after all, for the prophet Ezekiel had believed it to be both possible and true—that the fabled "dry bones" of African American spirituals would once again come to life.

But back to June 1967. I will always remember the youth group advisor at our Long Island synagogue calling all of us seventh graders together. He gave us a briefing on the war and then tore pages from the synagogue membership list, giving a page to each of us and teaching us how to call the members of the synagogue and ask for money for Israel. And thus it was, at the tender age of thirteen, using a dial telephone (also, of blessed memory), that I raised my first money for the State of Israel.

I remember that moment keenly. I was filled with a sense of duty and even grandiosity, for I believed that our little team of intrepid adolescent fund-raisers could actually make a difference, that we could actually save Jewish lives and even Jewish life.

June 1967 was the June of the year in which I became bar mitzvah—old enough to do mitzvot. In the true sense of the term, I actually did become bar mitzvah during the Six Day War.

There are other memories of that period for me as well. There were the junior high school bullies, whose *minhag* (custom) was to knock the tray out of my hands in the lunchroom. During the Six Day War they politely refrained from doing so, assessing the new situation in the Middle East and telling me with grim admiration, "Hey, you Jews really *can* fight, can't you?" There was the Israeli exchange student in my neighborhood whom I befriended primarily so he would walk my paper route with me and defend me against the myriad bullies who awaited my coming. Israel represented the tough Jew, and it was a toughness that I sought. To paraphrase the actor Ossie Davis's eulogy for Malcolm X: "Israel was our manhood." Or, at the very least, it was mine.

Israel, therefore, moved to the center of my consciousness as a Jew. I entered college weeks after the Munich massacre of 1972. I graduated from college weeks before Entebbe. Between those bookends in time there was the Yom Kippur War, the terrorist attacks at Maalot and Kiryat Shemonah and at the Athens airport (an attack that barely missed my parents, who were in the airport at precisely that time), and Yasser Arafat's pistol-adorned appearance at the United Nations. I founded the Jewish students' group on our fledgling college campus; I learned how to defend Israel in word and deed against both students and faculty members, many of whom were themselves Jewish and could spare not a tear for Israel and Jewish terrorist victims.

My vision for Israel and its future is wedded to its reality. I live with the grammatical knowledge that *Yerushalayim* (Jerusalem) is inexplicably in the plural form, that there is *Yerushalayim shel mattah* (the earthly, real Jerusalem) and *Yerushalayim shel maalah* (the idealized Jerusalem), and that there is a psychic and spiritual distance between the two Jerusalems. In the course of more than twenty-five visits to Israel of varying durations, I have come to love the distance between those realities, because that distance points to that which is still unredeemed in our lives, in Jewish history, and in existence itself.

Israel is at the center of my own personal spirituality. It reminds me that the spirit *is* flesh; that the spirit is land, though surely not only land and surely not all of the land; that a people can become resurrected from its ashes; that Israel is the fist we collectively shake in the faces of Hitler and Stalin. More than this, Israel is a "lab"—the living-out of the ideas that were in powder form during centuries of homelessness, but that were waiting to see if Jews, living in their own land, could add water and make them reality.

Finally, little about Israel moves me more than the fact that my two sons both feel at home in and with Israel—that they love the land and they can defend the State intellectually when circumstances warrant it, that they love visiting—and that within their souls, it is almost a second home, another neighborhood of the spirit.

It is often hard for me to explain to my non-Jewish colleagues and friends why this piece of land is so crucial, so central, so immediate to me and my family and my faith. But in those moments, when my articulation fails, it is the necessary stammering that comes out of a love that has lasted for two thousand years.

ARI L. GOLDMAN, a professor of journalism at Columbia University, is the author of three books, including the bestselling memoir *The Search for God at Harvard*. Born in Hartford, Conn., he was educated at Yeshiva University, Columbia, and Harvard. He lives in New York with his wife, Shira Dicker, and their three children.

"I am a Jew and like my ancestors, I long for Zion and Jerusalem. It doesn't have to be perfect. It just has to be. It is prayer that keeps the dream alive."

I did it again today. I prayed for Zion and Jerusalem. Hardly a day goes by, in fact, without my uttering some such prayer. You see, I am a *davener*.

A *davener* is someone who takes traditional Jewish prayer seriously, spending a few minutes or more a day in the ancient formulaic Hebrew prayers that are centuries old. I have to admit that I am not totally consistent, but I'm quite loyal to the practice.

Sometimes Zion will come up in the course of the daily *Amidah*, the silent meditation that together with the *Sh'ma* forms the core of daily prayer. "May our eyes behold thy return in mercy to Zion," I say.

At other times it may be in the grace after meals: "Rebuild Jerusalem the holy city speedily in our days," the prayer begins. "Blessed art Thou, O Lord, merciful restorer of Jerusalem."

What I love about these prayers is that they exhibit a certain purity, untainted by politics or even reality. They do not depend on one Israeli government or another. They have nothing to do with the debate over borders, territories, or the "security fence." Nowhere is Ariel Sharon or Ehud Olmert mentioned. Even David Ben-Gurion and Theodor Herzl are absent.

I love these prayers because my mother and my father said them even before there was a modern State of Israel. And their parents, my grandparents, said these prayers before them.

This is what these prayers mean to me: I am a Jew and like my ancestors, I long for Zion and Jerusalem. It doesn't have to be perfect. It just has to be.

I was born in 1949, the second year of Israel's existence. I have been privileged to see the dream become a reality. I've also seen Israel endangered in one war after another. I grew up hearing the promise of Gamal Abdul Nasser to "push Israel into the sea." In the days before the Six Day War, when Arab armies amassed at Israel's borders, I thought Israel was a goner. I thought the dream had died. I remember weeping on Yom Kippur 1973, wondering again how Israel could survive.

And I had my questions. I questioned the wisdom of the occupation of the Palestinian territories, was horrified by the 1982 invasion of Lebanon, worried about suicide bombers on one hand and Palestinian human rights on the other.

But through it all I've kept praying. "Return us in mercy to thy city Jerusalem and dwell in it, as thou hast promised," I say in the daily *Amidah*. "Rebuild it soon, in our days, as an everlasting structure, and speedily establish in it the throne of David."

Of course it is not enough just to pray. The modern State of Israel did not get built on prayers. It got built through incredible sacrifice, back-breaking hard work, extraordinary military prowess, economic ingenuity, and the steadfast support of Jews and others around the world.

I, of course, do more than just pray. I visit Israel regularly, contribute to the United Jewish Appeal and the Jewish National Fund, buy Israeli products, and speak out in defense of Israel on my university campus and to my legislators. Perhaps most important, I've raised three children who are Zionists. But I've also taught them to pray.

It is prayer that keeps the dream alive.

RABBI MORDECAI FINLEY is the rabbi and co-founder of Ohr HaTorah Congregation in Los Angeles. He is also the provost of the Academy for Jewish Religion, California, where he teaches liturgy, mysticism, Jewish ethics, and professional skills.

"I fell in love with the land—today I would say it was a mystical experience…. I felt a tie that was immense and inexpressible."

I was twelve years old in 1967 and I did not know that I was Jewish. My dad was born Catholic, but he left the Church as a teenager and became a socialist. Most of his fellow travelers were Jews, whom he admired greatly.

My dad was an American soldier in World War II, and his best buddy was a Jewish guy. My mother, whose grandparents were Orthodox, grew up in London in a nonobservant home. When my dad married my mom, he thought he was marrying into the Jewish people.

When my mom married my dad, she thought she was finally getting away from stifling English anti-Semitism and stiff English Judaism. I was brought up as a socialist, and I was told that Dad was born Catholic, Mom was born Jewish, and I could be anything I wanted. When I was in sixth grade, I read a book on the religions of the world and decided to become a Buddhist. On television, I saw Buddhists immolating themselves on the streets of Saigon and I decided to re-think the matter.

In May 1967 I saw my mother very distressed, uncharacteristically listening to the news station all day. I asked my folks what was going on. They told me about what was happening in Israel. I asked why that mattered to us. They sat me down and told me about the Holocaust and Israel. They had a world of knowledge they had not shared with me. They told me they had considered living on a kibbutz. They told me, definitely and inexorably: "You are a Jew."

I remember thinking: "Why didn't you tell me this before?"

As the Six Day War broke out, I wrote a letter to the Israeli consulate, volunteering to work on a kibbutz while the reservists were fighting (I had by this time read everything I could find about Israel and the Holocaust).

My first Jewish act was, as a twelve-and-a-half-year-old, volunteering to help out during that war. I forgot about those self-immolating Buddhists. I didn't want to see any more Jews being immolated by our enemies. You might say I became bar mitzvah a little early.

I was enrolled in Hebrew school, and at my bar mitzvah ceremony I announced that someday I wanted to live in Israel. In the summer of 1972 I finally went to Israel with Young Judea. I fell in love with the land—today I would say it was a mystical experience. My family and I had done much sightseeing across the United States, but in Israel I felt a tie that was immense and inexpressible. I had read Leon Uris's *Exodus* and James Michener's *The Source*. As we visited one place and one institution after another, I could hear voices and feel presences.

I came back to Israel in 1977 after three years in the U.S. Marines and I lived for about a year on a kibbutz. I became fluent in Hebrew and knew I would be back. I came back to California, finished my B.A., and made aliyah in 1980 with my then-wife. At the same time that I wanted to make aliyah, I wanted to become part of the growth of liberal Judaism in Israel.

We spent a year with our young son in Jerusalem, were accepted as candidates in a nearby kibbutz, and I applied to the Hebrew Union College to enter their Israeli rabbinate program. My Hebrew was fluent, I had an outstanding military record, and I had already been accepted to a kibbutz. To my dismay, the Hebrew Union College informed me of their policy not to accept applications into their Israeli program from American students, and that I had to return to the United States and finish my studies there and then come back to Israel. I understand that the policy changed soon afterwards, but it happened too late for me.

Fate took me in another direction. After we had our second son back in California, my wife and I divorced. I soon met a wonderful woman, fell in love, and remarried, and she raised my fine young sons with me. I finished rabbinical school, completed my doctorate, and had two beautiful children with my wife, Meirav. She and I founded a synagogue together. I also helped found a seminary here in California. I think we are adding some good to the Jewish people, trying to do the right thing.

My wife (who is Israeli) and I live an alternate life to the good one we have here. We often imagine what our lives would be like in Israel. I think of the Army service I would have done; we think of the communities we might have been a part of, the causes we would have supported. We do what we can from far away. Part of our hearts is always there.

In quiet moments, I can still hear the voices and feel the presences.

PETER HIMMELMAN is an Emmy-nominated TV composer, an acclaimed creator of children's music, and a critically lauded rock troubadour. Reviewing his latest recording, *No Depression* magazine marveled at how "Himmelman strips his music to its essence, tapping into a primal inspiration, investing melodies that have the sing-song simplicity of Buddy Holly or the Beatles with the yearning of a spiritual quest."

"I can quantify for you the reasons I love my wife and my children and still the list will tell you nothing. My connection to Israel is more than strong. It is based on things timeless, deep, and unknown."

When I was nine years old my parents took my three siblings and me to Israel for the month of July. We rented a house (more of a shack really) near the beach in Netanya. It was 1968, just a year after the Six Day War. Although we were strongly Jewishly identified, our family was not particularly religious, and so when I stood in front of the *Kotel* (Western Wall) for the first time and wept, I was confused. Here I was, this skinny kid with big ears who had no previously known spiritual proclivities; in fact, I had spent most of my summers collecting caterpillars and watching reruns of *Gilligan's Island,* and yet I was so overcome with a sense of awe that I cried. I must point out that crying in front of my older brother at a religious site was not something I took any pride in whatsoever.

Now at forty-seven, I still feel the power of that place. I sometimes wonder, though, if it's all just a function of a good brainwashing. Perhaps if, as a child, I had sung songs about, say, Saint Paul, Minnesota, and perhaps if, when I'd gone to school, the teachers had hung pictures of its lakes and spoke of it with reverence ... maybe if I'd seen the little blue and white boxes in people's kitchens collecting funds for its development, I'd feel the same connection to Saint Paul as I do to Jerusalem.

A few months ago, a Palestinian cab driver and I had a discussion about the Middle East. He said he couldn't understand the centrality of the Land of Israel to the Jewish people. He asked, "If G-d is omnipresent, why does there need to be any particular place to serve Him? See my prayer rug. I just take it out and anywhere I am I kneel to pray on it."

I felt that he was being disingenuous. Of course G-d is everywhere, but maybe even G-d has a home.

From the embryo of silence to the tomb of the unnamed
to the swirling wind of whispers in the valley of our shame
I can taste your tears and all the haunted words you never say

From the table in the temple to the mountains scorched and raw
To the point of savage ecstasy where the trees will shake with
    awe
I can taste your tears and all the bloody dreams you've locked
    away

From the monument of glory where G-d weeps night and day
On the dusty roads of twilight where men return to clay
I can hear you sing in a voice which rises upwards like a flame

Where the seeds they lay unopened in a field of rock and thorn
Where the ancients and the infants lay dying to be born
I can hear you sing in a voice which every angel longs to claim

Where the peregrines soar and a phantom mist shrouds the
    moon
I took a vow and I swore to wrap you 'round my soul like a
    cocoon
This night is like forever, I could never make it back to you too
    soon ...

—From "The Embryo of Silence," written in Jerusalem in 1992

I can quantify for you the reasons I love my wife and my children and still the list will tell you nothing. My connection to Israel is more than strong. It is based on things timeless, deep, and unknown.

SHARA YURKIEWICZ, Yale University '09, is majoring in biology and hopes to attend medical school. She is a member of the Jewish Life Fellowship at her university, which organizes religious and cultural events on campus.

"We visited the Kotel. I rested my hand against the millennia-old stones…. I felt connected with two thousand years of people for reasons that had nothing to do with religion…. Most of all, I felt that nebulous, fleeting category between earthly and heavenly. I felt spirituality."

I am nineteen years old, a college student, and a Jew. I visited Israel for the first time with Taglit-birthright in winter 2007. On the tour bus the first day, our guide opened with a question: "Why are you here?" He gave us four choices and told us we were not constrained to one: (1) to develop a better understanding of the culture and history of Israel, (2) to undergo a deep religious experience, (3) to meet new people, American or international, (4) to go on vacation. There were thirty-nine of us on that bus: some were nineteen years old, most were college students, and all were Jews. Our guide asked us to give a show of hands.

Self-consciously, first glancing around to make sure everyone else was playing, we raised our hands to symbolize our expectations about the trip. Not one person picked the second choice—to undergo a deep religious experience. The one factor we all shared in common—our religion—was the only factor that we did not want to further develop on this trip.

Spending almost a fortnight in the Holy Land made us acutely aware of the bond that united the thirty-nine of us and 13 million other Jews around the world. But what exactly composed that link if not a sense of religious conviction? We discussed spirituality under the stars outside of a Bedouin tent, and almost all of us agreed that religion was not necessary to be spiritual. But then what was spirituality? our group leaders asked.

The young Jews around the circle paused for a moment. We looked out over the landscape of the Negev desert and across the campfire that reflected the question in our eyes. Once again, slowly, self-consciously, we struggled to articulate the concept of soul. Our answers were neither clear nor consistent: one girl said she felt most spiritual at five a.m. alone on a misty morning run; others said that singing Havdalah melodies together around a single lit candle on the shore of the Mediterranean gave them a comfort that felt older than themselves.

I offered this explanation: "For me, you can't control when or where spirituality hits you, but you can tell immediately when it does. It's a feeling of being perfectly content with who you are and where you're going and what you represent. It's knowing that this feeling doesn't last more than a few minutes and may not return for days or years, but knowing that it will return. It will return because it's more than a feeling; it's something that transcends emotion. It exists, although we can only grasp it fleetingly and unpredictably."

On the third-to-last day of our trip, we visited the Kotel. I rested my hand against the millennia-old stones and the feeling I had described outside the Bedouin tent flooded my body. How many people placed their hands in the exact spot where mine rested now? How many people reached for something inexplicable beyond the stone that lay beneath my fingers? How many people felt perfectly content with the spot they were standing in, in front of the Wall and in front of the world? I felt connected with two thousand years of people for reasons that had nothing to do with religion. I felt no divine presence or holy spirit through the stone. All I felt was the hard touch of reality—of a people who survived for millennia of persecution, who kept traditions, sang thousand-year old melodies, laughed and cried collectively, and developed a common memory of the past and vision of the future. I felt humanity, not divinity. Most of all, I felt that nebulous, fleeting category between earthly and heavenly. I felt spirituality.

BRADLEY SHAVIT ARTSON (www.bradartson.com) is the dean of the Ziegler School of Rabbinic Studies at the American Jewish University (formerly the University of Judaism), where he is vice president. He is the author of six books, including most recently *Gift of Soul, Gift of Wisdom: Spiritual Resources for Leadership and Mentoring.*

"Israel's miracle is not only its deep and ancient roots. Today's vitality—cultural, social, intellectual, religious, and economic—also speaks to the continuing blessing of Jewish peoplehood."

Israel's existence is a miracle: After wandering in exile for almost twenty centuries, the Jewish people have returned to their homeland where they govern a Jewish democracy, speak the ancient language of the Torah and the Mishnah, and conduct their daily routine in the neighborhoods of Isaiah, King David, and Rabbi Judah Ha-Nasi. It is easy to take this collective resurrection for granted. Even after visiting Israel many times, I still forget how astonishing the establishment of Israel really is. Occasionally, however, a simple intrusion in my life can abruptly focus my amazement on that little state.

- A few years ago I received a small airmail package from Israel. My college roommate had moved to the Negev region (the desert region in southern Israel) shortly after graduation and was living on a kibbutz. One March, a few weeks before Passover, he mailed me a copy of the newly printed kibbutz Haggadah. It was beautiful. Although similar to many others I've seen, there were two striking differences: the text was entirely in Hebrew and the Haggadah emphasized agriculture and land over the traditional rabbinic concentration on liberation and commandment. Only in Israel, I thought, would such a Haggadah seem perfectly natural. Where else would a translation be superfluous, since even the youngest child at a kibbutz seder understands the Hebrew of the Bible and the Mishnah? (I am so used to evaluating the translation of American *haggadot* that this one seemed almost incomplete.) And where else would the emphasis on agriculture and the cycle of the seasons seem so natural? Restored to their own land and once again farming the soil, Israeli Jews experience a heightened sensitivity to the seasons and natural rhythms of growth and harvest. Within the confines of this little package, I was once again reminded of how unique Israel truly is.

- The great treasures that have come to light due to the careful studies and exploration of Israel's archaeologists—the most notable of which are the Dead Sea Scrolls—enrich our sense of belonging and of peoplehood wherever we live. The last time I was in Jerusalem, I went to the Israel Museum near the Knesset building. The exhibition of pottery, jewelry, and glass was from an unearthed tomb of the seventh century BCE. I passed each case fairly quickly until I was stopped by a spotlight illuminating a metal strip no larger than my thumb. Scratched onto this thin silver band were the ancient Hebrew words of the *Birkat Kohanim* (the priestly blessing). That little scroll, unearthed in Jerusalem, is the oldest existing fragment of a biblical text. I stood staring at this prayer, one that I recite every morning as part of the *Shacharit* (morning) service, and I began to weep. I wept at the mystery and majesty of finding my own spiritual expression rooted in almost three thousand years of Jewish living. Across the ages, a distant soul mate had found purpose, comfort, and identity in the same prayer that Jews today use to start our day.

- Having grown up relatively nonobservant, I took on the mitzvah of tefillin (phylacteries) as an adult. I recall telling my grandmother about the first time I saw someone wrapping himself in tefillin, and her surprised and encouraging response: she went into her closet and emerged holding a brown paper bag that contained her father's (my great-grandfather's) worn set of tefillin. A year ago a dear friend arranged to bring my tefillin to Jerusalem, where a *sofer* (scribe) installed new Hebrew scrolls, rendering the tefillin kosher for ritual use once again. This year I brought those tefillin to Jerusalem. Imagine the power of standing on the balcony of my hotel, with a view of the Old City of Jerusalem and its walls, as I wrapped myself in my tallit (prayer shawl), strapped my great-grandfather's tefillin around my arm and across my forehead, and began to recite the ancient prayers that faithful Jews have recited throughout the millennia. I had the sense that my great-grandfather had taken his precious tefillin, with all that they embody, and passed them across a chasm of a few generations until they could be lovingly received, and again become a vessel for connecting to God many decades later. In a sense, that link across the ages is precisely what being in Jerusalem means too. As I wore my great-grandfather's tefillin and recited the same prayers he would have recited each morning, I thought about what this moment would have meant to him and to his contemporaries—how they had prayed for the chance to see Jerusalem as the vibrant center of a sovereign Jewish community, and how he must have doubted whether he would have a great-grandchild for whom these mitzvot and *tefillot* (prayers) would still speak. I stood in his presence, and through his eyes I could see the miracle that Jewish continuity is, the unlikely miracle that Israel remains.

- Israel's miracle is not only its deep and ancient roots. Today's vitality—cultural, social, intellectual, religious, and economic—also speaks to the continuing blessing of Jewish peoplehood. Each year I get to visit the family of my college roommate, who made aliyah (immigrated to Israel) after graduation in the late 1980s. Each year I watch as his twins, Noah and Yonah, grow taller, stronger, more thoughtful, and more beautiful. They chatter to each other in Hebrew, and then smoothly transition to English to speak with their parents or with me. I marvel as my cousins' children, Adina and Doron, head off to their youth groups on their own. And I reflect that the miracle of Israel is no less its present than its past.

LYDIA KUKOFF was the first director of the Reform movement's Outreach program. An author, speaker, and consultant, she divides her time between Manhattan and the Upper Hudson Valley, where she is among the founders of the Chatham Synagogue Netivot Torah.

"Israel is special to me because, like Judaism, it is mine by choice, not by birthright. The challenge of making it my own enriches my life every day…. Israel is not the place I visit; it is the other place I live. Whether I am there physically or not, I am always interacting with it."

When I think about what Israel means to me, I go into a state of verbal and sensory overload. So many intense emotions, memories, experiences, and associations fill me simultaneously that it becomes difficult to single out one element. I love all the things about Israel that people who love Israel love: the layers of history, the beauty of the land, the very miracle of its existence.

Beyond that, Israel is special to me because, like Judaism, it is mine by choice, not by birthright. The challenge of making it my own enriches my life every day. Over the years, I have lived and worked there, learned its language and its ways, and developed deep friendships across the spectrum of Israeli society. Israel is not the place I visit; it is the other place I live. Whether I am there physically or not, I am always interacting with it.

Israel has a unique energy—an ability to create and re-create itself again and again. It comes from Jews who have gathered there from the four corners of the earth, returning to live in their ancient land, reclaiming and inhabiting ancient words as well as ancient places, while dealing with the challenge of being a modern country at the same time. For example, we know the word *matzileinu*, "our savior," from the siddur, but only in Israel can I walk on the beach and see a sign that reads "*ain matzil*" and know that there is no lifeguard on duty. To live in Israel is to live in that extra dimension. I am mesmerized by it.

Israel's creative energy is astounding, especially given the problems and trials it has continued to face since its beginnings. Wars, intifadas, and internal divisions cannot stifle its creativity.

Certainly in science and technology Israel has a high profile throughout the world. But there are two areas that resonate enormously with me. One is the arts and culture, through which dancers, writers, artists, filmmakers, and composers explore, in a way that is uniquely Israeli, the human and the Jewish condition. The other is the increasing interest that Israelis show in exploring their own Jewishness. I am not speaking of those who become fervently observant—the *ba'alei teshuvah* (those who have returned to traditional Judaism). Increasingly, I see "nonreligious" Israelis reclaiming holiday and life-cycle events and coming to own Jewish texts in a very personal way, aided by a number of new and creative grass-roots organizations.

I see a commonality between myself, an American Jew, and Israelis. We are all trying to live Jewish lives in the twenty-first century, trying to find an authentic way of living with the past in the present. I would like to see us share more of that challenge with each other.

May we come together to fulfill the words of Israel's first chief rabbi, Rav Kook: "to make the old new and to make the new holy."

Jane Friedman is the president and CEO of HarperCollins Worldwide.

"Israel is essential to my life today. It has drawn me closer to my family and friends. I have gained a larger community around the world. And it has connected me to my faith in a way I never thought possible. My only regret Is that it took me fifty years to get there."

It was the eve of my fiftieth birthday. I had been raised in a conservative Jewish household where we observed the tradition and celebrated the holidays—the High Holy Days, Hanukkah, Passover. And I had never been to Israel.

As this seminal birthday approached, I felt an intense desire to visit Israel. Fortuitously, my friend Joan Nathan—the distinguished cookbook author who had been an aide many years before to the former Jerusalem mayor, Teddy Kollek—decided to make this inaugural trip of mine her pet project. She immediately called her friend Colette Avital, who was the Israeli Consul General in New York at the time, and they began to plan an itinerary for my life partner, Jeff Stone, and me.

As soon as the El Al 747 touched down at Ben Gurion Airport, I felt as if I had come home. The city of Jerusalem welcomed me with the warmth of its Jerusalem stone and sun-drenched vistas; its incredibly fierce history, its wealth of cultures, and its extraordinary people.

I still feel this way each time I return. Visiting Israel has given new meaning to my life as a Jew. I now feel a connection to my heritage.

My first trip has had a lasting effect on me. I became determined to maintain this link and I have done so. I joined the Publishing Group of the UJA-Federation and became one of its leaders. I have been inspired by UJA's vital and humanitarian efforts in New York, throughout the United States, in Israel, and around the world. My hands-on experience of visiting many of the organizations funded by UJA—organizations that play a critical role in helping children, senior citizens, the displaced, the downtrodden, the abused, and the disabled to live in safety and with dignity—satisfies me greatly. I am now a co-chair of the Entertainment Division of UJA-Federation, the umbrella group of the arts. And I am continually renewing my commitment to UJA and the causes that it supports.

The Jerusalem International Book Fair has become another passion of mine. This biannual event is a natural way for me to marry my love of books with my love of Israel. In 2001 HarperCollins initiated the Jerusalem Fellowship Program for Agents and Scouts, a parallel program to the original Jerusalem Editorial Fellowship Program. Young agents and scouts can now visit Jerusalem to meet authors, editors, and publishers in the newly designated Rights Center at the Fair. There are also guided tours throughout the city and visits to Masada and the Dead Sea. The Fellowship allows me to share Jerusalem with the next generation of my publishing colleagues.

Through my association with the Jerusalem International Book Fair, I reached one of the most important moments in my life. In 2001 I was honored with the designation "Friend of Jerusalem" by Jerusalem's former mayor, Ehud Olmert. It seemed as if many aspects of my life came together at that moment as I was celebrated for my work within the publishing community, as a Jew, in Israel. I will never forget how I felt that day. The beautiful scroll now sits over my desk as a constant reminder of the importance of Jerusalem to me.

Israel is essential to my life today. It has drawn me closer to my family and friends. I have gained a larger community around the world. And it has connected me to my faith in a way I never thought possible. My only regret is that it took me fifty years to get there.

 RABBI HIRSHY MINKOWICZ is the founder and director of the Chabad center in Alpharetta, Georgia, a northern suburb of Atlanta.

"When I think about Israel and what it means to me, there is one word that says it best: holiness.... Even a basic look at the history of Israel from ancient times until today uncovers a constant divine protection and providence."

When I think about Israel and what it means to me, there is one word that says it best: holiness.

Imagine a place where everywhere you went, from the synagogue to the falafel stand, from the study hall to the airport, you knew and felt that you were in a holy place. That is Israel to me.

"A land the Lord, your God, looks after; the eyes of the Lord your God are always upon it, from the beginning of the year to the end of the year"—these are the words the Torah uses (Deuteronomy 11:12) to describe G-d's connection to the Land of Israel. A place that G-d assures us He is looking after every minute of the year and imbues with a unique sense of holiness and spirituality.

Even a basic look at the history of Israel from ancient times until today uncovers a constant divine protection and providence.

As a rabbi in suburban America, I have had the fortune of traveling on several community-wide trips with many Jews from our metro area, many of whom I had not met before. From the moment we set our feet down on the holy soil of Israel, there is a bond that forms between us that would typically take years to develop back home. Under the influence of the holiness of the land our souls seem to connect instantly.

Israel is G-d's special gift to us that He promised to our forefather Abraham. It is the eternal heritage of the Jewish people, and to me it is the source of all holiness entering this world.

May we merit the coming of the Messiah and the fulfillment of all the associated prophecies. "For out of Zion shall the Torah come forth, and the word of the Lord from Jerusalem" (Isaiah 2:3).

My ties to Israel extend deep into my roots and soar far into my future.

 MARSHALL J. BREGER is professor of law, Columbus School of Law, Catholic University of America. He served as special assistant to President Ronald Reagan to the Jewish community.

"For the significance of settling the land is not merely moral, political, and historical; it is also eschatological. As the modern Orthodox prayer book puts it, the creation of the state signifies the 'beginning of the dawn of our redemption'."

I think of Israel as a source of Jewish pride, as a place where a person can live a fully Jewish existence and contribute meaningfully to the unfolding of the Jewish narrative. But these are subjective feelings of *nachas* (pride).

To me the Jewish state has religious significance as well. "For you are crossing the Jordan to come to the land which the Lord your God is giving you; you must settle the land and live there" (Deuteronomy 11:31). This is, of course, where it starts. Without it, the nineteenth-century need to find a "solution" (Herzl's word, not Hitler's) to the Jewish problem would likely not have found expression in the arid plot of land astride the Syrian-African fault. Nor would those Jewish nationalists stirred by *Risorgimento* (the unification of Italy) in the age of the European nation-state have chosen Palestine as the site for a Jewish national home. (And indeed we know from the Sixth Zionist Congress what a near thing it was.) If not for the Jewish masses of eastern Europe moved by the text of the Hebrew Bible, our homeland may well have been Uganda.

When we ask, then, the question of what is the Jewish state today, we must begin with the biblical injunction. And in so doing, we must begin with the biblical promise as well. For the significance of settling the land is not merely moral, political, and historical; it is also eschatological. As the modern Orthodox prayer book puts it, the creation of the state signifies the "beginning of the dawn of our redemption."

It cannot be a state based, in the Lockean sense, on possessive individualism. It is as much nation as state. Even in its secular expression, the state of the Jews will by necessity reflect Isaiah Berlin's incisive term for the Jewish people—"a community of fate." This notion was well expressed by Justice Moshe Silberg, writing in the "Brother Daniel" case, which explored whether a Jew who converted to Christianity could claim Israeli citizenship under the Law of Return. In discussing the common bond among Jews, Silberg pointed out that "whether he is religious, non-religious, or anti-religious, the Jew living in Israel is bound, willingly or unwillingly, by an umbilical cord to historical Judaism from which he draws his language and its idiom, whose festivals are his own to celebrate, and whose great thinkers and spiritual heroes ... nourish his national pride." There is no way that a "people that dwells alone" can be post-Zionist.

In contrast, the nonideological Israeli society is one that wants to normalize or privatize all of social life: to disaggregate the collective into the atoms of its individualistic existence. Its paradigm is the Tel Aviv architect who told the *New York Times* some years ago that "hedonism is basically a very good drive to embellish your life." The resident of North Tel Aviv, we are told, "carefully cultivates a new Israeli aesthetic along the Mediterranean."

Now we all know that "normalization" was a specific goal of Theodor Herzl and the early Zionists. They wrote of building a society where Jews could own land, where a Jewish proletariat would live cheek by jowl with a Jewish professional class. It was Israel's national poet, Hayyiim Nahman Bialik, who is reported to have said, "Thank God, we are a normal people—we have thieves in our midst."

But there is a sense in which any version of a Jewish state—secular, socialist, religious—will be an ideological society, one organized to promote some overarching goal. The goal, of course, will differ radically from one person to the next, but the "community of fate" that encompasses the Jewish people could not envision a state that is based merely on liberal individualism. Thus whatever its faults, what was extraordinary about the collectivist Hashomer Hatza'ir experience was the effort to create a moral society, a secular version, one might say, of the religious Jews' effort at *imitatio dei* (the imitation of God). The same can be said of the aspirations of Vladimir Jabotinsky, who sought to refine the human personality to reflect ideals reminiscent of those of knighthood and chivalry. And of A. D. Gordon, who wished to transform the Jewish proletariat and create a new personality type through the dignity of labor.

Whatever the goal of the early Zionists, I do not believe that normalization can be the Zionist project for the future. Rather, if there is any eschatological meaning to the State of Israel, it is to be found in the effort to create a just society that justifies our inheritance.

If we are to continue to build a Jewish state in the next millennium, we must understand that part of what we mean by a Jewish state is to strive toward an ethical society for both Jews and non-Jews alike. Those who care about the Jewish state must remember that the biblical promise is contingent. The covenant between God and Israel is not a free pass. As the Bible teaches: "Justice, justice shall you pursue, that you may live and inherit the land which the Lord your God has given you" (Deuteronomy 16:20).

RABBI JANET R. MARDER is the senior rabbi of Congregation Beth Am in Los Altos Hills, California. She was the first woman to be elected president of the Central Conference of American Rabbis.

> "Israel is the only place in the world that offers me public Jewish space—an external environment that reflects my inner identity. I belong there, in a way that I belong nowhere else."

I first went to Israel in June 1974 for my first year of rabbinical school. I was twenty years old and had grown up in the sheltered suburbs of the San Fernando Valley. In every way, Israel was a shock to my system. Summer was hot and dry as a blast furnace; the Jerusalem winter was piercingly cold and damp. I lived in an apartment with no air conditioning or heating system. We had the choice of shivering through the night in a parka or enduring the headache-inducing fumes of a kerosene space heater.

We had to bring our own bags to the grocery store. The toilet paper was disconcertingly thin and scratchy. We had no oven or television or telephone; if there was an emergency we bought tokens at the post office to make a long-distance call. The radio played constantly on the bus; everything came to a stop so passengers could listen intently to the hourly news bulletins. Young soldiers strolled the streets, rifles slung over their shoulders; they checked my bag at the entrances of movie theaters and grocery stores and synagogues. I walked and hitchhiked everywhere, and always felt safe.

The buildings were made of pale stone that shone with a golden light. On Tisha B'Av thousands of people sat on the ground at the Western Wall, chanting in a mosaic of melodies from the Book of Lamentations, mourning the destruction of the Temple whose last remnant was before them.

The streets were full of *konditorei* (pastry shops) and stationery stores run by elderly Germans and Austrians. The receptionist at our school came from England. The gardener came from Yemen. Our Polish cantillation teacher told us that in the concentration camp, he chanted the Megillah (Scroll of Esther) on Purim for the other inmates because he knew it by heart. I stayed on a kibbutz and met *halutzim* (pioneers) who drained swamps in the Galilee. I ate humus for lunch every day in a restaurant run by Egyptian Jews. In the afternoons I tutored a little girl whose family came from Iraq. All of them told me their stories. All of them urged me to come home to Israel.

Because of these things, and others, I fell improbably and permanently in love. Some of what I love is the idea of Israel: a country created out of desperate necessity by Holocaust survivors, refugees from pogroms, idealists and kooks who believed in the impossible; the intense, dynamic collision of Jews of every color and culture and ideology; the noble dream of translating Jewish teachings and ideals into practical politics; the miraculous reestablishment of Jewish sovereignty after centuries of powerlessness almost led to our extermination.

Some of what I love is the reality of Israel: the automatic teller machine that spits out a receipt wishing me a happy Sukkot; the taxi drivers with *tehilim* (psalms) taped to the dashboard; street signs in Hebrew, named for sages and poets and great figures in our history; concerts that begin with the crowd singing "Hatikvah"; public lectures, literature, films, plays, and even rock music that wrestle with Jewish themes; the siren that announces Shabbat on Friday afternoons in Jerusalem; the buses that stop running, the quiet that falls over the city, and the streets full of people carrying flowers home or walking to synagogue. Israel is the only place in the world that offers me public Jewish space—an external environment that reflects my inner identity. I belong there, in a way that I belong nowhere else.

I am not blind to the other realities of Israel. There are loud cell phones and television talk shows where everyone screams at the same time; there is rudeness and vulgarity in the culture; there are painful economic and social inequities, political corruption, racism and bigotry; frightening voices of religious extremism and the denial of religious rights to Reform and Conservative Jews.

And always there is the shadow of war—past, present, and future—and the pernicious effects wrought by hatred and violence on the human soul. Israel's history has been shaped by the implacable enmity of its neighbors, but its own leaders have also displayed arrogance and blindness. A country founded on the highest moral principles has brought injustice and suffering to Israeli Arabs and Palestinians. Israeli political discourse, far more robust than among American Jews, wrestles every day with the agonizing implications of that dilemma.

I do not expect Israel to be perfect, as I do not expect the people I love to be perfect. I see them as they are, and I see the potential in them as well. I do my best to understand them. I rejoice in their strength; I grieve when they suffer or go wrong. My job is to keep on loving them, even when it is hard, and to help them in any way I can to become their best selves. They are ordinary, but they are also amazing; and they are mine, and because of that they are embedded in my heart.

For me Israel is a miracle, a source of religious meaning and spiritual inspiration. It is God's work accomplished through the hands of flawed and fallible human beings. It is beautiful in a way that transcends aesthetics. Along with beautiful sunsets and beaches, it is suffused with beauty of character and spirit.

Israel speaks eloquently to me of courage and endurance and self-sacrifice, of the love of children and the stubborn dream of peace. Israel testifies to our people's refusal to disappear from history. It is the assertion of our right to live. It is the only government in the world that cares for and protects that right.

Israel is the place where, even now, I believe that Torah can come to life. Here we Jews assert our collective will to transform reality in the light of transcendent moral truths. Here we Jews can build a country grounded in justice, compassion, and the pursuit of peace.

PART IV—
TIKKUN OLAM:

A Light Unto the Nations—Hopes for Repairing the World and Dreams of a Better World

"Thus said the Lord: Again there shall be heard in
this place, which you say is ruined ... in the
towns of Judah and the streets of Jerusalem ...
the sound of mirth and gladness, the voice of
bridegroom and bride ... for I will restore the fortunes of the land as of old—said the Lord."

Jeremiah 33:10–11

DR. MARC D. ANGEL is the senior rabbi of Congregation Shearith Israel, the historic Spanish and Portuguese Synagogue of New York City. Author and editor of twenty-five books, his most recent volume is *Foundations of Sephardic Spirituality: The Inner Life of Jews of the Ottoman Empire* (Jewish Lights).

"Israel is a bastion of hope in a world filled with despair. It is a wellspring of human dignity in a world filled with shameless hatred and strife."

A tiny nation, often misunderstood and maligned, changed the course of history for the good. This tiny nation produced the Bible and its prophets; sages and mystics; poets and dreamers. This tiny nation, generation after generation, in many ways has been the conscience of humanity, the litmus test of human civilization.

This tiny nation lived in a tiny land in antiquity. Its King David established Jerusalem as its capital city a thousand years before the dawn of Christianity and more than 1,600 years before Mohammed. It was seldom allowed to live in peace: other nations threatened, attacked, made war. It saw its capital city razed by vicious enemies, its Temples destroyed by Babylonians and Romans, its citizens ravaged and exiled.

This tiny nation, scattered throughout the world, faced persecutions and humiliations. Its men and women and children were confined to ghettos, deprived of elementary human rights, subjected to pogroms and pillage. Millions of them were murdered during the Holocaust.

Exiled from its land for nearly two thousand years, it always dreamed of returning to its ancestral soil and reestablishing its sovereignty. It prayed daily for the return. Many of its members made pilgrimages, and some remained living in the land throughout the generations, in conditions of poverty and oppression.

In spite of the persecutions it suffered and in spite of the callousness of so many nations of the world, this tiny nation maintained faith in One God and in the mission He assigned it to bring the lofty teachings of Torah to humanity. In spite of all its sufferings, this tiny nation maintained faith in humanity: it strove to make the world a better place for all human beings, with an eternal optimism that is truly a wonder.

This tiny nation, born 3,500 years ago, wove its way through history and refused to be destroyed or silenced. This tiny nation, scattered throughout the lands of the world, found the will and the courage to return to its historic homeland after nearly two thousand years of exile. The return home has been difficult. It has had to fight wars, withstand terrorism, overcome economic boycotts, endure political isolation, and combat hateful propaganda.

Yet this tiny and ancient nation, against all reasonable odds, has reestablished its sovereignty in its historic homeland; it has created a vibrant, dynamic, idealistic society, dedicated to the ideals of freedom and democracy. With its memory spanning the millennia, it has created a modern, progressive state.

My wife, Gilda, and I first visited this historic land in the summer of 1968, a year after our marriage. When we glimpsed the shoreline from the airplane window, we both found ourselves with tears in our eyes. We were not born in this land, we had never been there before, and yet we were returning—we and all the generations of our families were returning through us. "When the Lord turned back the captivity of Zion, we were as in a dream" (Psalm 126:1).

This tiny people is Israel. This tiny land is Israel. This nation of dreamers and visionaries, builders and farmers, sages and scientists, warriors and peacemakers—this nation is Israel. This tiny nation is a great nation. This tiny land is a holy land. "The tiny shall become a thousand, and the least a mighty nation" (Isaiah 60:22).

Israel is a bastion of hope in a world filled with despair. It is a wellspring of human dignity in a world filled with shameless hatred and strife.

To stand with Israel is to stand for the redemption of the people of Israel and humanity. To stand with Israel is to recognize the sheer wonder of the survival and contributions of the people of Israel. It is to affirm the preciousness of life over a culture of death; righteousness over hypocrisy; idealism over despair. This tiny nation in its tiny land is a testament to the greatness of the human spirit. It is a testimony to God's providence.

It is a privilege, beyond words, to dream with Israel and share its destiny.

"For Zion's sake I shall not be silent, and for Jerusalem's sake I shall not rest, until her righteousness go forth as brightness and her salvation as a flaming torch" (Isaiah 62:1).

JONATHAN D. SARNA is the Joseph H. & Belle R. Braun Professor of American Jewish History at Brandeis University, and the director of its Hornstein Jewish Professional Leadership Program. His most recent book is *American Judaism: A History*, which was selected as the National Jewish Book Awards Jewish Book of the Year in 2004.

"Forty, indeed, is the Hebrew numerical equivalent of the words 'God's hand' (*yad* YHWH). While Israel, over the forty years that I have been privileged to watch it, has not yet achieved messianic perfection, it has made remarkable progress on many fronts. Here's hoping that with the help of 'God's hand,' the progress that Israel makes over the next forty years will be even more dramatic."

In 1965, when I first visited Israel as a child, it was a small, third-world country. Plumbing was primitive, air conditioning was scarce, and good-quality meat was almost nonexistent. Poverty lined the faces of beggars and street peddlers. Rickety fume-belching buses and large taxicabs dominated the roads; automobiles were comparatively rare. In some cities, domestic animals roamed freely. None of today's limited-access highways existed. Even the trip from Tel Aviv to Jerusalem required long hours of travel on a winding narrow road. Jerusalem, when you finally arrived there, more closely resembled a large town than a capital city. Although home to 180,000 Jews, the city's dominant feature was the boundary separating Israeli Jerusalem from the Jordanian sector. Danger signs warned pedestrians to keep away from no-man's-land and disputed areas. Jordanian soldiers, their guns trained on the Israelis, stood in plain sight.

I have always been grateful to have seen Israel in its undeveloped adolescence. The realities that I encountered in 1965 spared me from the starry-eyed mythical Israel that so many American Jews of that time conjured up in their mind's eye. Israel, to them, was an extension of the American dream. It was a Jewish refuge where freedom, liberty, and social justice reigned supreme. It was an "outpost of democracy" that American Jews could legitimately, proudly, and patriotically champion. As for Israel's inhabitants, American Jews viewed them as bold desert pioneers and brawny Jewish farmers: brave men and women who overcame "the dangers of a wild frontier to bring law, order and civilization to a new land" (Debra Dash Moore, *To the Golden Cities: Pursuing the American Jewish Dream in Miami and L.A.*, p. 253). They worked hard, danced passionately, and looked suspiciously like Paul Newman and Jill Haworth did in *Exodus*.

The wonder is not so much that these dreams were eventually punctured but that they lasted as long as they did. The Israel of the American Jewish imagination embodied American Jews' most cherished hopes and fantasies, responded to their psychological and emotional needs, and helped them to counter the malicious slurs of their enemies. It became for them what the Soviet "socialist paradise" had been for some of their parents: a kind of Jewish utopia, a place where their fondest hopes and dreams might be realized. The problem, as I knew from having actually visited the country, was that these hopes and dreams obscured the larger reality: that Israel was a spirited third-world country, fraught with problems both internal and external, yet determined to claw its way up.

Four decades of war and terror have swayed American Jewish attitudes toward Israel. Some exchanged their utopian myths for demonic ones, hardly an unprecedented response to disappointment. Far more commonly, as Steven M. Cohen showed, American Jews continued to "proclaim a deep sentimental attachment to the country and a concern for its survival," but became more critical of Israel than before, and more willing to voice legitimate criticism of its actions. Certainly Israel plays a much smaller role in the lives of many young American Jews than it once did. *Slingshot*, a remarkable new resource guide for Jewish innovation that describes fifty "of the most innovative organizations, projects and leaders across the country," includes exactly one that deals with Zionism or Israel and forty-nine that do not.

This is a tragedy for many reasons, not the least of which is that it obscures the dramatic progress that Israel has made over its short history as it bounded from backwardness to prosperity and entered the first world. Somehow, despite all of the many problems that we may now acknowledge, Israel's cities boom and its deserts bloom. One need only visit Israel's neighbors to realize how remarkable the Zionist achievement has been.

On my most recent visit to Israel, exactly forty years since I was first there, I found that luxurious accommodations abounded, many featuring air conditioning, cable television, and whirlpool baths. Excellent restaurants and giant groceries overflowed with high-quality foods of every sort, meat included. A new bus lane speeded the way for modern buses and sleek taxis, while most people drove cars—late model ones—and they tended to drive them recklessly. Everywhere, new roads, some with elaborate tunnels, had reduced driving times appreciably. The trip from Tel Aviv to Jerusalem now took only an hour on a multilane highway, while Israel's first limited-access toll road cut driving times to the north even further. As for Jerusalem, its population had ballooned to include 647,000 Jews, making it the fifth-largest Jewish community in the world. In place of the ugly boundary that once disfigured the very heart of the city, there now stood beautiful homes.

To be sure, Israel still faces monumental challenges, from making peace with its Arab neighbors to keeping peace among its diverse communities of Jews. Israel's 1948 Declaration of Independence promises that the country "will be based on freedom, justice, and peace as envisaged by the prophets of Israel; it will ensure complete equality of social and political rights to all its inhabitants irrespective of religion, race or sex; [and] it will guarantee freedom of religion, conscience, language, education and culture." These promises, I know, remain tragically far from fulfillment.

But when I recall what Israel has already accomplished in my lifetime, the great distance that it has traveled from 1965 to 2005, I take heart. Forty years is a magical number among Jews: the Israelites wandered in the desert for forty years, and Deborah, David, Solomon, and Joash all reigned for forty years. Even the Messianic era, according to one rabbinic opinion, will only last for forty years. Forty, indeed, is the Hebrew numerical equivalent of the words "God's hand" (*yad* YHWH). While Israel, over the forty years that I have been privileged to watch it, has not yet achieved messianic perfection, it has made remarkable progress on many fronts. Here's hoping that with the help of "God's hand," the progress that Israel makes over the next forty years will be even more dramatic.

SHOSHANA S. CARDIN was the first female chair of five national organizations including the Conference of Presidents of Major American Jewish Organizations. She was once referred to as "the chief of staff of American Jewry."

"It is my firm belief that when Israel no longer needs to focus on survival and defense, all peoples on this globe will benefit from the research and scientific advancements that will emanate from Israel."

Perhaps Israel means so much to me because I was born there—in the land known to Jews as Eretz Yisrael or the Yishuv—not yet the State of Israel, rather it was British-mandated Palestine, according to travel documents. Medical facilities were such that doctors advised my parents to go to a country that was more advanced in medicine, and so we arrived in the United States, not to stay, but to return to Eretz Yisrael when my mother's health was no longer in question.

The status of Jews in the Yishuv remained a major focus of our house, as my mother had siblings and parents who lived there and who wrote frequently to update us on the status of Jewish–British relations and Arab–Jewish relations. All of our activities in Baltimore, where we lived, were Zionist-oriented. My parents were members of Poalei-Tzyion and Pioneer Women; my brother and I were members of Habonim, a Zionist youth group; and daily conversations reflected both the dream of an independent Jewish state and the challenges in the Yishuv. We raised money; we broadcast Sunday radio shows highlighting the progress, agricultural and otherwise, that was occurring in Eretz Yisrael. We participated in community events promoting an independent Jewish state.

And then the United Nations vote established the State of Israel for the entire world to see. The joy, the elation, the tears—all the emotions came to bear, as the hoped for, prayed for, and labored for independent state of and for the Jewish people was within reach.

Little did we know that all that had preceded was simple in comparison to what remained to be done. For those of us labeled as Zionists, we had succeeded to a degree.

Most American Jews were not involved or concerned. But now that I could and did claim Israel as my homeland, my energies and activities continued to be directed to helping Israel: raising funds, both philanthropic and Israel Bonds; public speaking at synagogues and community meetings; enlisting others to visit Israel (which I have done more than a hundred times); and serving as an advocate for Israel.

My personal life as an American Jew improved because of the State of Israel. The victorious Six Day War elevated the status of Jews in America, as well as enhanced the self-esteem of individual Jews who had been hesitant to identify as Zionists.

Israel has legitimized the Jews of the Diaspora. Because of its existence Jews everywhere have a homeland, a place that pulls us ever back to our roots and one in which the world can see a nation with a proud heritage of freedom and democracy, fighting for a democratic way of life. Like someone who is Polish or Irish or French, I can point to a place on the map and say that it is my native land. Though the struggles in the Middle East have brought much sorrow to each of us, we also feel much joy at the strength, dignity, and perseverance of the Israelis. Our children have grown up not as displaced persons, but forever connected spiritually and emotionally to this hard-fought-for land. My husband and I took our four children to Israel as often as possible, and all of our grandchildren, with the exception of two very young ones, have visited Israel at least once. I still have cousins living in Israel whom I visit almost every time I travel to Israel, and friends with whom I exchange e-mails and phone calls, all of which enable me to feel very close to daily life in Israel, in Binyamina, Jerusalem, and Ramat Gan.

The status of life in Israel and the viability of the State are integral to my daily life, in both Jewish and non-Jewish settings. It has been and remains my belief that my future as an American Jew, and that of my children and grandchildren, depends on the continued existence and success of the State of Israel. It is my firm belief that when Israel no longer needs to focus on survival and defense, all peoples on this globe will benefit from the research and scientific advancements that will emanate from Israel.

Rabbi Arnold Jacob Wolf is rabbi emeritus of K.A.M. Isaiah Israel Congregation in Chicago and a leading voice in Israeli peace movements through his involvement in Breira and Brit Tzedek v'Shalom. He was the founding rabbi of the experimental Congregation Solel in Highland Park, Illinois, and is responsible for five books of Jewish thought.

"I love Israel as the prophets did—demanding that Israel be the Covenant People and staking my life on its sacred destiny."

I fear for my country when I remember that God is just. Not only after Viet Nam and Iraq but also after Haiti and Granada and all of

Latin America. My country has blood on its hands and I shudder for its future. Are we to be the last empire in the world and one, therefore, destined to fall in deserved ignominy?

But I also know that the United States is the freest nation in the world, that from every corner of the globe people are struggling to enter our borders. We are not innocent but we remain a desperate hope for all manner of the persecuted and the submerged of humankind.

So with Israel! Our Jewish homeland is not free of sin: occupying someone else's land for decades; resisting peace while pretending to embrace it; marginalizing its own Palestinian citizens; ignoring United Nations directives; widening the gap between its rich and poor; characterized by increasing corruption and dangerous polarization. Israel has not yet fulfilled its noble dream of linking humane Jewish values and modern democratic government.

Yet Israel still lives in our consciousness for what we dream of its becoming: a refuge and a model, a homeland and a holy place where swords are broken and communities joined. Martin Buber and Theodor Herzl are not yet forgotten; the greatest works of Jewish imagination and of Jewish scholarship come from Jerusalem even now. The kibbutz is in difficult transition, but its example is lasting and still powerful. No country can be more precious to us or closer to our hearts than Israel.

That devotion has always been true for me. In the 1930s my uncle and teacher, Rabbi Felix Levy, became the first Zionist president of the Central Conference of American Rabbis and took leadership in passing its first pro-Zionist (Columbus) platform. In the 1940s I was the first Hebrew Union College student to win the preaching prize for a strongly Zionist sermon. In the 1950s my congregation sent all its Hebrew students to Israel for a summer at no cost to their families. During the Six Day War, that congregation also mortgaged its synagogue building and sent the borrowed money to Israel. In the 1970s I headed Breira, a project of Israelis and American Jews that supported peace in two secure and mutually guaranteed states.

I love Israel as the prophets did—demanding that Israel be the Covenant People and staking my life on its sacred destiny. I lived to see the Jewish state reborn. May my grandchildren live to see it not only survive but also flourish in peace as the fullness of its promise under God's providence and with a human creativity unprecedented and undreamed.

DANNY SIEGEL is a poet, author, lecturer, and founder and chairman of Ziv Tzedakah Fund.

"Call me a romantic. Since I am a poet, that's a compliment.... Side by side with the terror, hatred, and international condemnation for whatever Israel does, I have to keep the magic, holiness, the miraculous, and the lyricism of the land and the people in my mind, heart, and soul ... always."

I don't recall being a morning person when I was in college back in the early 1960s. If there was an exam or a paper due, I could pull an all-nighter with the best of them.

Things changed radically on one of my early trips to Israel. I've been back almost fifty times, ever since my rabbi took me with him in 1959. I was fourteen years old, and the country was eleven years old.

Sometime during those early days—I cannot remember exactly when—I discovered dawn in Jerusalem. In late June, the first glimmers of light can be seen around 4:00 a.m., and I was hooked. I began walking by 4:45 for two hours—anywhere. Most of the time I had no route planned. I just opened the door and headed in whichever direction my feet (the Almighty?) took me.

I still do it on many mornings, and always on Shabbat. Groups of tourists, or a friend or two would go with me, with a guarantee that they would be back in plenty of time to get to any synagogue that caught their fancy. They could pray with the Turks in Yemin Moshe, the *chazzan* (cantor) and choir at the Great Synagogue, or the neighborhood *shul* (synagogue). I always take with me *Rehovot Yerushalayim* ("The Streets of Jerusalem"), that marvelous paperback that explains the origin of all the street names in the city. That way I can turn left and reach back in my mind three centuries, or walk straight ahead to the next corner and find myself in the heyday of the Talmud.

Call me a romantic. Since I am a poet, that's a compliment. And that's exactly the point. This is not to say that I am not glued to the radio every time the news comes on if I am visiting friends or in transit in a taxi. Of course I am. I listen to the news, watch the news, read the news in the Hebrew papers. But that is never enough. Side by side with the terror, hatred, and international condemnation for whatever Israel does, I have to keep the magic, holiness, the miraculous, and the lyricism of the land and the people in my mind, heart, and soul ... always.

Sometime in the mid-1980s I wrote:

I think
(now that I look back)
I'd rather drive a taxi
in Jerusalem
than be the King
of all of South Dakota ...

Am I naïve, oblivious to the real lives of the people? Not so. One day, while I was having a leisurely cup of coffee on Ben Yehuda Street, I wrote:

The downtown triangle of streets is seething with Jews—
Loud chattering geniuses, drivers, merchants, and kids,
Pharmacists from Germany, scholars,
Kibbutzniks on a spree, saints,
Men shaking in yarmulkas over a Coke,
The round and the blind, the muscle-bulging
Of our people, foaming beggars,
And open-shirted name-brand macho Sabra men.

I see them, hear them, listen to them, talk to them and argue with them, buy my newspapers from them. They are in my consciousness morning, noon, and night. A few even pass by me as dawn breaks and I am out and about on my morning stroll.

But there is still more to the human side of Israel. For more than thirty years I have sought out Israel's *tzaddikim*, The Good People. These are the individuals, young, old, men, women, and children, religious, so-so, and secular—you name it—that are doing The Good Things for others.

I call these individuals "mitzvah heroes," and they are easy to find because they are everywhere. On the surface, some of them even appear to be " ... drivers, merchants, and kids ... and open-shirted name-brand macho Sabra men." Mitzvah heroes are the ones who spend their days organizing masses of volunteers to retrieve perfectly good leftover food from hotels and wedding halls to feed hungry people. Mitzvah heroes say, "I have to do something" and wind up sending packages of "goodies" to thousands of soldiers. These paradigms of *yiddishkeit* (a deep sense of Jewishness) and humanity bring refuge and relief for victims of domestic violence, extend loans with zero interest for people living on the economic edge, and provide opportunities for individuals with every conceivable kind of disability. Giants of *tikkun olam* (repair of the world), they find masseurs and masseuses to give free massages to survivors of terror attacks. They mend broken and breaking hearts and ease the minds of those who falter and lose their way.

All of them care with such vigor and human and Jewish creativity—it is at once awe-inspiring and eminently accessible. For every heartache, dissonance, and broken spirit, they will find a solution.

I am "hooked." I need to find them, be with them, and do at least something with them.

They are the visionaries who remind us that there is a Heavenly Jerusalem, as well as the Jerusalem of schwarma stands, shoe stores, and garages. And what applies to Jerusalem Above and Below extends beyond the city's limits to the very ends of the earth. Just read the last twenty-six chapters of Isaiah. Theirs is the same "unrealistic" vision as that of the biblical prophets from centuries ago.

Unrealistic? Spend time with the Mitzvah heroes and it may seem less fantasy than possibility.

Am I living disconnected with reality? To the contrary, the reality of Israel as I see it is reality and fantasy, vision, and prophecy inextricably mixed together.

Am I living with my head in the clouds?

For sure. I wouldn't have it any other way.

RABBI SHARON BROUS is the founding rabbi of IKAR (www.ikar-la.org), a vibrant spiritual community in Los Angeles.

"My prayer for those who love this tiny country of so many tears and such delicious chocolate is that we never lose the will to reengage, to reimagine what is possible in a country built on the foundational principles of the Jewish people: that every human being has innate dignity and worth, that justice must prevail over chaos, that peace is always possible."

My friends call me a chocolate Zionist because I actually believe that Israeli chocolate tastes better, just because it comes from Israel. Hearing little children speak in Hebrew makes me cry—I am overwhelmed by the miraculous revival of a language that should have been lost two thousand years ago. My heart soars when I read about Israeli forces traveling to Turkey as immediate responders in the aftermath of a devastating earthquake, and I weep with pride and joy when I hear about innovations in medicine—from neonatology to gerontology—born out of the inexhaustible dedication of Israeli doctors and scientists.

But I also cry when I hear "Hatikvah." I cry for the questions it evokes: What has happened to that great hope when 900,000 Israelis choose to live abroad? And what would it take, as one of my teachers once said, for all the people of the land—Ashkenazim and

Sephardim, Russians and Ethiopians, Druze, Bedouin, and Palestinians—to be able to say that they are *am hofshi, be'artzeinu* (a free people, in our own land)? I cry when I read the news, wondering how it happened that our beloved country came to be detoured and even devoured by endless corruption and sexual assault scandals, bruised perhaps irreparably by the personal and political failures of its leaders. And I cry when I hear that 1 million Israeli children go to bed hungry each night, and that Israel has one of the greatest gaps between the haves and the have-nots in the modern industrialized world.

But most of all I cry for the intractability of the conflict with the Palestinian people. My heart breaks again and again over the terror, violence, and hatred that too often characterize the Palestinian response to Israel. I weep for the thousands of lives lost to this long war. At the same time, my heart breaks over our unwillingness to look long and hard at what Israel and those of us who love it have neglected to do in the pursuit of peace. I weep over the last forty years, during which the occupation has not only sown misery and hopelessness for the Palestinian people, but has also cost Israel so much in blood and soul.

Haim Gouri taught us that we are a people of "ups and downs, euphoria and pathos, pride and pique. Everything about us is drastic.... Every day there is a sudden sunrise and an equally dramatic sunset, but there is no twilight." *Hazal* [the ancient Sages] wrote: "The Jewish People is compared to the dust of the ground and to the stars of the sky. When they sink, they sink down to the dust; when they rise, they rise into the stars."

My prayer for those who love this tiny country of so many tears and such delicious chocolate is that we never lose the will to reengage, to reimagine what is possible in a country built on the foundational principles of the Jewish people: that every human being has innate dignity and worth, that justice must prevail over chaos, that peace is always possible. I believe that we can still build an Israel that reflects the best of what our people has to offer the world. And it is this prayer that makes the tears that I shed over Israel tears of pride and joy, and tears of grief, but never, never tears of despair.

ARTHUR GREEN is currently the rector, and was the founding dean, of the Hebrew College Rabbinical School. A scholar and theologian rooted in the mystical tradition, his more recent books include *EHYEH: A Kabbalah for Tomorrow* (Jewish Lights) and *A Guide to the Zohar*.

"I see Israel, the state and the society, as the great collective accomplishment of the Jewish people in the twentieth century.... But the essential moral failing of Israel—its inability to deal fairly with the rights and even the full humanity of the other people with whom it shares a homeland—remains deeply troubling."

I first visited Israel in 1961, six years before the Six Day War and Israel's conquest of the Old City of Jerusalem. In those days you could go up to the belltower of Notre Dame Monastery, right on the city divide, and for a fifty-*grush* fee you could get a look over the Old City wall and peer into its marketplace. During that first visit, a year of study and teaching, the holy Jerusalem of my dreams and fantasies was transformed into a real place. I loved the real Jerusalem—its people, markets, parks, and cafes.

But it was no longer the Jerusalem of my prayers, of perfect wholeness, of messianic dreams. That Jerusalem, I decided, must reside over there, inside the Old City wall, a place I could not reach.

When I went back after the war, I was able to walk through those markets, seeing the difficult conditions in which Jerusalem's Arabs lived and feeling the hostility behind their masks of commerce-driven friendliness. The markets were beautiful in their own backward way, and I was drawn to them frequently. But they were not holy; the air I breathed in them was not that of redemption. Old Jerusalem, too, became real, even profane, as I came to understand the deep conflict between its diverse inhabitants.

Where, then, was holy Jerusalem? I looked up at the Temple Mount, beyond the Western Wall, and decided that was where the true Holy City lay. Respecting both strict *halakhah* and Muslim sensibilities, I decided I would not go up there, and I still have not done so, despite perhaps thirty trips to Jerusalem since then. But the truth is that it is neither Jewish nor Muslim strictures that have held me back. I fear that this Jerusalem, also, might turn out to be profane, and then there would be no holy place on earth at all. I cannot allow that to happen.

This self-imposed taboo is a metaphor for much of my relationship with Israel. I so wanted to believe in it fully—in the rightness of our cause, in the high humanitarian ideals it represented, in the "purity of arms" of its soldiers, in the writing of poetry in Hebrew once again, in the clearing of swamps, the eradication of mosquitoes, and the raising of health standards throughout the Middle East, for Jew and Arab alike. This was the Israel of my childhood dreams, the Israel I believed in fully when watching Abba Eban address the United Nations, when hearing about David Ben-Gurion's interest in the Bible and in Buddhist meditation, when corresponding in childish Hebrew with pen pals in Pardes Hanna, when reading the first Hebrew novel I mastered, S. Y. Agnon's *In the Heart of the Seas*, the tale of a fantasy journey to the Holy Land, many centuries ago.

That Israel got lost, of course, in the clash with reality. If it continues to exist somewhere behind a wall, that wall stands deep within my own heart. Meanwhile, I have indeed come to love the real Israel, the one I visit so frequently and where I have many friends. I love the richness and naturalness of its Jewish culture, so much of which is borne by the Hebrew language itself. I love the directness of human encounter you have there, as though you are always dealing—and arguing—with half-familiar members of your own extended family. I love the closeness of Jewish historical memory that Israel represents, so dulled and almost forgotten among luxury-bathed American Jews.

But that love combines with a deep sense of betrayal, disappointment, and hurt that I also feel when visiting Israel. In recent years, I have refused to visit Jewish settlements across the Green Line. My feeling since 1967 has been that this territory belongs to the Arabs, and should be kept in trust to be given to them when they are ready to make true peace. Settling that land in seemingly irreversible ways, creating "facts on the ground," as they were called, betrayed the Zionist dream. It (combined with ongoing Arab intransigence, of which there is plenty, I know) has made a two-state solution nearly impossible. Without a two-state solution, I believe, Israel is impossible and will not survive.

Even inside the State's borders, the ongoing discrimination against Arabs, who have been treated at best as second-class citizens for half a century, is a terrible stain on the moral reputation of the entire Jewish people. The inability of most Israelis, both individually and institutionally, to treat the Arab population with dignity, even to the point of learning their language, marks a major failing in the Zionist enterprise. One would have thought that post-Holocaust Jews would know what it is to be a minority, and would treat others in our midst as the Bible tells us to treat strangers. But this has been far from the case.

I believe that it is very late. Great damage has already been done. Is it too late? Is it still possible to reverse direction? Could responsible leadership in Washington, Jerusalem, and Ramallah force a change, giving us a peaceful Israel behind safe borders, one not consumed by Holocaust-driven fears and not playing into and intensifying the hatred by which it is surrounded? I have to believe that time has not yet run out, but that belief gets harder to maintain, day by day. Meanwhile, I see Israel, the state and the society, as the great collective accomplishment of the Jewish people in the twentieth century. Its astounding success—material, cultural, scientific, and in several other realms—reflects the tremendous strengths and resources that are our people's legacy. But the essential moral failing of Israel—its inability to deal fairly with the rights and even the full humanity of the other people with whom it shares a homeland—remains deeply troubling. Whether this inability was caused by the intransigence of the other side; whether it was fueled by memory and fear left over from the Holocaust; or whether it was the predictable legacy of Jewry as an ancient covenantal community that never cared enough about the lives of those who stood outside it—only history will be able to judge.

 RABBI DAVID A. TEUTSCH is the Wiener Professor of Contemporary Jewish Civilization and director of the Levin-Lieber Program in Jewish Ethics at the Reconstructionist Rabbinical College. He has served in various leadership roles in the Reconstructionist movement, including president of the Reconstructionist Rabbinical College and as editor in chief of the seven-volume Kol Haneshamah prayer book series.

"We need to do what we can to move our land to a messianic future where Israel's daily life will reflect the principles and values about which we pray. That is the task of redeeming our land that stretches before us. That is our hope—*hatikvah*."

As far back as I can remember, I have sung about Yisrael every time I worship: Israel as the historic homeland of the Jewish people. Israel as a place of messianic dreams of justice, peace, and plenty. Israel as the home of the Jewish heart.

On my first visit there as a college student, I observed how different the biblical Hebrew I had learned in school had become from contemporary Hebrew, with its own grammar and vocabulary. The archaeological site where I dug was near new buildings and highways. The energy and bluntness of the Israel of 1970 was a far cry from the elaborate courtesies of Abraham's conversations. This Israel was thriving far after "historic birthplace" and much before "messianic future." The dynamism of the new land was palpable, but it took some adjusting before I could face the messy if exciting reality in which I found myself.

Israel still felt like a fragile and embattled land back then, just a few years after the 1967 war. Since then it has become economically and politically more secure, and the Palestinians have emerged as a powerful political force in the world as well. Growing tension exists between the commitment to equality, harmony, and justice recorded in Israel's founding documents and the gap there between rich and poor; between Israeli Jews, Muslims, and Christians; between secular and *haredi*. Those of us who love Israel wrestle with these internal issues as well as the struggle for land and peace that dominates the news.

The Israel of the past and future is far easier to deal with. But my current concern—like that of all who love our little nation—is the contemporary Israel. Joining with like-minded people, I work for the triumph of the ideals that drove Israel's creation. Sometimes the news is depressing, but this land is woven into my soul as the homeland of my people. I remind myself that we need to do what we can to move our land to a messianic future where Israel's daily life will reflect the principles and values about which we pray. That is the task of redeeming our land that stretches before us. That is our hope—*hatikvah*.

STEVEN BAYME serves as National Director, Contemporary Jewish Life for the American Jewish Committee and is the director of its Koppelman Institute on American Jewish-Israeli Relations.

"Israel is redefining the meaning of Jewish peoplehood not only by being the latest and, in some measure, most exciting chapter in the annals of Jewish experience, but also by upholding the promise of fulfilling a vision of Jewish statehood that provides both for the rights of all its citizens and for the renewal of Judaic civilization in the homeland of the Jews—a daunting challenge, and one that we have only begun to address."

The birth of Israel in 1948 changed the map and meaning of Jewish peoplehood in irrevocable and overwhelmingly positive ways. The return of the Jews to sovereignty and statehood after two thousand years of statelessness constitutes both the success narrative of the modern Jewish experience and the challenge to the entire Jewish people of shaping its own future destiny. The return of the Jews to ancestral homeland entails a Jewish commitment to constructing a new model of state and society in which Judaic and democratic principles coexist and reinforce one another. In effect, Israel is redefining the meaning of Jewish peoplehood not only by being the latest and, in some measure, most exciting chapter in the annals of Jewish experience, but also by upholding the promise of fulfilling a vision of Jewish statehood that provides both for the rights of all its citizens and for the renewal of Judaic civilization in the homeland of the Jews—a daunting challenge, and one that we have only begun to address.

There have been other, perhaps more tangible, transformations in the map of Jewish peoplehood resulting from the creation of Israel. Politically, Israel serves as a statement of permanent Jewish refuge. Recall, by contrast, the testimony of Chaim Weizmann before the Royal British Peel Commission in 1938 to the effect that the world was then divided between places that did not allow Jews to live and places that did not allow them to enter. This situation was rectified by Israel's creation. Everyone has their own "if only" concerning the Holocaust. For me, "if only" there had been a Jewish state in 1938, the dimensions of the Holocaust would have been sharply reduced although by no means eliminated.

Demographically, we are currently witnessing an Israeli demographic ascendancy over the Diaspora. Since the Babylonian exile in 586 BCE, if not earlier, until the twenty-first century, consistently more Jews had been residing in the Diaspora than in the Jewish homeland. That demographic pattern at present is being reversed by Israel's positive birthrate coinciding with attrition in the Diaspora. Although this transformation reflects the very real problem of Diaspora Jewish assimilation, it also reflects a process of normalization in which Israel increasingly becomes the critical, although by no means exclusive, expression of Jewish peoplehood in the contemporary world.

Lastly, Israel has transformed the meaning of Jewish identity in the modern world. To be a Jew in the twenty-first century entails a connection with Israel—repository of Jewish memories, scene of the daily sounds and actions of a vibrant Jewish people, and locale of future Jewish aspirations.

To be sure, the unfinished agenda remains daunting. Israel confronts her own demographic dilemma of preserving a Jewish majority as key to remaining both a democratic and a Jewish state. The secular–religious divide within Israeli society warrants a new social contract between Jews in which different ideologies of Jewish expression may compete harmoniously rather than intensify polarization between Jews.

American Jewry, too, has much to address in its relationship with Israel. In sharp contrast to the Holocaust, which has, regrettably, become the one chapter of Jewish history that virtually everyone is mandated to know, the study of Israel has failed to penetrate the curriculum of the Jewish school system. As a result, knowledge and understanding of Israeli history, politics, and culture is at best minimal even among the best-educated of American Jews. Barely a third of American Jews have even set foot in the State of Israel, notwithstanding the relative affluence and propensity to travel so common among American Jews generally. Orthodoxy constitutes a significant exception in this regard inasmuch as visits to Israel and one-year study programs have become normative for Orthodox Jews and thereby cement ties with the Jewish state. The Taglit-birthright israel program constitutes an important statement on the centrality of Israel to contemporary Jewish identity. However, the larger reality of young American Jews today is that increased distancing from Israel is part of a greater distancing from matters Jewish generally. In that sense, assimilation and Jewish continuity constitute the primary challenges facing the Jewish community. The relationship to Israel remains part of that greater dynamic and overall challenge.

These are real issues and need to be confronted honestly and wisely. Yet as Israel approaches the end of her sixth decade we can point to a Jewish state whose permanence and legitimacy have been established, and that has opened its doors and spared no efforts to absorb endangered Diaspora Jewries. The rescue of Ethiopian Jewry, for one, should forever set to rest the canard of Zionism as racism. For this and many other reasons, Israel's place in history as the first Jewish state in over two millennia should inspire Jews everywhere for decades and centuries to come.

RABBI ELLIOT NELSON (FORMERLY KATZNELSON) DORFF, PHD, is rector and Distinguished Professor of Philosophy at the American Jewish University (formerly the University of Judaism) in Los Angeles. His ties to Israel include cousins Beryl Katznelson and Rachel Katznelson Shazar, wife of the second president of Israel, as well as a first cousin and her family now living there. His twelve books include *The Way Into* Tikkun Olam *(Repairing the World)* (Jewish Lights).

"My ties to Israel are thus both real and ideologically messy. My hope for its future, though, is not messy at all. I dare to hope that Israel will find a way to make peace with its neighbors; that it will find a way to accomplish the very difficult task of being both a Jewish state and a democracy granting freedom of religion to all its citizens, including its Jewish ones; and that it will flourish materially, intellectually, culturally, and spiritually."

My wife, Marlynn, created a curriculum about Israel for Catholic high schools in Los Angeles. The first lesson includes a map of the Middle East without the countries' names. The instructions say: "There are fourteen countries in the Middle East. How many of them do you think are Jewish?" Typical answers range from ten to fourteen. The next page says, "Only one of these countries is Jewish. Which one do you think it is?" The most common answer is Saudi Arabia because it is the biggest! That Israel is in the news almost daily has clearly made it much more important—for non-Jews as well as Jews—than its size or numbers alone would warrant.

So why am I committed to a Jewish state in Israel? A year spent there, multiple trips, and much thinking about it have made my ties to it strong, complicated, and complex. I am not committed to it because the majority of the world's Jews live there, for that has not been true since 586 BCE, and it is not true today. It is not because I think that all Jews should move there, for if Jewish history tells us anything, it is that we dare not put all of our eggs in the same basket, even if that basket is Israel. Most surprisingly to me, it is not even because I could live my life religiously there with the greatest sense of fitting in, for I am neither an Orthodox Jew nor a secular one, and living as a Conservative/Masorti Jew is really hard there. In fact, one of the things that bothers me a lot about Israel is that people of any other faith can choose to be married by any clergy member they choose, but Jews have to use an Orthodox rabbi for their weddings. Only Jews could have created a country where there is freedom of religion for everyone except Jews!

Despite these complications, my commitments to Israel are real. They stem from multiple, intersecting elements. One of those elements is history, for it is in Israel that both the biblical and mishnaic history of my people developed; we can even visit some of the sites. Legally, the United Nations granted Jews a homeland there in 1947, and so I think that we have an internationally recognized legal right to be there.

Language is another part of my connection to Israel, for it has resurrected the language of the Bible, the Mishnah, and the siddur (prayer book), albeit in a new, vibrant form. Israel's marking the Sabbath and holy days by the Jewish calendar is another part of my attachment to it. The fact that a significant minority of the world's Jews live there, including members of my extended family, is clearly another part of my tie to Israel. Part of it is also that I appreciate the educational import of Israel, for I have witnessed how experiences in Israel awaken a Jewish spark in many, many Jews, one that prompts them to commit themselves to contributing to a strong Jewish future and to live more seriously themselves as Jews. Ultimately, though, I have to confront some very difficult claims to explain the root of my tie to that piece of geography—theological claims about God's gift of this land to Abraham, Isaac, Jacob, and their descendants. Do I really believe that? What should I make of Christian and Muslim counter-claims?

My ties to Israel are thus both real and ideologically messy. My hope for its future, though, is not messy at all. I dare to hope that Israel will find a way to make peace with its neighbors; that it will find a way to accomplish the very difficult task of being both a Jewish state and a democracy granting freedom of religion to all its citizens, including its Jewish ones; and that it will flourish materially, intellectually, culturally, and spiritually. Moreover, I am committed to doing what I can to realize that dream. I take steps to make those hopes real every time I contribute to Israeli causes, teach American Jews and non-Jews about Israel, help to send Americans to visit there, and engage in dialogues with Israelis to help them think about how Israel can become the ideal that we all fervently want. I also take steps to strengthen Israel when I work to strengthen the Jewish Diaspora, for only if Diaspora Jews know about Israel and feel committed to it can we hope that Israel will continue to get the political, financial, cultural, and demographic support it needs to exist as a thriving Jewish state.

AARON PRESS TAYLOR is a student at Brandeis University where he transferred after three semesters at Yeshiva University. He is an alumnus of the Reform youth movement and its various leadership programs, and has spent significant time in Israel.

> "Nothing short of frigid temperatures can raise goose bumps like the words sung in 'Hatikvah,' '*od lo avda tikvateinu*'—'our hope is not yet lost'…. Part of it all is helping to fulfill the Jewish hope that Israel will ultimately stand as a beacon, just and upright in its values among the nations."

As a youngster in a diverse New Jersey suburb, I took diversity for granted. I went to a public school and learned that while my own heritage was important, so, too, was learning about others and aspiring to see the unique colors and character of the world's far corners.

I felt proud to be Jewish but took Jewishness for granted before moving to Spokane, Washington, where Jews were far less abundant. My father converted to Judaism when I was seven. We lit Shabbat candles, frequented the synagogue, celebrated holidays, and discussed the meaning of being Jewish. I was raised to value my Jewish heritage; that my great-grandparents made Horowitz-Margareten matzah and that like all the unique and interesting people around me, as a Jew, I, too, was sort of special.

My maturing appreciation for both diversity and Judaism naturally makes negotiating identity more complex. My relationship with Israel—built up over a year of study in both Haifa and Jerusalem, living with both Druze and Jews, independent exploration, hours of reading and ongoing contemplation—only complicates this task further.

And so, I was a Jewish college student in Manhattan, soaking in the diversity of its neighborhoods like Little Italy, Chinatown, and Harlem. I participated in a vast array of Jewish cultural events and synagogue options. So, why would I care about Israel? As a Jewish American, American Jew, or whatever, don't I have it all?

To this question, posed most often introspectively, I can only offer a perpetually fluctuating response. In my limited experience in traveling abroad, I have been lucky enough to see fantastic sites, encounter various cultures, and learn from each new way to appreciate and experience life. I won't argue that Israel's Elite café tops Costa Rican coffee, or that compared to French cathedrals, Israel's average *batei knesset* (synagogues) offer a superior aesthetic. Instead I can rely only on the irrational devices of a usually rational, sometimes even agnostic, mind. While I can concede that the diversity on a crowded subway platform is interesting, I cannot help but gravitate toward the Hebrew I hear uttered by Israeli partygoers nearby.

While I find the Sacré Coeur in Paris to be stunning, I am more spiritually stirred beside the few remaining pillars of a two-thousand-year-old synagogue atop Masada. While experiencing New York City's most diverse thoroughfares is indeed humbling and awesome, it is not because they are strangely familiar like the streets of Tel Aviv, Afula, Jerusalem, or Sderot, where Ashkenazim, Sephardim, Ethiopians, and Russians greet each other with "Shalom." And as I strive to champion the rights of all humankind, it is my responsibility as a Jew to pursue justice. Nothing short of frigid temperatures can raise goose bumps like the words sung in "Hatikvah," "*od lo avda tikvateinu*"—"*our hope is not yet lost.*"

I cannot have it all if I disregard the centuries-old dreams and aspirations of my people and ignore Israel's compelling nature in our own time. I cannot have it all by willfully negating the anthem's assertion—*"nefesh yehudi homiyah"*—that the Jewish soul still yearns. Part of it all is helping to fulfill the Jewish hope that Israel will ultimately stand as a beacon, just and upright in its values among the nations.

 **RABBI AVRAHAM (AVI) WEISS** is the founder and dean of Yeshivat Chovevei Torah, the modern and open Orthodox rabbinical school. He is the senior rabbi of the Hebrew Institute of Riverdale, New York, a modern and open Orthodox congregation. Rabbi Weiss is national president of AMCHA—the Coalition for Jewish Concerns, a grassroots organization that speaks out for Jewish causes and Israel.

"Only in a Jewish state do we have the political sovereignty and judicial autonomy that we need to be the *or la-goyim,* a light to the nations to establish a society from which other nations can learn basic ideals of Judaism."

Stepping into the arrivals area of Ben Gurion Airport during the second Lebanon War, I felt a sense of homecoming. The sight of my friend Yossi Shonfeld waiting for me lifted my heart. But as I looked at Yossi, I saw a deep sadness in his eyes as he told me about a terrible loss in his home community of Nehalim. Daniel Gomez, a helicopter pilot, son of Miriam and Patrick Gomez, the doctor of the community, had been killed in battle, leaving his wife, Sarit, who was six months pregnant. At his funeral the next evening after midnight, thousands of people stood silently weeping as Sarit rose and cried over and over at his grave, "I love you, Daniel. I'll take care of our child down here, and please, you take care of him from heaven."

As a young man born at the tail end of the Holocaust, I saw the State of Israel as the ultimate response to the Shoah. Never again would Jews be defenseless. Israel and its army would be there to protect Jews everywhere. I understood Israel's *chok ha'shevut* (Law of

Return), granting any Jew immediate citizenship, as a deeply religious statement. Never again would Jews in distress have nowhere to go.

As I've grown older, my understanding of the relationship between Israel and the Jewish people has evolved from viewing Israel merely as a physical haven for Jews. It has become one based on the idea of chosenness. The idea of our chosenness has always been associated with our sovereignty over the chosen land and it is critical to understand the meaning of this concept.

There are some Jewish thinkers who posit that chosenness is a statement that the Jewish soul is innately superior. Personally, I find this problematic, as this could create a sense of second-class citizenry for the rest of humanity. Judaism is based on a primary principle that every person is created equal in the image of God.

Mainstream Jewish belief maintains that chosenness means that our mission to bring Torah ethics to the world is of a higher purpose. Our task is to function as the catalyst in bringing about a redeemed world. The movement of chosenness is not from the particular to the more particular, but rather from the particular to the universal. Chosenness is, therefore, not a statement of superiority, but of responsibility.

From this perspective, Israel is important not only as the place that guarantees political refuge; not only as the place where more mitzvot can be performed; not only as the place where, given the high rate of assimilation and intermarriage in the exile, our continuum as a Jewish people is assured. It is rather the place—the only place—where we have the potential to carry out our mandate as the chosen people. In exile, we are not in control of our destiny. Only in a Jewish state do we have the political sovereignty and judicial autonomy that we need to be the *or la-goyim*, a light to the nations to establish a society from which other nations can learn basic ideals of Judaism.

Of course, Jews living in the Diaspora can make significant individual contributions to the betterment of the world. And there are model Diaspora communities that impact powerfully on Am Yisrael and humankind. But I would insist that the national destiny of the Jewish people can only be played out in the Land of Israel. Only there, as a nation, do we have the possibility to help repair the entire world.

When we talk about nations, it is crucial to recognize that the best model of nation is family. The Book of Genesis is about broken families that become whole. Only when the family comes together, as occurs at the end of Genesis, can the Book of Exodus and the story of our nationhood begin. And, for me, the test of family is not how its members love each other when they agree, but how they love each other when they disagree.

With this in mind, I am keenly aware that not everyone shares my vision for Israel. Many Israelis seek a state that is *ke-khol ha-goyim* (like the other nations) rather than *or la-goyim* (a light to the nations). And even among those who support the *or la-goyim* ideal there is disagreement as to what this means. This schism within our family on these issues is so great that it poses a threat to the very survival of the State.

Chosenness means that God covenantally promised that the Jewish people is eternal. It does not mean, however, that in every generation the Jews as a people would be sovereign in a Jewish state. Our destiny in some ways depends on us. It depends on our ability to learn from one another, and, for that matter, it depends on our ability to learn from other nations. How we deal respectfully with disagreement and with different visions is critical as we move forward. How and if we survive depends on us.

It is true that this is a disconcerting thought. It would be comforting to know that Israel's existence is guaranteed. All we would have to do is be. Once understanding that we must do our part to remain sovereign in the land, we realize that we must be worthy of the land. Being is not enough, doing is necessary.

What, then, can we do for Israel while living in the *golah* (Diaspora)? The Talmud records that from the exile a person ought to be a *doresh Tzion*, a seeker of Zion (Rosh Ha-shana 30a). For me, a *doresh Tzion* is someone who recognizes that his or her life as a Jew in the Diaspora is incomplete. It is the person whose goal is to live in Israel. It is the person who, while living outside Israel, does tangible acts to connect to the land—visiting Israel, buying Israeli products, calling friends in Israel, advocating for Israel, supporting the redemptive mission of the people of Israel in the Land of Israel. Only someone who lives in Israel is a complete Zionist, but in the exile we can constantly yearn to be there. To paraphrase Rav Nahman of Bratslav, wherever I am walking I am walking to Israel.

The word Zion is associated with *metzuyan*, which means to excel. *Tziun* is the mark, the center, the place from which the core values of Judaism emanate. The place of dissemination of these values is Israel.

But this is no simple emanation. The rabbis point out that just as light (*or*) of day ascends slowly (and, I would add, is occasionally blocked by the clouds), so, too, the redemptive process may be slow. It sometimes seems to be standing still, even moving backwards, but ultimately it progresses. Yet Israel is, and will continue to be, a great country, as long as we keep the message of Zion alive—as long as we strive toward excellence. In Israel we do so as Zionists, in the Diaspora as *dorshei Tzion*.

(I call the Jew in the Diaspora who is disconnected from Israel a *bar Tzion*. Just as a young person is bar or bat mitzvah when reaching the appropriate age even without a ceremony, so, too, every Jew, even one who feels no connection to Israel, is in fact subconsciously linked and hence could be called a *bar Tzion*.)

Every moment, I keep hearing Sarit wailing. Enough. Enough. The time has come for mothers and fathers to care for and raise their children here on earth. The time has come for Israel to be not only reactive as it defends its citizenry and Jews everywhere, but also proactive as Israel affirms the ultimate mission of Judaism, to be *or la-goyim*. Then, and only then, will the dream of Zion be realized.

STANLEY P. GOLD is the president and CEO of Shamrock Holdings.

"My dream for Israel is for it to retain its lofty place as a source of ongoing inspiration for Jewish communities around the globe and to continue its rich tradition of practicing *tikkun olam*."

The modern state of Israel is a miraculous achievement for the Jewish people and, personally, an immense source of inspiration and pride.

On a recent stroll down Tel Aviv's glamorous Rothschild Boulevard, I overheard a local tour guide provide the following description of a unique structure:

"This home in the Bauhaus district of Tel Aviv was built for an Ethiopian by a man named Berlin who came from Poland. The structure became a landmark Chinese restaurant headed by a renowned Israeli chef who cooked nonkosher food while splitting the dwelling's space with a religious Israeli organization providing kosher food for the needy."

This vivid description made me think of an Israel that has become home to nearly half of world Jewry; an Israel that is tolerant, modern, and normal; and that has demonstrated *tikkun olam* as a core value. Surely David Ben-Gurion must be smiling somewhere.

My own journey of deep personal connection to Israel began in the early 1980s. I came to Israel as a committed Jew and returned home as a committed capitalist. In the late 1980s Shamrock Holdings, the private investment firm that I founded with my partner and long-time friend, Roy E. Disney, started its activities in Israel with three modest investments. I recall that several people in the financial community called me at the time to inquire about the motivation for the Disney family's charity work in Israel. Several years later, these three investments produced a five-fold return on capital and I recall, even more fondly, thinking that I and the Disney family would be happy to engage in this kind of charity for a long time to come.

Over the years I have continued to be a firm believer that the highest contribution that we in the Diaspora can make to Israel's existence and well-being is the building of a sound economy for the

Jewish state. The creation of business and jobs, the training of senior management, the institutionalization of incentive compensation predicated on proper corporate governance are important milestones for any first world economy. They are especially important milestones for Israel as it perpetually strives to maintain its place among the community of developed nations.

Through Shamrock's deepening investment activities in Israel over the past eighteen years, I am fortunate to have participated in the ongoing development of the Israeli economy. I have marveled at the ingenuity, drive, ability to execute, and hunger to succeed that our Israeli employees and managers have demonstrated over the years. It is now well known that Israel has a first-rate legal system and accounting transparency on par with the Western world, and its educated work force is second to none.

Israel can and should be a tremendous source of pride and inspiration to Jews worldwide—and not only because of its accomplishments in the economic, technological, and scientific spheres. Jews worldwide can stand tall in the knowledge that Israel is among the first nations to send emergency search and rescue crews to earthquake victims in Turkey, tsunami victims in Asia, and terror victims in Kenya. In many ways, Israel reflects the collective consciousness and best efforts of world Jewry.

My dream for Israel is for it to retain its lofty place as a source of ongoing inspiration for Jewish communities around the globe and to continue its rich tradition of practicing *tikkun olam*. I wish for Israel to continue strengthening its relationships with Jewish communities worldwide and to welcome their contributions to the Jewish people. I dream of an Israel at peace with its neighbors, living tranquilly in the community of nations

RABBI GOLDIE MILGRAM is the executive vice president of ReclaimingJudaism.org and a 2006 Covenant Award finalist for excellence as a Jewish educator. She is the author of *Meaning and Mitzvah: Reclaiming Judaism through Prayer, God, Torah, Hebrew, Mitzvot and Peoplehood* and *Reclaiming Judaism as a Spiritual Practice: Shabbat and Holy Days* (both Jewish Lights).

"It is utopian Zion, this Israel is a dream we pursue, a garden in space and time we create whenever possible, a laboratory for learning and living. Israel irritates many, simply by existing, but perhaps like sand in a pearl, from this dream even sustainable peace may come."

February 2007. We landed at Ben Gurion Airport with my father, Samuel Milgram, age eighty-eight. A scooter-like wheelchair we'd rented awaited him along with a guide accustomed to physically challenged visitors. While I'd been to Israel numerous times, this would be my dad's first and likely only trip, made possible when a new antibiotic had removed the bone-marrow infection from which Dad had suffered since "the war." My father never complained of his disability; his only explanation was that while clowning around on a moving truck when he was on duty, he'd accidentally fallen off.

That first Jerusalem night, jetlagged, I awoke at 3 a.m. to notice his door ajar. Dad was not in his room?! Alarmed, I ran to the lobby only to find my ever-gregarious father chatting with the security guard, a friendly Druze man we'd met on arrival.

"Your father," the Druze man explained, "is sharing about the concentration camp site where he was wounded." Camp?! What new detail was this? My father shrugged and as always quickly changed the topic.

He declared with admiration: "This great man was a soldier for Israel; he has much to tell us." I had noted the guard's missing fingers, scarred arm, and reconstructed left hand. Wounded war veterans, both.

"Dad, what's this about a camp?" He knew my attention was now tuned to the detail about his life just revealed. He sighed.

The Druze man continued, "Soldiers know family must not be burdened with our war memories; it is enough they willingly live with us as damaged people." I persisted: "All these years you were giving us a cover story?"

Dad spoke, ever so softly. "We arrived at an assigned furlough destination and I could not believe my eyes—walking skeletons in the town and there, beyond a gate, piles of them. 'Who are you, what happened?' I asked. They looked at me with hollow eyes. It was the townspeople who explained, "Jews." No one had yet told us such things as genocide were happening. I did not see an enemy truck aiming straight for me. I was crushed against a wall."

The Druze man added, "Your father does not forgive himself for getting wounded and not being able to stay to help them." My father began to weep softly, saying, "I failed them."

The Druze man looked at Dad, then at me: "But he did not fail—his unit carried the first portable radar in that war, he helped liberate that camp. Kind sir, dear woman, look around you carefully on your travels here, marvel at what your people did—they came back here fueled by loss and beside us built their dream. How rare and impressive, instead of wreaking revenge, instead of this land the Ottomans so laid waste, they created a garden. And reading and learning; initially their books were scarce, how excited they would be when someone arrived with a book. Some would walk across the street reading, they loved to learn."

He went on. "Those who slipped in here during and after your father's war, I will never forget their haunted faces, weak bodies, yearning for missing and murdered family. I remember how it seemed they would dig everywhere they more or less safely could, weeping and leaping as they found their roots in mounds that proved to be ancient ruins. In our village we later learned their family's fates, horrible, horrible—what your father saw.

"Still our children and grandchildren dream, of peace. I know this region, peace has never been the way of things—conquerors will come and go, there will be more ruins. Or perhaps your people will invent sustainable peace, they are always inventing something. Last year they invented bees that don't even miss one flower when they do their seasonal visits. Yields more honey—I've bought some from that kibbutz myself."

He paused, as though searching. "I remember back then the dream of the Jews had a different name, not Israel; they talked of Palestine and more often of Zion."

So it is that a Druze man described to me what Israel, indeed, means to me. It is utopian Zion, this Israel is a dream we pursue, a garden in space and time we create whenever possible, a laboratory for learning and living. Israel irritates many, simply by existing, but perhaps like sand in a pearl, from this dream even sustainable peace may come.

 **Ariel Beery** is the editor and publisher of *PresenTense* magazine, founder and director of the PresenTense Institute for Creative Zionism, co-editor of blogsofzion.org, and a frequent contributor to various publications across the Jewish world on contemporary affairs and Zionist thought. Articles by Ariel can be found on www.arielbeery.com.

"My Zionism might be different from my grandfather's Zionism, but it is predicated upon the same fundamental understanding: We Jews are not just a spiritual community—we are a people, one that will only fulfill its collective potential with a state in which we can hammer out the details."

A small, ten-inch hammer with a light wooden handle hangs in a green handkerchief with a white line pattern that is nailed to my wall. I collected it from my grandfather's house at the age of nine or so, after he died, and before the house and all of its general possessions were returned to the kibbutz in northern Israel on which he lived. Those were still the years of the collective, the years in which children lived together in a single house separated from their parents, when

food was served in the general dining hall, when holidays were celebrated together on a grassy field. Other than the fact that children
lived away from their parents, it was an ideal I wish I could return to
today.

Chaim Beery, born Chaim Koledjanski in what the Austrian
writer Stefan Zweig called the "Age of Security" before World War I,
came to Kibbutz Beit Alfa together with my grandmother and a group
of young pioneers from his village of Brestoviche, Poland, in 1936.
My father likes to tell me that half of the inhabitants of the village
were communists, and half were socialist Zionists—members of the
youth movement my father, mother, siblings, and I would later join,
Hashomer Hatzair. Zionists came to Israel over mountains and across
oceans. The communists didn't; they perished in the Second World
War, a war they thought their international comrades would save
them from.

I myself grew up in the relative comfort of downtown New York
City, two blocks away from the legendary punk oasis CBGBs when
CBGBs had something to be legendary about. In my public school at
least half of the teachers were Marxists and half were social demo-
crats, but other than the occasional anti-Semitic comment, that's
where the similarity to my grandfather's time ends. I should be grateful for it, my parents told me. They themselves left Israel before I was
born to ensure that their children wouldn't serve in the army. America
was and is not Poland, and it was and is not Germany even when
Germany was good, they say, and they're right.

But America was always foreign to me, despite being born and
raised here. The Founding Fathers—George Washington, James
Madison, and Thomas Jefferson, whom I learned about in my history
lessons—were not my Founding Fathers. Abraham, Isaac, and Jacob
were. Abraham Lincoln was no Moses. The history of my people is
much longer than the history of the European settlement upon the
island on which I was born. It struck me as sort of cute when we'd
take field trips to the Liberty Bell and my classmates would revel in a
history that would fill hardly a few pages in the books chronicling the
story of my people. Christmas and St. Valentine's Day and Easter further reminded me that my own place was elsewhere: America was a
nice hotel I was staying at, but it would never be my home.

My home is the land in which my people can finally—after over two thousand years of living under the rule of various majority populations—be the narrators of its own story, and not the objects of someone else's prejudices or machinations. My home is in the land that, for all its problems, sets the backdrop for the stories my people tell at every holiday—the land my grandfathers and grandmothers risked life and limb to escape to, the land that, at the age of nineteen, I immigrated to and spent three years defending.

Until my service in the army I hadn't really thought about why Israel was so important to me—it was just a gut feeling, that buzzing notion you get in your lower abdomen as you draw close to the person you feel just right with. When I got there, my Israeli friends and peers constantly asked me: "Why did you come? What, it wasn't good for you in America?" And I would answer, as I still answer now: Human beings are no good alone. Even though no community is perfect, we humans need others to surround us as a community if we're to ever get anything done. Once we recognize this point—and thereby see through the mirage of individualism that sets the pace in the United States—all that remains is to ask: Which community would you like to be part of? I felt this question had already been answered for me.

I wanted to be part of a community that has proven its strength by maintaining its support network throughout untold hardships, one that has withstood the storms and has proven time and again that it can provide immeasurable value to its members. I wanted to be part of a community whose members band together, who care more about having the community be all that it can be than about who will win at being all that one can be, alone. And so I chose to become a full member of the Jewish community—that is, to put my life where my identity is, not willing to have other kids my age lay their lives on the line for the defense of my homeland, my place of refuge, while I drank college away.

Today, living in America, those same friends ask me: "Why did you leave if you are such a Zionist?" And here is where my relationship to Israel differs from that of Ben-Gurion: Though I love Israel, and plan on living there fully one day, I do not think that each and every Jew must live in Israel. The very existence of the State is enough to qualitatively change the Jewish experience.

Throughout our history, Jews always represented such a small percentage of our host countries, and therefore our voices were not loud enough. In the Diaspora, we have never fully realized our potential; while excelling in science and business, we were fundamentally alienated from the communities in whose midst we lived. The same creativity of a few individuals that developed new paradigms in fields from psychology to physics had been effectively barred from creating and enacting new paradigms in government and civil service. Our yearning for Zion was like a departed soul's yearning to return to a physical body, the yearning to arise and walk again. Israel, like any physical body, is imperfect—and yet like a body it serves as the tool for the perfection of the soul.

Israel's existence, however, has changed that—and Zionism has changed in Israel's wake. While Jews can now participate in all levels of life in the United States, those policies that will ultimately guide the country's spirit will forever remain foreign and controlled by the majority. Israel, by its very existence, and due to the very real challenges that it faces, provides the opportunity for Jews from all over the world to apply their creativity to solving human problems as Jews: to apply Jewish values and the Jewish spirit to every aspect of life, from the holiest of holies to the most rank and mundane. My Zionism might be different from my grandfather's Zionism, but it is predicated upon the same fundamental understanding: We Jews are not just a spiritual community—we are a people, one that will only fulfill its collective potential with a state in which we can hammer out the details.

RABBI STANLEY M. DAVIDS, rabbi emeritus of Temple Emanu-El of Atlanta, is president of the Association of Reform Zionists of America. He and his wife, Resa, reside in Jerusalem and Santa Monica, California.

"Our people has yet to demonstrate that we have the capacity to translate prophetic imperatives into the governing norms of a just, democratic, pluralistic Jewish society."

As David Hartman [the leading Modern Orthodox theologian and philosopher] famously insists, the hardest place in the world to be a Zionist is on the streets of Jerusalem. A city of poverty and of poetry, Jerusalem seems to epitomize the fractured and factitious nature of life in the Jewish state. Bumper stickers proclaim, "Keep your distance," but no one ever keeps anything resembling the kind of distance that would grant breathing room and even a degree of respect to another person—either on the streets or on the sidewalks.

From the *haredim* who seem constantly concerned about getting somewhere else very quickly, to the Arab women taking their driving lessons on Saturday morning, to the Bratslavers and Chabadniks who actually believe there is beauty to be found in plastering over the cityscape with their posters of hope and defiance, to the habitués of the Aroma cafe on Emek Refaim who savor their cigarettes while watching fellow citizens stroll toward the Shabbat *minyan* of their choice, to the Bell Park where Muslim children dominate on Friday and Jewish children on Saturday—Jerusalem scorns those who would seek to paint her image with simple descriptions.

For me and for my wife, Resa, our aliyah could only have been made to Jerusalem, the very heart of Zion. We love its unsettling vibrancy. We thrive in its institutions of study and of faith. Our Shabbat table is regularly adorned not only with old friends and with family from around the world but also with new friends whose backgrounds and passions continually open up for us new opportunities to understand our world.

I was born in 1939. My first memory of the world "out there" was when I stood with my family on the front steps of our home in Cleveland Heights, watching the outpouring of grief over the death of President Roosevelt. I was nine when my Hebrew teacher allowed me to hold in my hand a real coin that bore the letters spelling out the name of the reborn Jewish state. June 5, 1967, was the first time I ever wept when singing "Hatikvah," joining with a stunned and grieving group of Jewish leaders in the Israeli Embassy in Washington. On February 21, 2004, Resa and I touched Israel's soil for the very first time as *olim*.

My Reform Zionism is far from fulfilled, despite the existence of the State. Our people has indeed reentered history, determined to exercise control over our own destiny. But we do so at a time when we continue to stagger from the unimaginable losses of the Shoah—losses that not only have been a human tragedy, but that have also reduced our numbers, shattered most of our communities, and left us vulnerable to a devastating loss of faith. And we do so at a time when the very openness of a post-modern, post-nationalist pluralistic Western world calls into question on the part of many of our young people why it is that Jewish survival in general, and the survival of a Jewish state in particular, should have any resonance for them. We do so at a time when the rising political, cultural, and economic powers are China and India—vast countries whose populations have little awareness of and concern for the millennial Jewish narrative. And we do so at a time when our people has yet to demonstrate that we have the capacity to translate prophetic imperatives into the governing norms of a just, democratic, pluralistic Jewish society.

My Reform Zionism will be fulfilled when a coercive state-sponsored Orthodoxy in Israel will yield to a multifaceted Jewish state in which the rights of all genders and minorities—ethnic and religious—will be fully protected and respected. My Reform Zionism will be fulfilled when issues of education, human welfare, economic equality, and justice will have a level of priority comparable to defense and security. My Reform Zionism will be fulfilled when a reasoned and just political and diplomatic process yields a two-state solution that will free up our energies to take advantage of the unmatched human resources at our disposal.

My Reform Zionism will be fulfilled when American Reform Jews fully integrate Jewish nationalism and peoplehood into our identities. My Reform Zionism will be fulfilled when young American Reform Jews embrace programs and possibilities that allow them to spend extended periods of time studying and working in Israel. My Reform Zionism will be fulfilled when American Reform Jews come to see the Hebrew language as an irreplaceable doorway into the Jewish future.

My Reform Zionism will be fulfilled when Israeli Jews understand and celebrate the reality that their future and their identities are irrevocably intertwined with the fate of the Jewish people worldwide. Not one. Not the other. But all of us together.

So I go out into Jerusalem's streets, take a deep breath, and realize once again what a sacred privilege I have.

STEVEN M. COHEN is research professor of Jewish social policy, Hebrew Union College–Jewish Institute of Religion, New York. He is also the director of the JCCA/Florence G. Heller Research Center.

"I wonder how many of the next generation are walking away from a serious engagement with Israel, if only because we have failed to welcome, let alone encourage and invite, the expression of serious skepticism, criticism, and opposition."

"There was no such thing as Palestinians. When was there an independent Palestinian people with a Palestinian state? It was either southern Syria before the First World War, and then it was a Palestine including Jordan. It was not as though there was a Palestinian people in Palestine

considering itself as a Palestinian people and we came and threw them out and took their country away from them. They did not exist."
—**Prime Minister Golda Meir, June 15, 1969.**

"The Palestinian people today have all the attributes of nationhood. They have national consciousness. They have territorial continuity where most of the Palestinians live. They have a Palestinian history of decades, marked by struggles and wars. They have a diaspora with a strong affinity to their birthplace. They have national awareness of a common disaster, common victims, sufferings and heroes. The nation has a vision, its own literature and poetry. The Arab Palestinian nation is perhaps the nation with the most obvious signs of identity and the strongest national unity, among the Arab nations."
—**Lova Eliav, Secretary General of Mapai, November 1968.**

The college campus of the late 1960s is remembered as marked by protests, debate, and contentiousness, largely focused around the Viet Nam War. But the war in Viet Nam was not the only war to spark debate and controversy on campus. The Six Day War brought pro-Palestinian and pro-Israel sympathizers into conflict, with Arab students on one side, Israelis on the other, and leftist Jews on both.

Among the American public, it was a time when sympathy with Israel was at its height. Among American Jews, it was a time of extraordinary pro-Israel attachment, expressed in surges in travel and the largest aliyah over a sustained period (1968–1973). But on campus things were more complicated, as the most respected voices condemned American imperialism and the use of military force, and held out admiration for national liberation struggles by third world peoples resisting neocolonial domination by the West.

Jewish college students at the time—I was an undergraduate at Columbia University—could choose one of four ways to relate to Israel. First, they could choose to ignore publicly engaging with the issue—an option probably taken by most. Second, they could side with those who questioned Israel's very right to exist. My namesake on campus, a leader of Students for a Democratic Society (SDS), in a

well-attended public debate with me advocated the creation of a secular, democratic binational state; not surprisingly, I took a somewhat
different position. Third, Jewish students could adopt what was then
the official policy of the Israeli government, as expressed in Golda
Meir's remarks above. It was one that saw all right and justice on the
side of Israel, and rejected any legitimacy or moral standing whatever
to the other, be they Arabs in general or Palestinians in particular. I
imagine such "Israel right or wrong" students existed, but truth be
told, none at Columbia coalesced to form a recognizable campus
group or organized any programs expressing a position in line with
Israeli official policies.

The fourth alternative, one that I and many of my friends
embraced, was embodied in the quote above by Lova Eliav, the Labor
Party's Secretary General and Golda Meir's likely successor—that is,
until his views on the Palestinians provoked Meir to shunt him aside.
The pro-Israel activists at Columbia, and on campuses all across the
country, espoused a Zionism that endorsed both the Jewish and
Palestinian "national liberation movements," in the favored terms of
the day. We took umbrage at Israel's treatment of the Palestinians and
advocated a two-state solution to the conflict, as I did in that debate
with the "other" Steven Cohen from SDS.

Given the tenor of the times, the choice we made is not particularly remarkable. But what is remarkable is the identity of those who
inspired, funded, and supported the youthful critics of Israeli government policies: the educational arm of the Jewish Agency and World
Zionist Organization. The American Zionist Youth Foundation
(AZYF) provided pro-Israel campus organizations, such as the one I
helped lead at Columbia, with program budgets, speakers, intercam-
pus connections, and ultimately $100-a-month "stipends" for leaders
such as myself. The AZYF brought us the likes of Lova Eliav on campus speaking tours. In this context, it's important to note that the
AZYF was a wholly owned subsidiary of the Jewish Agency's Youth
and Hechalutz Department, then chaired by retired General Morele
Baron (formerly head of education for the Army and later a Meretz
Knesset member) and under the political aegis of the Labor Party.

In essence, a semi-official Israeli body, with close ties to the
Israeli government and leading American Jewish funders, helped pro-

vide American Jewish students with the option of combining deep Zionist commitment with a sharply critical stance toward key positions of the Israeli government in matters of war and peace. The policy was effective politically, as seen in our successful advocacy on the campus; and it was effective educationally, for I am not the only lifelong Zionist and *oleh* (immigrant to Israel) to come out of that environment of contentious Zionism. We contended both with the campus-based anti-Israel forces and with the unwise and morally questionable policies of the Israeli government; and we contended as well with our emerging identities as leftists, as Zionists, and, of course, as Jews.

If the policy of encouraging contentious Zionism was effective then, it is also instructive today. Today, to our detriment, no significant Jewish communal or educational agency promotes pro-Israel contention and controversy—either on the campus or in the "real" Jewish community. We cannot ignore the sorry fact that Israel is no longer a source of Jewish mobilization for most Jewish young people. Rather—as so many of them frequently tell us—the perception that communally involved Jews demand allegiance to Israeli policies, whatever they may be, serves as a barrier and obstacle to Jewish communal involvement. Jews under thirty-five years old see organized Jewry as, in their words, "coercive," in squelching any morally charged questioning of Israeli policies. Insofar as we fail to invite American Jews into the rich and compelling debates in which Israelis themselves engage, we miss the opportunity to engage many more in the national life of the Jewish people.

As I reflect on an entire adulthood with Israel and Zionism at the core of my being, I think back with gratitude to the likes of Lova Eliav and Morele Baron, whom I recently have had the privilege of thanking personally for providing me and so many others with the Zionism of debate, controversy, and contention. As I do so, and as I think of the absence of doubt, divisions, and debate in the pro-Israel American Jewish community, I wonder how many of the next generation are walking away from a serious engagement with Israel, if only because we have failed to welcome, let alone encourage and invite, the expression of serious skepticism, criticism, and opposition.

RABBI MOSHE WALDOKS is the spiritual leader of Temple Beth Zion, an independent congregation in Brookline, Massachusetts. He is well known as the co-editor of *The Big Book of Jewish Humor*, now in its special twenty-fifth anniversary edition.

"As a passionate lover of Israel and its people, I feel compelled to opt for a vision of peace and security rather than alarmism and despair."

My first encounter with Israel, the reality, followed the 1967 Six Day War. As a student I traveled to Israel for my junior year in 1968. I eventually stayed for three years and finished my undergraduate work at the Hebrew University. Those were heady days for Israel; the post-1967 euphoria, the reunification of Jerusalem, and the sense that Israel's existence was vindicated and assured when the near-"miraculous" nature of the swift victory led to the rise in aliyah of Jews from the United States and elsewhere. The liberation of the territories on the west and the east was seen as divine providence, and only a few voices raised a specter of caution over taking in millions of Arabs into the Israel body politic.

In those days I was enthralled and attracted to the new Jewish militancy that inspired the settlers of the West Bank, Hebron, in particular. I recall the Shabbatot spent in the *mimshal tzvai* (the military headquarters) that served as the home to the nucleus of the Hebron resettlement movement before the creation of Kiryat Arba, a suburb of Hebron. Having been raised the son of a Revisionist Zionist from the pre–World War II Polish Ukraine who arrived with my mother in 1949, two weeks before my birth, I had attended the ceremony for the reinternment of Ze'ev Jabotinsky's remains to Israel when Levi Eshkol succeeded David Ben-Gurion as prime minister in the early 1960s.

The Hebron settlers exuded an exotic combination of Zionism and religious faith, of muscles and moorings in tradition that seemed so different from the inhabitants of my pre-1967 Brooklyn yeshiva world. They smelled of redemption, not exile. They were heralds of a messianic future that would overcome the bitter *galut* (exile) of the Jewish people. But after a few years of unmitigated admiration, I began to feel uncomfortable with the settler style, its in-your-face braggadocio. Walking to the Cave of the Patriarchs, tallit and Uzi swinging from their shoulders, they sang as they walked through the Arab market, making a clear statement of domination as they prepared to offer up praises to the God of Abraham. Rarely were there efforts to engage these fellow children of Abraham beyond quotidian necessities.

In the early 1970s I hearkened to a new voice, one that led me to question whether the Hebron settlers were potential redeemers of the land or simply transplanted *golus yidn* (Diaspora Jews) forever creating divisions between Us and Them, erecting fences and wired ghetto walls, first for themselves and then, in the years to come, for their Arab cousins. This voice talked of returning the territories to Arab rule and establishing a confederation of Jordan, Israel, and Palestine, a Middle Eastern Benelux. It was an idea so based on hope for a different future that it overcame many of the triumphalist urges that were part and parcel of my upbringing. This voice proclaimed that in the real world, there needn't be winners and losers, "Us vs. Them"; rather, it augured the possibility of coexistence, cooperation, and confederation. The years of 1968 to 1971 are still recalled by many Israelis as the "best years" ever experienced by the country.

I returned to the United States to enter a doctoral program at Brandeis University. My ongoing attachment to Israel and its people continue to this day, and a few years back my brother and his family made aliyah to Jerusalem.

I see myself as being somewhat in the middle of the spectrum of Israeli opinion. I sustain a hefty pride for all of the achievements of the State of Israel over the last sixty years. I am always amazed by the robustness of Israeli life, the capacity people have to continue to live their lives amid abnormal pressures. While I miss the culture shock that I experienced in my first encounter with Israel in the 1960s (Jerusalem had only one traffic light, at the corner of Jaffa and King George Streets), I am pleased that Israelis enjoy many of the creature comforts I enjoy in Boston. I am also wary of the tendency to see Israel as somehow not strong enough for the necessary compromises that will have to be made, hopefully in the near future, to ensure a two-state solution, or in the voices of the early 1970s: a confederation of Israel, Jordan, and Palestine that will fuel a truly democratic vision for the Middle East. A vision created by ballots, not bullets.

In the throes of the current situation in Iraq, Iran, and throughout the world, this seems like a pipedream. But as a passionate lover of Israel and its people, I feel compelled to opt for a vision of peace and security rather than alarmism and despair. It is very disturbing that those who profess the most fervent faith and adherence to tradition seem to lack the deep-seated security that *netzach yisrael lo yeshakeir*—the eternity of Israel is no falsehood.

DR. DAVID M. GORDIS is president and professor of Rabbinics at Hebrew College and founding director of the National Center for Jewish Policy Studies (formerly the Susan and David Wilstein Institute of Jewish Policy Studies). He has lectured and written extensively on the subjects of Jewish life in America and Israel, Israel–Diaspora relations, and Judaism in America and Israel.

> "As we celebrate Israel's reality and reflect on its past, we should remind ourselves that we are still at the threshold, and that Israel and the Jewish people have much to aspire to and to work toward as we move ahead to further realization of our vision for our people and for our world."

I was eight years old when the State of Israel was established. Though very young at the time, I have vivid memories of sitting glued to the radio and listening to the reports from the United Nations at Lake Success, New York, voting on the partition of Palestine and enabling the establishment of Israel. Which country would put the vote over the line? And I clearly recall an excursion to what was then Idlewild Airport (now JFK) in Queens, New York, to see the first airliner bearing the Israeli flag on its tail and the emblem of El Al on its fuselage. It was a magical moment!

I also have clear recollections of the schoolyard at the Yeshivah of Flatbush, where I attended elementary school, at which the establishment of Israel was celebrated and the announcement was made that, from that day on, only the *sefardit*, or Sephardic pronunciation, of Hebrew (the one used in Israel) would be used at the yeshiva. It was clear, even to a youngster, that something epochal was happening, transforming the Jewish world from the unrelieved bleakness of the Holocaust and the war years into a hopeful transfusion of Jewish vitality. This was a powerful new and living assertion that the Jewish people lives.

It's now almost sixty years later. Since my first trip there as a college student, I have been to Israel for brief or extended visits more than fifty times, many of which were related to professional responsibilities there. Israel has been central in all of my activities—academic, communal, and public policy. Without question, for the Jewish people and for me personally, the establishment of Israel is the most remarkable feature on the landscape of modern Jewish history.

It is unique to me and my contemporaries that our lives have embraced both the moments of most profound Jewish despair and highest Jewish exaltation—Holocaust and rebirth. But time has a way of tempering our awareness and consciousness, and there is great risk that memories will become submerged and that what should be continuing sources of reflection and wonder are taken for granted. We need to remind ourselves of the radically transformative impact of Israel on every dimension of Jewish life: identity, culture, scholarship, influence, self-image, world presence, and vitality. Jews are no longer a marginalized footnote to history; we are active participants in shaping human experience. Even if our Jewish community in the Diaspora continued to exist, how radically different it would be without Israel!

Reality is always very different from vision, and the reality of Israel is certainly far more complex than the idealized vision aspired to for two millennia. We are a fractious people, assertive and articulate, and it is in itself a miracle that the articulation of diverse ideological, religious, and political views is possible within the context of a sovereign Jewish state. Israel is—thank God—a living reality, and as such is a work in progress. As we celebrate Israel's reality and reflect on its past, we should remind ourselves that we are still at the threshold, and that Israel and the Jewish people have much to aspire to and to work toward as we move ahead to further realization of our vision for our people and for our world.

 **Rabbi Robert B. Barr** is the rabbi of Congregation Beth Adam, a humanistic congregation in Loveland, Ohio.

"I bought myself a T-shirt. It was green with blue lettering. It was the Hebrew version of the classic American slogan of the time—'War is unhealthy for children and other living things.' It spoke to me of hopes and dreams and of an Israel that was safe and secure."

For some people, the first time they step off the plane onto the tarmac at Ben Gurion International Airport feels like coming home. Others say that the experience overwhelmed them and moved them to the depth of their being.

The first time I stepped off an airplane onto Israeli soil I was tired, hot, and scared. Tired—that's simple—it was a long flight and I was unable to sleep. Hot—it was late June and the black asphalt of the tarmac was as hot as the desert sun above my head. Scared—well, I was twenty years old, had never been away from home, and had just flown halfway around the globe to a tiny country surrounded by hostile nations.

As I looked around the tarmac, I was both excited and nervous. What had I gotten myself into? Would I survive a year in this country? Could I be successful in my studies? Was I up to this challenge? My mind raced and for the first few weeks I didn't know the answer to any of those questions. Gradually, I settled in and grew comfortable in my new home, excited by my studies and energized by my experiences.

That year in Israel was transformative and significant for me. In my rabbinic studies, I was challenged to think about my values, beliefs, and understanding of Judaism. Living in Israel, a place I knew only through filmstrips and books, I was gradually transformed from a stranger in a foreign land to a Jew comfortable in a homeland for my people. I came to value and appreciate the small nation more than I ever thought possible. I grew to love Jerusalem, the city I lived in, and came to know its smells and sounds. No longer was it just a picture in some book; it was alive and remarkable. The past and future slammed together with such intensity in that city that my ears and eyes would ring with wonder. It was magical and intoxicating, and yet the sense of danger always lingered, was always there in the background just out of sight.

While I lived in Jerusalem, Yitzhak Rabin was prime minister of Israel and I frequently walked past his house to get to my apartment. Even in 1976, a peaceful year, there was much security. Though I felt safe, it was a constant reminder of the realities that Israel faced. Frequently, when I passed the prime minister's home late at night, I would be stopped and questioned about who I was, where I had been, and where I was going. One morning on my way to school, there was even more security than usual. Dr. Henry Kissinger was inside meeting with Prime Minister Rabin. I hoped and imagined that they were discussing ways of creating lasting peace in the Middle East. I stood with a crowd of people and waited as long as I could to see one or the other of these men, but neither emerged. I was late for class and lasting peace remained elusive.

As nervous as I was upon my arrival, one year later I was equally sad as I prepared to leave Israel. I cleaned my apartment, packed my duffel bag, and mailed my books back to the United States. Ready for departure, I went out for one last excursion with the hope of finding something special for myself, some lasting memory of my time in an amazing country.

In retrospect it seems a little silly, but I bought myself a T-shirt. It was green with blue lettering. It was the Hebrew version of the classic American slogan of the time—"War is unhealthy for children and other living things." It spoke to me of hopes and dreams and of an Israel that was safe and secure. For years I wore that T-shirt, and every time I did I was taken back to my home in Jerusalem. Regrettably, the colors began to fade and the T-shirt wore out long before its message had been realized. I hated throwing that T-shirt away; it was as if I was giving up on the words written there. Today, that T-shirt is a memory and lasting peace remains a dream.

 RICHARD ELLIOTT FRIEDMAN is the author of: *Who Wrote the Bible?*; *The Hidden Face of God*; *The Hidden Book in the Bible*; *The Bible with Sources Revealed*; and *Commentary on the Torah*. He is the Davis Professor of Jewish Studies at the University of Georgia and Katzin Professor of Jewish Civilization Emeritus of the University of California, San Diego.

> "So I, as a Bible scholar, have a lofty dream of Israel as aiming for something awesome and having a mission to make that awesome goal a reality.... Israel must be now what it has stood for from its very beginning: a people seeking to bring blessing to every family on earth."

My perspective is biblical. The cases in the Bible in which God is pictured as giving the reasons for commanding anything are few. But a supremely notable exception is the gift of the land. For the Bible's first eleven chapters, it doesn't focus on Israel but rather on the whole world. Divine–human relations don't work out: expulsion from Eden, flood, Babel. And so, the biblical text narrows to Abraham. God's first words to him are the instruction to go to the Land of Israel. God gives the reason for this command: "And all the families of the earth will be blessed through you" (Genesis 12:3).

It's in God's first words to Abraham and God's first words to Isaac (26:2–4) and God's first words to Jacob (28:10–14). If you still might miss it, it's repeated during the appearance of the three visitors (18:17–18) and after the near-sacrifice of Isaac (22:16–18).

I wrote in my commentary on the Torah that the text never tells us what this blessing is supposed to be. Is it that the people of Israel are to bring blessing by being a light to the nations, showing how a community can live: caring for one another, not cheating one another, not enslaving one another, and so on? Or are they to bring blessing by doing things that benefit all: inventions, cures, literature, learning?

It doesn't say. But at a minimum it must mean that the people of Israel are not to live only for themselves. Israel's destiny must be bound up in the destiny of all humankind.

How central is this? The first occurrence of the word "torah" in the Torah is: "There shall be one torah for the citizen and for the alien" (Exodus 12:49). Later, in the same chapter in which we find the commandment to "Love your neighbor as yourself," we discover that this includes non-Israelites: "The alien who resides with you shall be to you like a citizen of yours, and you shall love him as yourself" (Leviticus 19:34).

But what if others are hostile? The people of Israel had enemies, then as now. The measure of Israel's commitment to the families of the earth is its attitude toward those who attack them. The Torah instructs that Israel should surely defend itself from its enemies but not hate them. It commands, "Don't abhor an Edomite ... " (Deuteronomy 23:8). Edom (what is now southern Jordan) had a perfectly awful history with Israel, yet Israel is instructed not to hate them. It goes on to say, "Don't abhor an Egyptian ... " You would think that if one people enslaves another people, this would be a perfectly good reason for the enslaved people to hate the enslaving people. But the Torah says otherwise, and Jews keep taking drops of wine from their Passover cups to express empathy toward an oppressor.

So I, as a Bible scholar, have a lofty dream of Israel as aiming for something awesome and having a mission to make that awesome goal a reality. Our Torah doesn't begin with Moses, or even Abraham, but with the creation of the whole world. While some interpret the idea of "the chosen people" to mean the exclusion of others, and while some still repeat the anti-Semitic canard that "Jews keep to themselves," Israel has, from its beginnings, stood for the opposite tendency. Even while enemies demonize Israel—identifying the Jewish state as apartheid, racist, colonial, segregationist, terrorist, involved in ethnic cleansing, and so on—I stand in awe of Israel's principles, from the Torah to Theodor Herzl and David Ben-Gurion, that embody the opposite image.

Israel must be now what it has stood for from its very beginning: a people seeking to bring blessing to every family on earth.

 ROSANNE MILLER SELFON, a native of the fourth oldest community in the United States, Lancaster, Pennsylvania, and a lifelong Reform Jew, currently serves as president of Women of Reform Judaism, the women's agency of the Union for Reform Judaism.

"The time has arrived for a democratic Israel to stand fully upright. It is time for Israel, our beloved homeland, to become a light unto itself, a land whose heart and mind open equally to all Jews, a land where religious pluralism can thrive and equal treatment and representation for all Jews will become a reality. All Jews will know that Israel is theirs. Not a single Jew should feel excluded."

Israel, the modern state, and I were born the same year: Israel in May and I in October. We share a deep commitment to our faith, our heritage, and our people. Little did we both realize that our seemingly disparate paths would cross often as we entered middle age.

Throughout my classical Reform "Sunday School" education, I was told about a land far, far away from Lancaster, Pennsylvania. That land was the birthplace of my ancestors, people whose Torah names I repeated often in Hebrew prayers. There were places located in that land that I had only imagined. Was the Jordan River as big as the Susquehanna? Did Abraham's Cave of Machpelach resemble American caves I knew? Where was Solomon's Temple? Would Safed be as mystical for me as it was for the kabbalists? I had dreamed of those places. Mostly I had wondered if they were real, and if I would ever see them.

Years pass quickly, with life mandating immediate choices while delaying the fulfillment of far-away dreams. Like the typical

Jewish female of my era, I went to college, married my high school love, began teaching, gave birth to two fabulous daughters, and immediately joined the Reform congregation where I was reared. Neither time nor resources existed for travel. We were busy just living.

However, volunteering and relationship-building within our local community occupied my hours. Activism opened new doors. I began a serious, intentional Jewish journey as an adult. First through volunteerism, and then through study and teaching, living an educated Jewish life became a driving force. Only my family consumed more attention and love.

Originally that volunteerism focused on my local sisterhood. Participation in Women of Reform Judaism (WRJ), formerly the National Federation of Temple Sisterhoods (NFTS), encouraged learning about the modern State of Israel. Of course, those ancient sites could be found within modern Israel's borders. But developing progressive communities in Israel engaged me. Preschools in congregations whose names I couldn't pronounce needed North American sisterhood support. Emerging progressive synagogues would only grow if native-born Israeli rabbis were ordained. We, North American Reform sisterhood women, accepted responsibility for raising scholarship funds for Israeli rabbinic students as well as raising awareness of those liberal congregations and kibbutzim.

As my sisterhood involvement grew, my need to visit Israel grew. I wanted to see Hebrew Union College, located on prestigious King David Street in Jerusalem. Sisterhoods had raised thousands of dollars to help build the Beit Shmuel Guest House and Cultural Center of the World Union for Progressive Judaism attached to HUC. I wanted to see our name, NFTS, on the dedication plaque. I yearned to share coffee with friends at a cafe on Ben Yehuda Street. I wanted to follow the paths our daughters, Lysa and Amanda, had walked during their National Federation of Temple Youth (NFTY) trips to Israel. I wanted to experience an ancient dig and touch ancient soil. I wanted to visit ancient and modern Israel alike.

My first visit finally materialized in 1995. My husband, David, and I celebrated our twenty-fifth wedding anniversary by traveling to

Israel on a congregational trip. The trip fulfilled my every dream. "Israel is a country of great contrasts," I wrote over and over again on postcards back to the States. I can vividly recall my initial impressions. I marveled that an ancient wall became a leaning post for cell phone users. Small cars and long tour buses expertly maneuvered alleyways where Israel's prophets had walked. The Western Wall was smaller than I had imagined, but it was mine; it was every Jew's remnant of days long gone.

I grappled with understanding how Israelis seemed to thrive despite the stressful, life-threatening daily environment. I couldn't imagine teaching my daughters how to use gas masks. I developed an intense respect for Israelis. Sabras are tough because their lives demand tenacity. Survival isn't an option; it is, quite obviously, a necessity.

Israel mirrors a modern miracle. I feel great pride for this little country. I had first felt that pride during the Yom Kippur War. I remember David and me, as teenagers, attending a local community meeting, each pledging our small amount of savings. Seeing modern Israel magnified our pride. Israel became a home away from home. We are part of this place where names are now real, where faces are now familiar, and where blessings and struggles also belong to us.

When I now travel to Israel as President of Women of Reform Judaism, I am no longer a casual tourist. As a friend recently commented, I am a "change agent." It is my obligation to strategize, to create awareness, to raise funds, and to support paths to progress. Israel and I have reached our "mature" years; our initial growing pains have subsided. The time has arrived for a democratic Israel to stand fully upright. It is time for Israel, our beloved homeland, to become a light unto itself, a land whose heart and mind open equally to all Jews, a land where religious pluralism can thrive and equal treatment and representation for all Jews will become a reality. All Jews will know that Israel is theirs. Not a single Jew should feel excluded.

I envision an Israel, as did Prime Minister Yitzhak Rabin, where equality and respect are fundamental values that apply to all. I dream of an Israel that affirms Joshua's account, a land overflowing with milk and honey. That is the Israel of my dreams. As our prophets and sages said, it shall come to be.

 ELLIOT RATZMAN is assistant professor of religion at Swarthmore College. He is a contributing editor to *Heeb* magazine, and author of the forthcoming memoir *After Zion*. He can be reached at elratzman@gmail.com.

"Israel is the arena in which our politics and ethics are tested…. We should soldier on, committing to an imperfect State, working at times with insufferable people in trying conditions."

Moses Hess, the first theorist of Zionism, in his brilliant book *Rome and Jerusalem*, first figured out in 1862 why today's Israel matters. Writing during a time of intense Polish and Italian nationalism, Hess made the case that the genius of the Jewish people constituted the most original and substantial form of national liberation. Judaism's genius was its ideal of social justice, and the Jewish tradition is the constellation of community and material practices that transmits this essence through time. When the Jews return to their ancestral homeland and create the just society, *Israel* will serve as a model for all oppressed nations by putting into practice Judaism's blueprint for social harmony. What vision could be more attractive?

Hess's insight over and against his colleague Karl Marx was that humans naturally group themselves into familial, tribal, and national units. Rather than advocate tribalism or attempt to peddle universal liberation in anemic, abstract terms, Hess made a convincing case that authentic universal social justice begins with national projects. One cannot have a "brotherhood of nations" without healthy nations.

This framework fits well with my own experience of Israel and Zionism. The Israel of my youth consisted of tourist photographs of happy kibbutzniks harvesting fields, stories of resourceful, resolute, and ingenious sabras (native-born Israelis) and promises of safe havens for threatened Jews everywhere. Israelis were mysterious and tough like the kids who spent the summer at our rural Indiana summer camp. I understood in naïve black-and-white terms that Israel was beset by enemies, haters, and anti-Semites. Later, I admired Israel's progressive activists and intellectuals from afar and looked forward to serving as a foot soldier for the cause of peace and reconciliation.

After studying in Jerusalem for several years, my utopian notions dissolved. The kibbutzim were dour and uninspiring. Israeli students were clueless about the conditions of their own country. Every kabbalist I met was uncomfortably bigoted and undemocratic. Even the Israeli peace movement was woefully unorganized and uncreative. Nevertheless, Israel matters despite disappointing.

Israel is the arena in which our politics and ethics are tested. On one hand, this means that Israel is where Jews are responsible for fighting for equal rights for all of Israel's citizens and for reconciling with our Arab cousins; we must resist the temptations of chauvinism and myopia that come with power. On the other hand, Israel is the challenge for we Jews who prefer our politics pure. We cannot erase the mistakes the State has made regarding its Arab neighbors and citizens or forget the injustices of the occupation. But the response to this should not be the refusal to see anything good in Israel—we must resist the temptation of purity. We should soldier on, committing to an imperfect State, working at times with insufferable people in trying conditions, acting to make Hess's noble vision of a model just society more than a dream.

As Jews in a fantastically successful Diaspora, we have to negotiate our relationship to this troubled other country. As American Jews, the qualities that have catalyzed our success—the values of individualism, social justice, and liberalism—have also resulted in creating a generation disillusioned with Israel. The culture of Diaspora Judaism creates individuals with strong democratic characters who are wary of getting involved with traditions like Zionism; strong individuals may not make strongly committed joiners. To keep the best and brightest Jews engaged with Israel, we need to foreground ways of being committed, but critical, Zionists, emphasizing the prophetic and prophetic aspects of Jewish patriotism.

I am engaged with Israel because as a Jew, I cannot turn away from the responsibility I have to Israel, with all of its warts. Agreeing with Hess, to be the most splendid universalist, I have to begin with my own particularity.

RABBI NILES ELLIOT GOLDSTEIN is the founding rabbi of The New Shul in Manhattan and the author or editor of seven books. His most recent work, *Gonzo Judaism: A Bold Path for Renewing an Ancient Faith*, was honored by *Publishers Weekly* as one of the top ten religion books of 2006.

> "The *mikveh* is ultimately about renewal and rebirth. It is a timeless ritual that, for me at least, reached its most powerful expression in the Holy Land. And it is just this process of revitalization, purification, and renewed wholeness that the Land of Israel itself now craves so desperately and deeply."

During my first year of rabbinical school, I lived in Kiryat Shmuel, a beautiful neighborhood in Jerusalem. Every Friday afternoon, my routine was the same: I'd buy food for Shabbat in the local markets, go to rugby practice at the Givat Ram stadium of Hebrew University, and then clean up for services. There were many synagogues near my apartment, and almost each week I'd try out a new one with friends.

Several of the shuls had a *mikveh* (ritual bath) attached to them. I'd been in a *mikveh* only once before, while I was a college student in Israel three years earlier—an unusual one that had been built into the cleft of a mountain in the Galilee. It had been a very powerful experience, but it had never occurred to me that ritual immersion would ever become a regular part of my religious and spiritual life—especially of my Shabbat preparation. Taking a shower after rugby practice paled in comparison.

There was a *mikveh* down the street from my apartment, in the basement of a synagogue named Yad Tamar, that I particularly liked. Though I was invariably viewed by the other bathers with some degree of suspicion (since I did not look the part of the typical, ultra-Orthodox *mikveh* user), I always looked forward to my weekly immersion. Shabbat started to seem somehow different, somehow purer—or perhaps I was the one who had changed. When I moved back to the United States to continue my rabbinical studies, it became too difficult to go to a *mikveh* every Friday; there just weren't enough of them close to me. And, to be fully honest, I probably grew lazy.

I longed for that neighborhood *mikveh,* so I tried to bathe myself each week in its memory instead of its waters—as well as my memories of Jerusalem.

In classical Jewish writings, the waters of a *mikveh* are referred to as *mayim chayim,* "living waters." They must come from a natural source, like a spring, stream, or rainwater, and they must completely envelop the Jew who enters them. Not even the hair on a person's head should float above the surface. It was just this feature— the idea of envelopment, of engulfment—that made going to the *mikveh* such a meaningful, and at times transcendent, experience for me. As many of us wrap prayer shawls around ourselves before we begin to worship, so, too, do the waters of the *mikveh* wrap themselves around our bodies as we descend the steps of its pool.

The *mikveh* is ultimately about renewal and rebirth. It is a timeless ritual that, for me at least, reached its most powerful expression in the Holy Land. And it is just this process of revitalization, purification, and renewed wholeness that the Land of Israel itself now craves so desperately and deeply.

May the waters of the *mikveh*—the waters of life—seep over and into every Israeli city, every street, every home, and every living soul.

PETER EDELMAN, a law professor at Georgetown University Law Center, is currently the board president of the New Israel Fund. He served as law clerk to Supreme Court Justice Arthur Goldberg and legislative aide to the late Senator Robert F. Kennedy, and was Assistant Secretary of Health and Human Services in the Clinton Administration.

"I believe that the Israel I love should be and *must* be an Israel of justice for all its citizens, and an Israel that believes in the power of words as its first defense before using its necessarily strong military might. That is my Judaism and it is my Zionism."

Like many American Jews of my generation, I grew up with mixed messages. My father came from a long line of rabbis, but as the son of immigrants he wanted to be a "regular" American, too. My parents sent me to Talmud Torah and Camp Ramah, but their own actions spoke otherwise. We were clearly proud to be Jewish, but they went to synagogue only on the High Holy Days, and in our home observed only Pesach and Hanukkah. We were ardent armchair Zionists, but Israel was half a world away from our daily lives, and our actual connection to all of that was tenuous. I was out of law school by the time my father learned he had lost an uncle and other relatives in the Holocaust.

Fast-forward to the first intifada. The Israeli response disturbed me. I didn't find Yasser Arafat attractive, but I began to see that there is a case for a Palestinian state based on Israel's national security interests, wholly apart from Palestinian nationalism. I became involved in Americans for Peace Now. Having been in Israel only once, in 1968, I began going at least once a year. I was hooked.

Why? I am a walking cliché, but sometimes clichés are profound. There is a multi-millennial history, but it boils down to this: in the twentieth century, we paid with the lives of 6 million Jews to convince the world that there has to be a home for the Jewish people. I feel passionately about that.

We Jews come in dozens of flavors. Put two of us in a room and there will be three views. But one rather bright line is between those who think that we should never say a bad word about Israeli government policy and public attitudes and those who believe and say out loud that maybe the very preservation of the State of Israel depends on a robust public discussion of issues of peace and justice. Needless to say, I am of the latter persuasion.

I grew up somehow into being a person whose self-definition is heavily tied to the idea of *tikkun olam*, whether in Darfur or New Orleans, and certainly in Israel. My very Judaism is woven with the warp and woof of Israel. I believe that the Israel I love should be and *must* be an Israel of justice for all its citizens, and an Israel that believes in the power of words as its first defense before using its necessarily strong military might. That is my Judaism and it is my Zionism.

My special passion, as to both the United States and Israel, is the ever-growing disparity between the rich and the poor, and the disproportionate likelihood that minorities whose race or ethnicity perpetuates their position on the periphery will find themselves on the economic edge. The poverty rate in Israel is twice what it is in the United States, where having one person in eight living below the poverty line is itself totally unacceptable.

So I find myself, nearing the end of the first seven decades of my allotted time on this planet, working as a fervent Diaspora supporter of the State of Israel to bolster those people there who also work for *tikkun olam*. As board president of the New Israel Fund for the past five years, I am immersed in helping to gather financial support for the efforts of those in Israel who act for justice in their country.

I am American, and I am deeply involved in the ongoing struggle for justice for all in my own country. But I am also a Jew, and for me, above all else, that means doing everything I can to help my Israel live up to the promises reflected in its prophetic history and, so recently, in its modern Declaration of Independence.

RABBI DAN EHRENKRANTZ is president of the Reconstructionist Rabbinical College in Wyncote, Pennsylvania.

"The vision: make the world a better place through the creation of a model society in the State of Israel based on Jewish history, wisdom, and creativity."

I grew up in Habonim camps with a socialist-Zionist, kibbutz-oriented ideology. When I say "grew up," I mean it quite literally. The growth I experienced during the two months of each summer seemed to equal or surpass whatever growth had occurred during the prior ten months of the year.

At age twelve I prepared for my bar mitzvah by living with my grandfather for a few weeks and studying with him. This study consisted of learning my grandfather's version of Judaism as it could be communicated to a twelve-year-old. What I learned from my grandfather reinforced my Habonim camping experiences.

As a child, my grandfather was a Hasid in eastern Europe. His father, my great-grandfather, was a *maskil*, a learned and dedicated Jew who was a member of the enlightenment movement and couldn't bear to see his children raised within the superstitious shtetl environment. He came to the United States planning to find a job and bring his wife and four children to America where their learning could take place in an environment of intellectual freedom.

World War I intervened, and my grandfather, his mother, and his three siblings had to fend for themselves through war, pogroms, and hunger. Their youngest sibling, Esther, didn't survive the ordeal. After the war, the family was reunited in the United States. My grandfather was thirteen years old, but his childhood was long past.

My great-grandfather became the principal of the Talmud Torah of B'nai Abraham, then of Newark, now of Livingston, New Jersey. His professional life was dedicated to the education of a new generation of Jews. The Judaism my great-grandfather left Europe to help create was a Judaism revitalized through creative engagement with the rest of the world. The movement dedicated to the renewal of Jewish life was Zionism.

My grandfather and great-grandfather shared a passion for a Judaism whose heartbeat was in Israel. Both pre-1948 Palestine and post-1948 Israel presented an opportunity for Jews to create a society built on a vision of justice and righteousness that the Jewish people had carried with them for centuries. The trials and successes of the nascent state of Israel, both military and sociocultural, represented movements toward or away from a messianic vision of a world at peace.

My bar mitzvah study brought me into this worldview. It is impossible to heal the world without starting with yourself and your family. But it is essential to go beyond your family to the community, the nation, and ultimately the world. The Jewish people have inherited an obligation to work toward building a just society. Israel in general, and the kibbutz movement specifically, are at their core and at their best dedicated to this work.

My camp experience, which was imbued with the spirit of the early 1970s and contained virtually no reference to Jewish life and history prior to 1948, merged with the story of my family and the four-thousand-year-old story of my people. The vision: make the world a better place through the creation of a model society in the State of Israel based on Jewish history, wisdom, and creativity. I carried this vision from the age of twelve and in many ways I still carry it today.

The first time I actually went to Israel was after I had graduated college. I lived in Israel for a year prior to entering rabbinical school. The dream and vision encountered the reality. In many ways the reality was more awe inspiring than the dream ever could have been. And in many ways the dream was forever tempered by the reality.

Israel is still the place where my dreams of Jewish life are most nourished and where the realities of Jewish life have their highest stakes. Israel is the place of the most potential damage and the most potential good, for both the body and soul of the Jewish people. I have experienced the blessing and the curse, the life and the death of modern Israel.

My life is intertwined with the life of Israel and Israelis. The land, oceans, smells, and rhythms; the challenges, successes, failures, and potential. All are a part of who I am and who I hope to become.

May the One who makes peace in the heavens help make peace for us, for all Israel, and for the entire world. Amen.

 LAURIE L. PATTON is professor of early Indian religions and chair of the Department of Religion at Emory University, Atlanta, Georgia.

"I came to Judaism in an unfolding process of recognition. As a non-Jew, I kept encountering moments of profound healing in Jewish contexts.... The same process of recognition was true for Israel.... Israel is more complex to me now—and at times its moral possibilities seem more nascent than actual."

My keenest images of Israel are the sunken porch gardens. In different streets in Jerusalem, Tel Aviv, Haifa, or Netanya, you can look down from the sidewalk and see porches descending several flights. As your eye travels downward, you can see open windows revealing glimpses of colorful libraries and sending forth the last notes of a concerto. Israel is a country where you could wind down and down into the earth, only to have more and more flora and fauna greet you with each step you take.

I came to Judaism in an unfolding process of recognition. As a non-Jew, I kept encountering moments of profound healing in Jewish contexts. They were so powerful, and eventually became so numerous, that I began to realize that it was time for me to think about becoming a Jew by choice. In a way, becoming Jewish was like winding down further and further into my own soul, only to discover more color and life with each step I took.

The same process of recognition was true for Israel: getting on the plane from New York in 1995, two years before I started the formal process of conversion, everyone spoke Hebrew to me because they assumed I was Israeli. At that time, Israel seemed to me what the philosopher Emmanuel Levinas (1906–1995) thought it was: a place of moral possibility. As a professor of comparative religions and Indian mythology, I thought Israel was a chance to shape an authentic religious pluralism. Israel was a chance to cultivate a shared acceptance of and embrace of the most painful and joyous of all of our pasts. When I first came to Israel, in 1995 and 1997, I visited Neve Shalom, and I met Palestinians and Israeli Arabs and Christians and Israeli intellectuals working toward a just peace. I walked through Jerusalem and marveled at the sunken porch gardens. With flowers winding up unexpectedly from the depths of the earth, everything seemed possible.

I have been a Jew by choice for eight years. I became bat mitzvah; I chant Torah and *haftarah*; I married a Jewish man. I teach comparative religions throughout the Jewish community here in Atlanta and beyond. I am working on a second book of poetry that follows the Jewish liturgical year of *parshiyot* (weekly Torah readings). I have lived and taught in Israel as a Fulbright lecturer in Tel Aviv and Jerusalem. From a safe place in America, I watched the second intifada and the Israeli withdrawal from Gaza. Also from the safe American summer of 2006, I corresponded by e-mail with friends whose family was being bombed in Beirut; minutes later I heard an update from a friend whose family was near the train station being bombed in Haifa. A friend said that her parents in northern Israel had found a safe place to go, but they were mostly afraid about the fate of the sunken garden in their kibbutz.

Israel is more complex to me now—and at times its moral possibilities seem more nascent than actual. But I have had the best arguments about Israeli politics, taught my best tutorials on world religions, and learned the most midrashim in those sunken, secret, fertile places scattered over all of Israel's cities. I know now that those cellar gardens are places not only of possibility, but of privilege and pain.

DR. ROBERT WEXLER is the president of the American Jewish University (formerly the University of Judaism) in Los Angeles, California.

> "For me, Israel exists simultaneously in its heroic past, its precarious present, and its visionary future.... Most appealing by far is the dream of Zion yet to be. I maintain my still unshaken belief that, one day, the idealism of Ahad Ha'am or Abraham Isaac Kook will arise to infuse the values of the State and its people."

For me, Israel exists simultaneously in its heroic past, its precarious present, and its visionary future. I regularly encounter Israel by walking the land, meeting its people, studying ancient texts, reading its history, and carefully contemplating the ideologues who attempted to give the Zionist state its focus and texture.

I am not naïve about the internal and external dangers that haunt the Israel of my generation. Nevertheless, when I am there, my imagination still sees the tragic King Saul fallen in battle on the hills of Gilboa; I see the estimable Maccabees challenging the soldiers of Antiochus; I encounter Rabbi Isaac Luria in the mystic byways of Safed; I envisage the bumptious Theodor Herzl entertaining the German Kaiser, and I hear the autocratic voice of David Ben-Gurion declaring the establishment of the Jewish state.

Even the social and political difficulties of the present do not obscure the innate warmth of a fractious people or the welcoming embrace of my own family and friends. The growing poverty, the intractable religious divisions, the deteriorating educational system, the political corruption, and the waning empathy of the outside world may disappoint and disconcert me, but they never dampen my fundamental enthusiasm for the existential miracle that is the modern State of Israel. Despite all its shortcomings, this chaotic Jewish democracy arose out of the ashes of incomprehensible despair and has kept faith with its prophetic mission to gather in the exiles of our people.

Most appealing by far is the dream of Zion yet to be. I maintain my still unshaken belief that, one day, the idealism of Ahad Ha'am or Abraham Isaac Kook will arise to infuse the values of the state and its people. Centuries of painstaking Jewish ethical debate will come to inform the moral, social, and political climate of Herzl's *medinat hayehudim* (state of the Jews). Centuries of authentic Jewish creativity will thrive in a state that truly serves as the center of a world of Jewish culture.

 **RABBI RAMI M. SHAPIRO** is an award-winning storyteller, poet, and essayist, and director of the Simply Jewish Foundation. His books include *The Sacred Art of Lovingkindness: Preparing to Practice* and *Hasidic Tales: Annotated and Explained* (both SkyLight Paths).

"I don't believe in chosen peoples and promised lands. I don't think God plays favorites or deals in real estate. But I do believe—no, I know, I experience—that there are certain places on this planet that hold deep promise for personal and planetary transformation and renewal. Israel is one of these places."

I'm writing this while sitting on the steps overlooking the Western Wall of the Jerusalem Temple. I have just prayed at the Wall, slipping a number of tiny prayer sheets into the cracks in hopes that …

Wait a minute; this can't be right. I don't believe God is a being separate from the universe who hears prayers and grants or ignores our heartfelt requests. I believe God is the source and substance of all reality who manifests as and transcends creation.

I believe the power of prayer is its capacity to shift my consciousness from *mochin d'katnut* (narrow mind) to *mochin d'gadlut* (spacious mind), from selfishness to selflessness; from the part and partial to the whole and holy. I pray not to be heard, but to hear; not to be present to God, but to be revealed as God, the One who is all things. I come to Israel to receive this revelation.

I don't believe in chosen peoples and promised lands. I don't think God plays favorites or deals in real estate. But I do believe—no, I know, I experience—that there are certain places on this planet that hold deep promise for personal and planetary transformation and renewal. Israel is one of these places.

When I walk the streets of Jerusalem and allow the city to work her magic, shifting me from narrow mind to spacious mind, I walk with Solomon and feel the call to wisdom; I walk with Jesus and feel the call to love; I walk with Mohammed and feel the call to surrender.

When I walk the Bahai Gardens of Haifa, I walk with Baha'u'llah, the nineteenth-century Persian prophet, and hear the call to universal justice. When I walk the winding streets of Safed, I walk with Joseph Cordovero (1522–1570) and hear the call of the Ineffable.

For me, Israel is all about walking with God and God's prophets. I am less concerned with the Israel of David Ben-Gurion and more with the Israel of Elisha ben Avuyah (yes, the first-century heretic and iconoclast—there is nothing more Jewish than that). For me Israel is more about the Wall, the Dome of the Rock, the Church of the Holy Sepulcher, the Garden Tomb, and the Shrine of the Book than it is about politics, warfare, or the rapture.

The promise of modern Israel is the hope that it can live up to the promise of timeless Israel.

I believe that humanity is in the early hours of a spiritual renaissance, and I come to Israel to hear the clock tick. I come here to be reminded of the new covenant promised by God in Jeremiah, a covenant written on our hearts revealing a God within calling us to godliness without.

I walk streets with diverse people, some praying for the old times, others for the end times. I pray for the new times. So I walk and I listen and I hope that my next step will be my first step in God, with God, as God.

PART V—AN AMERICAN HISTORICAL PERSPECTIVE:

THE WORDS OF THE FATHERS AND MOTHERS

"For the sake of Zion I will not be silent, for the sake of Jerusalem I will not be still, till her victory emerge resplendent and her triumph like a flaming torch."

Isaiah 62:1

The people whose thoughts and dreams appear in this book are the "descendants" of many American Jews who, in years past, responded to the challenge of Zionism and the creation of the modern State of Israel. They had many different perspectives on the Jewish state. Some believed simply in the historical connection between the Jewish people and the Land of Israel (often called Palestine in the pre-state era). Some came from a religious perspective and were explicit in their belief that the Land of Israel was part and parcel of the Jewish people's unique covenant with God and saw the creation of the state as the fulfillment of the divine promise; others saw it as a place of refuge for persecuted Jews, and as a necessity to protect beleaguered Jewish communities around the world. Some saw it as the reassertion of Jewish forcefulness in the wake of a millennium of Jewish vulnerability; others saw the establishment of a Jewish state as the creation of a national cultural center for the Jewish people that would be in the vanguard of creating a Jewish future. And some people expressed their ambivalence and struggle with the very idea of Jewish sovereignty—appropriate for a people whose very name and land is Yisrael, those who struggle with ultimate meaning. Let us hear their voices to enrich our understanding and appreciation of our own views.

"Wake, Israel, wake!"

EMMA LAZARUS was a nineteenth-century American Jewish writer and activist best known for her poem "The New Colossus," which adorns the base of the Statue of Liberty. The descendent of an old Sephardic family, her poem "The Banner of the Jew" stands as a song of early American Zionism.

The Banner of the Jew

Wake, Israel, wake! Recall to-day
The glorious Maccabean rage,
The sire heroic, hoary-gray,
His five-fold lion-lineage:
The Wise, the Elect, the Help-of-God,
The Burst-of-Spring, the Avenging Rod.

From Mizpeh's mountain-ridge they saw
Jerusalem's empty streets, her shrine
Laid waste where Greeks profaned the Law
With idol and with pagan sign.
Mourners in tattered black were there,
With ashes sprinkled on their hair.

Then from the stony peak there rang
A blast to open the graves: down poured

The Maccabean clan, who sang
Their battle-anthem to the Lord.
Five heroes lead, and, following, see
Ten thousand rush to victory!

Oh for Jerusalem's trumpet now,
To blow a blast of shattering power,
To wake the sleepers high and low,
And rouse them to the urgent hour!
No hand for vengeance—but to save,
A million naked swords should wave.

Oh deem not dead that martial fire,
Say not the mystic flame is spent!
With Moses' law and David's lyre,
Your ancient strength remains unbent.
Let but an Ezra rise anew,
To lift the Banner of the Jew!

A rag, a mock at first—ere long,
When men have bled and women wept,
To guard its precious folds from wrong,
Even they who shrunk, even they who slept,
Shall leap to bless it, and to save.
Strike! for the brave revere the brave!

"We believe that if an end is to be made to Jewish misery and to the exceptional position which the Jews occupy—which is the primary cause of Jewish misery—the Jewish nation must be placed once again in a home of its own.... And we hold that this does not mean that all Jews must return to Palestine."

RICHARD JAMES HORATIO GOTTHEIL (1862–1936) was an Orientalist and an early American Zionist. He served as president of the American Federation of Zionists, president of the Society of Biblical Literature, and vice president of the American Jewish Historical Society. He was also the founder of the Zeta Beta Tau Fraternity, affectionately known as "ZBT," which was originally a Zionist society. He uttered these words in 1898, at the same time as the first Zionist Congress in Basel, Switzerland. (Gottheil, true to his time, refers to the Land of Israel by its Roman, Ottoman, and British designation of Palestine.)

We believe that the Jews are something more than a purely religious body; that they are not only a race, but also a nation; though a nation without as yet two important requisites—a common home and a common language.

We believe that if an end is to be made to Jewish misery and to the exceptional position which the Jews occupy—which is the primary cause of Jewish misery—the Jewish nation must be placed once again in a home of its own.

We believe that such a national regeneration is the fulfillment of the hope which has been present to the Jew throughout his long and painful history.

We believe that only by means of such a national regeneration can the religious regeneration of the Jews take place, and they be put in a position to do that work in the religious world which Providence has appointed for them.

We believe that such a home can only naturally, and without violence to their whole past, be found in the land of their fathers—in Palestine.

We believe that such a return must have the guarantee of the great powers of the world, in order to secure for the Jews a stable future.

And we hold that this does not mean that all Jews must return to Palestine.

This, ladies and gentlemen, is the Zionist program.

We take hope, for has not that Jewish Zionist said, "We belong to a race that can do everything but fail."

From "The Aims of Zionism," 1898

"A center of Jewish culture and a safe refuge for the homeless."

RABBI KAUFFMAN KOHLER (1843–1926) was one of the ideological fathers of American classical Reform Judaism. As such, he was closely aligned with the anti-Zionist position of early American Reform. Nevertheless, in 1919 even he—a non-Zionist—could utter these words that would affirm the place of the Land of Israel in the Jewish spirit. It is ironic that this "non-Zionist" would echo the Zionism of the Zionist thinker Ahad Ha'am (1856–1927), who saw the Land of Israel as the cultural center of the Jewish people, as well as that of Zionist pioneer Theodor Herzl, who saw the land as a necessary Jewish refuge from persecution.

Let Palestine, our ancient home, under the protection of the great nations, or under the specific British suzerainty, again become a center of Jewish culture and a safe refuge for the homeless. We shall all welcome it and aid in the promotion of its work. Let the million or more of Jewish citizens dwelling there ... be empowered and encouraged to build up a commonwealth broad and liberal in spirit to serve as a school for international and interdenominational humanity. We shall all hail the undertaking and pray for its prosperity.

"You know that I am not a Zionist, but that does not prevent me from appreciating the noble idealism of those associated with this movement."

OSCAR SOLOMON STRAUS (1850–1926) was a diplomat, author, public servant, and jurist. A member of the prominent German-Jewish Straus family, he eschewed mercantile interests in favor of a political career. He served as minister to Turkey under President Grover Cleveland and secretary of commerce and labor under President Theodore Roosevelt. As the first Jew to hold a cabinet post, Straus always remembered his responsibilities to Jews, both in America and worldwide.

You know that I am not Zionist, but that does not prevent me from appreciating the noble idealism of those associated with this movement—an idealism which is very near akin ... to the spirit that actuated the founders of our republic, who drew their inspiration from the prophets of Israel and the Hebrew commonwealth.

Reprinted in Alfred Kolatch (ed.), *Great Jewish Quotations* (Middle Village, NY: Jonathan David Publishers) 1996, p. 451

Just as we contemporary American Jews long for words of Jewish solidarity from Jewish public figures, so, too, did our ancestors. They got what they wanted and needed from two famous, pioneering U.S. Supreme Court justices. It was through their presence that the Supreme Court to this day has a so-called "Jewish seat." But more than that, these two justices—**Louis D. Brandeis** (1856–1941) and **Felix Frankfurter** (1882–1965)—embraced Zionist sympathies. This was particularly true of Brandeis, who went so far as to identify Zionism with the true American spirit. Like the university that would ultimately bear his name, his life and career bear testimony to the fact that there need be no separation of loyalties between a person's Jewishness and a person's Americanism

LOUIS D. BRANDEIS

"Let no American imagine that Zionism is inconsistent with Patriotism. Multiple loyalties are objectionable only if they are inconsistent.... Every American Jew who aids in advancing the Jewish settlement in Palestine, though he feels that neither he nor his descendants will ever live there, will likewise be a better man and a better American for doing so."

Perhaps the most extraordinary achievement of Jewish nationalism is the revival of the Hebrew language, which has again become a language of the common intercourse of men. The Hebrew tongue, called a dead language for nearly two thousand years, has, in the Jewish colonies and in Jerusalem, become again the living mother tongue. The effect of this common language in unifying the Jew is, of course, great; for the Jews of Palestine came literally from all the lands of the earth, each speaking, excepting those who used Yiddish, the language of the country from which he came, and remaining, in the main, almost a stranger to the others. But the effect of the renaissance of the

Hebrew tongue is far greater than that of unifying the Jews. It is a potent factor in reviving the essentially Jewish spirit.

Let no American imagine that Zionism is inconsistent with Patriotism. Multiple loyalties are objectionable only if they are inconsistent. A man is a better citizen of the United States for being also a loyal citizen of his state, and of his city; for being loyal to his college or his lodge. Every Irish American who contributed toward advancing home rule was a better man and a better American for the sacrifice he made. Every American Jew who aids in advancing the Jewish settlement in Palestine, though he feels that neither he nor his descendants will ever live there, will likewise be a better man and a better American for doing so.

Note that Seton-Watson [British historian, 1879–1951] says:

America is full of nationalities which, while accepting with enthusiasm their new American citizenship, nevertheless look to some center in the old world as the source and inspiration of their national culture and traditions. The most typical instance is the feeling of the American Jew for Palestine which may well become a focus for his déclassé kinsmen in other parts of the world.

There is no inconsistency between loyalty to America and loyalty to Jewry. The Jewish spirit, the product of our religion and experiences, is essentially modern and essentially American. Not since the destruction of the Temple have the Jews in spirit and in ideals been so fully in harmony with the noblest aspirations of the country in which they lived.

America's fundamental law seeks to make real the brotherhood of man. That brotherhood became the Jewish fundamental law more than twenty-five hundred years ago. America's insistent demand in the twentieth century is for social justice. That also has been the Jews' striving for ages. Their affliction, as well as their religion, has prepared the Jews for effective democracy. Persecution broadened their sympathies. It trained them in patient endurance, in self-control, and in sacrifice. It made them think as well as suffer. It deepened the passion of righteousness.

Indeed, loyalty to America demands rather that each American Jew become a Zionist. For only through the ennobling effect of its strivings can we develop the best that is in us and give to this country the full benefit of our great inheritance. The Jewish spirit, so long preserved, the character developed by so many centuries of sacrifice, should be preserved and developed further, so that in America as elsewhere the sons of the race may in the future live lives and do deeds worthy of their ancestors.

From "The Jewish Problem and How to Solve It," 1915

FELIX FRANKFURTER

"Considering the contributions of the Jew in the history of mankind, a contribution directly related to the fact that the Jewish people lived in that strange and wonderful place called Palestine, make it not unimportant to the future of civilization that they be given the opportunity of seeing what more was in them for the benefit of mankind, but giving them the opportunities of a free life in that small territory."

Dick Casey [Australian politician and diplomat, 1890–1976] asked me to see him again and he turned up at nine o'clock and although he said he had to leave at about twenty minutes past ten, he did not leave until nearly half past eleven. He wanted to talk with me about Palestine and his relations with the Jewish Agency people. He said: "I feel hostility on the part of the Jewish representatives whenever I see them, and I don't know why they would feel that way, so I come to you as the one man in the world who can make me understand their problems and possibly shed light on their attitude toward me personally." I told him I was greatly surprised, indeed dumbfounded to hear that any personal differences should have arisen between him and the Jewish leaders in Palestine, that this is the first I heard of it, and ... that however much they had made him feel their dissatisfaction with him, I am sure it had nothing what ever to do with him as a person, but rather that he now symbolizes the long experience they had had with the British government in frustrating their hopes. I said that in order to understand the Palestine problem he would have to understand—what is very difficult for any outsider to understand—the position of the Jews throughout the world (he interrupted at this point to say that that was exactly where he would like me to begin), or indeed for any member of a majority to understand the position and conditions of a more or less oppressed minority—the difficulty of an Englishman to understand what, as a matter of pure reason, is at times, or appears to be the behavior of the Irish or of the Indians.

I then tried to make Casey comprehend something of the position of the Jew in history, the resulting psychological state—at times aggressive, at times too deferential—and the resulting sensitiveness and preoccupation with grievances, or so it would appear to a person like himself who has no grievances because the Fates had been good to him.... I traced, as best I could, the relation of Palestine to the Jewish problem in the world, told him that perhaps the best way for him to understand the Zionist aspirations would be to read the speeches of that unsentimental, cool headed Scot, Lord Balfour, who was the author of the Balfour Declaration, and who thought that considering the contributions of the Jew in the history of mankind, a contribution directly related to the fact that the Jewish people lived in that strange and wonderful place called Palestine, make it not unimportant to the future of civilization that they be given the opportunity of seeing what more was in them for the benefit of mankind, but giving them the opportunities of a free life in that small territory, without dislodging the Arabs, considering the fact that such a vast domain for the Arab world was wrestled from the Turks and given to the Arabs after the last war.

My sum total impression was that poor Dick Casey never in his life gave a thought to the position of the Jew in the world in general, or to Zionism in particular, that he suddenly is confronted with problems for which he has no background, and which, being only a small aspect of his total responsibility, come to him as a nuisance and the Jews who bring these problems, as unreasonable nuisances.

From Joseph P. Lash, *The Diaries of Felix Frankfurter: With a Biographical Essay and Notes* (New York: W. W. Norton, 1975), pp. 152–153

"Zionism is an ideal.... It may appear to one as the rebirth of national Jewish consciousness, to another as a religious revival, whilst to a third it may present itself as a path leading to the goal of Jewish culture; and to a fourth it may take the form of the last and only solution of the Jewish problem."

From its earliest inceptions, Conservative Judaism has maintained a strong, overarching identification with the Jewish people as the very matrix for Jewish belief and activity. Part and parcel of that approach would be an unquestioning and unwavering Zionist commitment—here set out by Conservative Judaism's intellectual "father," **Solomon Schechter** (1847–1915).

I will state here clearly the reasons for my allegiance to Zionism. I am not claiming or aspiring to the role of leadership in this movement. The following remarks have only the value of representing the opinion of one of the rank and file, stating clearly his views of a great number of fellow Zionists. Zionism is an ideal, and as susceptive of different aspects. It may appear to one as the rebirth of national Jewish consciousness, to another as a religious revival, whilst to a third it may present itself as a path leading to the goal of Jewish culture; and to a fourth it may take the form of the last and only solution of the Jewish problem. By reason of this variety of aspects, Zionism has been able to unite on its platform the most heterogeneous elements, representing Jews of all countries, and exhibiting almost all the different types of culture and thought as only a really great and universal movement could command. That each of its representatives should emphasize the particular aspect most congenial to his way of thinking, however, they all agree, namely, that it is not only desirable, but absolutely necessary, that Palestine, the land of our fathers, should be recovered with the purpose of forming a home for at least a portion of the Jews who would lead there a normal life.

First published in pamphlet form, December 28, 1906

"When a Jewish Commonwealth has become into being, when outcast Jews have found peace, when the Hebrew language and literature have taken root in their native soil, the Tradition will have a fresh chance at free, spontaneous unfolding."

In the "pantheon" of the Conservative rabbinate, perhaps no rabbi occupies the place of **Rabbi Milton Steinberg** (1903–1950). His tragically short life was a love song to God, Torah, and Israel. While his best-known book is the perennially popular historical novel *As a Driven Leaf*, about the life of the heretical sage Elisha ben Avuya, his other major literary gift to the Jewish people was his short primer *Basic Judaism* (1947), which has guided countless numbers of people into Jewish life and is still used in many introduction to Judaism classes. Here, in an excerpt from that precious literary legacy, is his interpretation of the meaning of Zionism. For him, as for all Jews at that time, Israel was not "yet" Israel; it was still British Palestine.

The consciousness of Palestine pervades every phase of the Jew's religious life. The Scripture he reads, the prayers he recites, the rabbinic literature he studies are full of allusions to it. And as for Jewish rites and observances, having been fashioned in the Holy Land, they reflect their native scene. Like other faiths Judaism takes cognizance of the cycle of the seasons. But the calendar it follows is Palestinian in form and inspiration. Passover marks the ripening of the first grain, Pentecost the garnering of the first fruits, Tabernacles the final ingathering—all as they occur in the Holy Land. Always Palestine sets the pitch of Judaism's awareness of the agricultural and pastoral.

Land and language are sacred, last of all, for their place in the vision of the future.

Except for extreme modernists, all religious Jews regard Palestine and the Hebrew tongue as involved in some fashion in the destiny of Israel and mankind.

Many a traditionalist believes that the reconstitution of Israel on its ancestral soil is a precondition to the Messianic era. When the dispersed Jews of the world have been brought home by the Messiah, Torah will go forth from Zion, the word of the Lord from Jerusalem, swords will be beaten to plowshares and spears to pruning hooks.

Less rigid traditionalists and the bulk of modernists see the future in a less mystical light. To them Palestine and the Hebrew language contribute in natural course to the triumphant outcome of the human adventure.

For long centuries the growth of Judaism has been hampered by dispersion and persecution. But when a Jewish Commonwealth has become into being, when outcast Jews have found peace, when the Hebrew language and literature have taken root in their native soil, the Tradition will have a fresh chance at free, spontaneous unfolding. Its circumstances will be favorable as they have not been in two millennia. And not in Palestine only, but throughout the world. For Palestine then will be an unfettered heart pumping the blood of health and vigor to all the Jewries of the dispersion.

Who knows what revelations the people of revelations shall have to speak at that time? This much is certain: the Jewish people everywhere will be the stronger for the Homeland and its revived Hebrew culture, and therefore the better able to labor for the advent of that ideal society which it was the first to project and after which it has striven so long and mightily.

From Milton Steinberg, *Basic Judaism*
(New York: Harcourt, Brace, 1947), pp. 97–98

"Give so that the Jewish people may live."

JUDAH MAGNES (1877–1948) was a Reform rabbi, communal leader, and early Zionist. His growing traditionalism led him to break with Reform Judaism and ultimately to move to Israel. There, he became the chancellor and first president of the Hebrew University of Jerusalem and advocated for a single-state (Jewish and Arab) solution to the problem of Palestine.

With my own eyes, I have seen the misery, the slow starvation of thousands. The Jews of America are sharing in prosperity as never before. Will they do their duty by their fellow Jews? Give, I beg of you, to the old men and women, to the young wives whose husbands are at war in the different armies, to the numberless sick who have been brought down by privation, to the children who still play and sing despite the cold and the hunger that menace them. Give so that the Jewish people may live.

> From a letter to M.J.H. Rosenberg, December 21, 1915, asking that the Joint Distribution Committee raise $10 million for war relief

"We have passed beyond the stage of quarreling over the place of Palestine in Jewish life and are deeply interested in its fate."

RABBI FELIX LEVY (1884–1963) was a Reform rabbi who served as rabbi of Emmanuel Congregation in Chicago, Illinois, from 1908 until his retirement in 1955. As president of the Central Conference of American Rabbis, he was almost single-handedly responsible for moving that Reform rabbinic body from its classic anti- and non-Zionist ideology into a more assertive embrace of Zion.

We have passed beyond the stage of quarreling over the place of Palestine in Jewish life and are deeply interested in its fate. As the suffering of Polish Jewry united us, as the hostility of Hitler closes our ranks, so the present juncture in Zion must bind us together. We cannot be indifferent on purely Jewish grounds to the report of the Royal Commission. World religious Jewry has never spoken; we have left that to others, so-called secular organizations. Now is the time to prove to the world that American religious Jewry is one in its regard for Palestine. Religionists comprise the major portion of the United States Jewry and their collective voice will make a profound impression upon the world as well as hearten our brothers in the ancestral home-land.

From his presidential address to the CCAR, 1937

"Well, Harry, I, too, have a hero."

EDWARD (EDDIE) JACOBSON (1891–1955) occupies a near-legendary place in American Jewish history. He was a longtime friend of President Harry S. Truman as well as his partner in a haberdashery in Kansas City, Missouri. When Truman became president, Jacobson used their personal relationship as a way to educate the president on the refugee and Palestine partition issues. In March 1948 he persuaded the reluctant president to see Chaim Weizmann and help the nascent Jewish state come into being. (Truman finally agreed to have an audience with Weizmann, telling Jacobson: "All right, you bald-headed son of a bitch, I'll see him.") We might say that it was the most important act of Jewish "nudging" in history.

Harry, all your life you have had a hero. You are probably the best read man in America on the life of Andrew Jackson.... Well, Harry, I, too have a hero, a man I never met but who is an old man and a sick man, and he has come all the way to America to see you. Now you refuse to see him because you were insulted by some of our American Jewish leaders.... It doesn't sound like you, Harry.

Reprinted in Kolatch, p. 228

"There is but one solution for national homelessness. That is a national home."

In the "contest" for the designation of the greatest Reform Zionist leader,
there is an admirable competition between Rabbi Abba Hillel Silver and
Rabbi Stephen S. Wise. For this reason they are among the very few Reform
rabbis whose names adorn streets or communities in Israel.

ABBA HILLEL SILVER (1893–1963) spent most of his illustrious career as the
rabbi of The Temple-Tifereth Israel in Cleveland, Ohio, where he deftly
combined scholarship and activism with the tasks of a congregational rabbi.
He is best known for his presence at the General Assembly of the United
Nations on May 8, 1947, when he presented the case for an independent
Jewish state before that world body.

There is but one solution for national homelessness. That is a
national home…. From the infested, typhus-ridden ghetto of Warsaw,
from the death-block of Nazi-occupied lands, where myriads of our
people are awaiting execution by the slow or the quick method, from
a hundred concentration camps which befoul the map of Europe,
from the pitiful ranks of our wandering hosts over the entire face of
the earth, comes the cry: Enough! There must be a final end to this,
a sure and certain end.

 … I believe that the Committee of Inquiry should most certainly
visit Palestine. Written documents are important, but infinitely more
instructive are the living documents, the visible testimony of creative
effort and achievement. In Palestine they will see what the Jewish
people, inspired by the hope of reconstituting their national home
after the long, weary centuries of their homelessness, and relying
upon the honor and the pledged word of the world community, has
achieved in a few short years against great odds and seemingly insur-
mountable physical handicaps. The task was enormous—untrained

hands, inadequate means, overwhelming difficulties. The land was stripped and poor—neglected through the centuries. And the period of building took place between two disastrous world wars when European Jewry was shattered and impoverished. Nevertheless, the record of pioneering achievement of the Jewish people in Palestine has received the acclaim of the entire world. And what was built there with social vision and high human idealism has proved a blessing, we believe, not only to the Jews of Palestine, but to the Arabs and other non-Jewish communities as well.

That the return of the Jews to Palestine would prove a blessing not only to themselves but also to their Arab neighbors was envisaged by the Emir Feisal, who was a great leader of the Arab peoples at the Peace Conference following the First World War. On March 3, 1919, he wrote:

> We Arabs ... look with the deepest sympathy on the Zionist movement. Our deputation here in Paris is fully acquainted with the proposals submitted yesterday by the Zionist Organization to the Peace Conference, and we regard them as moderate and proper. We will do our best, insofar as we are concerned, to help them through. We will wish the Jews a most hearty welcome home.... I look forward, and my people with me look forward, to a future in which we will help you and you will help us, so that the countries in which we are mutually interested may once again take their places in the community of civilized peoples of the world.

Your committee of Inquiry will conclude, we are confident, that if allowed to develop uninterruptedly, the standards of life which are being developed in Palestine, the concepts of social justice and modern scientific methods, will serve as great stimulus to the rebirth of progress of the entire Near East with which Palestine and the destinies of the Jewish national home are naturally bound up.

"That the Jewish people should practice non-violence in a Christian world of violence is asking a little too much of those who have suffered most in the war and who are more truly homeless than any group on earth."

RABBI STEPHEN S. WISE (1874–1949) was, like Abba Hillel Silver, a brilliant orator and a congregational rabbi. His career was suffused with activism on behalf of the entire Jewish people, as well as playing a major role in creating the social justice agenda that would come to define Reform Judaism. He was the founding rabbi of The Free Synagogue (now Stephen Wise Free Synagogue) in New York, which was created on the principle of freedom of pulpit and pew. He collaborated with Louis D. Brandeis and Felix Frankfurter in creating the text of the Balfour Declaration of 1917, and his Zionist activity continued unabated for more than three decades beyond that.

I agree with you that there are disturbing things happening in Palestine, but it's Britain that is responsible for violence. The government that prevents Jews from entering into Palestine is guilty of violence, most especially seeing that those, who choose to enter, are the survivors of the Hitler horror.

My people would not be worth their salt if they were ready to remain out of Palestine because of a White Paper or because the English have decided that they may enter Palestine only with certificates. That the Jewish people should practice non-violence in a Christian world of violence is asking a little too much of those who have suffered most in the war and who are more truly homeless than any group on earth.

From a letter to John Haynes Holmes, 1946

I have been thinking very carefully about the ... question which you put to me—namely, whether Jews ought not to help the so-called

Arab refugees at this time. There are a number of reasons why I think this should not be done. Let me state them as I see them—of the two hundred and fifty million dollars asked for by the U.J.A. [United Jewish Appeal], not more than one hundred and fifty million has been forwarded. It is going to be hard sledding to get the rest of the funds so desperately needed, and I tremble to think how great will be the difficulty of securing even comparable sums in 1949, in view of the possible beginnings of a very real recession.

As for helping the Arabs, I wonder whether you noted that the moment some Arabs deserted their Palestinian homes—they were driven out—the British government, through dear Mr. Bevin, made a generous offer of one hundred thousand pounds for their help and relief, though Britain had never given one penny for the Jews, however terrible their need. Far from giving relief, throughout the war, and especially after the White Paper, they denied Jews the right to enter into Palestine and save themselves from Nazism.

Two things should be remembered, which people who have not carefully studied the Palestine situation do not quite understand. The Palestine Arabs have not warred against the Jews, are not warring against them now. Under the cruelest coercion, some of them have been compelled to take up arms against us, lest they perish at the hands of their fellow-Arabs—I mean the extra-Palestinian Arabs from the so-called Christian Lebanon and from the Arab states, Iraq, Syria, Transjordan, Saudi Arabia, Egypt. If today the Arabs were free, they would effect a lasting truce, indeed peace, with the Jews of Palestine or the Jewish state, to which they are more deeply indebted than anyone can know who has not seen, as I have seen on three different widely separated visits to Palestine, the transformation in economic and social standards which Jews have achieved for the Arabs, and only incidentally for themselves. The fullest assurance was given to the Arabs or Palestine, after the Arabs of neighboring lands began to war against the State of Israel, that they were safe, that their rights and status would be respected. But the coercion of the Arab states compelled them to flee, against their own will and judgment. If and when the Arabs return to their former homes in Palestine, they will find that no wrong has been done to them, and they will enjoy every right within the Jewish state which is the lot of the Jews who dwell therein.

I feel this way about any organized gifts to the Arabs. It seems an acknowledgment of wrong, for one thing. It is we who have been wronged. I feel so strongly about this. The Arab states took part in the discussion for weeks and weeks preceding the Partition decision of November 29. Immediately thereafter, they began to war upon Israel. If we now set out to help the Arabs, who have chosen to flee—I repeat, under the coercion of fellow-Arabs—there will be involved an acknowledgment of wrong on our part, which we have not committed.

Letter to Fanny Mayer Korn, October 20, 1948

"One must understand that the ideas of the people and land of Israel are so deeply embedded in Jewish existence that even the secularized Jew still responds to them, sometimes in a manner he himself may not have considered possible."

Silver and Wise would raise up disciples among Reform rabbis, especially after the late 1930s when Zionism became more acceptable in Reform ranks. Consider these words from one of American Reform Judaism's most persuasive Zionist leaders, **Rabbi David Polish** (1910–1995). A rabbi who served congregations in Connecticut, Iowa, and Illinois, Rabbi Polish would ultimately found Beth Emeth—The Free Synagogue in Evanston, Illinois, to serve as a platform for his independent ideas. A great social activist (on one occasion, the Reverend Dr. Martin Luther King, Jr., slept at the synagogue in Evanston because he could not find a hotel), as well as a proponent of Reform's reclamation of tradition, he is notable for a rabbinate that embraced Zionism at a time when such views were still in the minority.

The land of Israel has also been endowed with a special character by the Jewish people. To live in the land was always considered a supreme objective of life. Throughout the Middle Ages, Jews made pilgrimages to Palestine, risking the terrors of highway brigands and of pirates at sea. At no time since the expulsion of the Jewish people following the destruction of the Second Commonwealth was the land empty of a Jewish community. At no time did the Jewish people relinquish its claim to the land, and every day pious Jews the world over would face toward Jerusalem and pray: "May our eyes behold Thy return to Zion in mercy." The attachment to the land represented more than a physical or a political impulse, and it was informed with overwhelming religious and spiritual content. Even with the emergence of the Zionist movement, which is generally regarded as a response to the eruption of European nationalism, Jews were willing to settle for nothing less than Palestine as the Jewish homeland.

Thus one cannot cope with the question of Israel unless he understands that there are spiritual and psychological factors which may be hidden from view by the exigencies of Israel's struggle for existence. One must understand that the ideas of the people and land of Israel are so deeply embedded in Jewish existence that even the secularized Jew still responds to them, sometimes in a manner he himself may not have considered possible. This was, in fact, true of large numbers of presumably alienated Jews in May and June of 1967.

But there are other factors as well, and they must be dealt with as the historical ground of reality out of which Jewish life flows. If the yearning for the land of Israel animated the Jew as a theological principle, it was given special impetus by the realities of the exile that had been imposed upon him. For some years, the land of Israel was a cherished goal even in times and places of security, few though they may have been. It should come as no surprise that large numbers of Jews would (and indeed did) abandon any hope of national restoration in return for freedom and endurance in the Diaspora. Early American Reform Judaism was predicated upon the idea that the Jewish exile had come to an end and the hope for Palestine was a vestige of the medieval past. The plunging of the world back into the age of barbarism soon dispelled this short-lived illusion. Not all Jews are Zionists, but the rise of Hitler convinced most that the state of the world as inhospitable to Jews had not really changed. A Hebrew poet, Zalman Shneour, apprehended this prophetically when in 1903 he wrote: "The Middle Ages are approaching."

From David Polish, *Israel—Nation and People* (New York: KTAV, 1975), pp. 111–112

"To continue developing, to expand what it has already given, thus enriching still further the total human heritage, [Judaism] must have its own place of creative development. For Jewish civilization, that place is Israel."

The Reform movement knew that the attainment of its goals for equality in the State of Israel depended on the creation of a Reform Zionist movement. That vision was fulfilled in 1977, with the creation of the Association of Reform Zionists of America (ARZA). They could have chosen no better founding president than the indefatigable **Rabbi Roland B. Gittelsohn** (1910–1995). Rabbi Gittelsohn first drew national attention when he became the first Jewish chaplain in American history to be assigned to the Marine Corps. He received three medals of honor for his service in the Iwo Jima campaign and delivered the dedicatory address at the Jewish section of its cemetery. A noted author and activist, Rabbi Gittelsohn was the founding rabbi of Central Synagogue of Nassau County in Rockville Centre, New York, and spent several decades as the rabbi of Temple Israel in Boston, Massachussets.

What is the Zionist movement really about? What are its basic purposes and aims?

(1) Only the re-establishment of a Jewish State can effectively cure the virus of anti-semitism, from which we Jews have suffered so grievously. We shall then, as a people, have an address as well as an agency in the council of nations to protect our rights wherever they may be threatened.

(2) Individual Jews whose lives are made intolerable in other lands will have a place to which they may go and in which they may live, free of persecution.

(3) The survival of Judaism and the Jewish people will be rendered more probable. During the past two millennia, the internal drive of the Jewish community to persist was constantly reinforced by the external pressures of anti-semitism. With those pressures relaxed, with ghetto walls crumbled and entrance of Jews into the larger world facilitated, with the threat of total assimilation thereby immeasurably increased, there is grave danger that, lacking a concentrated center, Jews and their continuing heritage may cease to exist as identifiable historic entities.

(4) To survive and develop creatively, a civilization must have a locus, a laboratory or hot-house, if you will, where it can be the primary culture of its people, where new strands and strains may be tested and refined.

Zionists insist that Judaism is not a dead fossil. If it were to disappear from the stage of history tomorrow, of course whatever it has already contributed to civilization would persist as part of the mainstream. But there would be no further Judaic infusions. Civilizations do not evolve in vacuums; they develop out of the living experience of specific peoples, in specific places and times. Each such people, like every individual, has its own unique thread to weave into the fabric of civilization, expressive of its collective nature and personality. To continue developing, to expand what it has already given, thus enriching still further the total human heritage, it must have its own place of creative development. For Jewish civilization, that place is Israel.

Ironically, not only Israel's enemies, some of its staunchest friends also misconstrue the full dimension of Zionism. Take my good friend Ben Halpern, for example. One of the ideological leaders of American Zionism, he recently wrote: "Reduced to its simplest terms, Zionism aims to make a normal—that is, an ordinary—nation of the Jewish people." Nonsense! This reduces Zionism not to its simplest terms but to a caricature. We Jews have never been an ordinary people; this has been a seed of our problem in history. The minute that Israel, God forbid, becomes ordinary or normal, it will cease being a Jewish state.

Theodor Herzl, founder of modern Zionism, knew this. He anticipated a state that would be "an outpost of civilization against barbarism." He said that Zionism must mean a revival of Judaism before it could produce the revival of a Jewish State. A. D. Gordon, seminal shaper of Labor Zionism, knew this too. He reminded his contemporaries: "We Jews were the first to teach the world that human beings are created in the image of God. The purpose of a Jewish State," he added, "must be to refashion the entire Jewish people in a divine image."

David Ben-Gurion, one of Israel's architects and its first Prime Minister, also understood the full meaning of Zionism. He wrote: "The State of Israel will be judged not by its riches or military power, not by its technical skills, but by its moral worth and human values .... Merely to be like all other peoples is not enough."

From Roland B. Gittelsohn, *Here Am I: Harnessed to Hope*
(New Jersey: Vantage Press, 1988), pp. 148–150

"I was profoundly conscious of the need for a place of refuge, not only for Jews but for others of all faiths and nationalities whom Hitler had marked for destruction."

BERNARD M. BARUCH (1870–1965) was an American financier, stock market speculator, statesman, and adviser to presidents Woodrow Wilson and Franklin D. Roosevelt. Despite his sizable contributions to American economics (he was the creator of, among other things, the idea of rent ceilings), he may have done his best "work" from park benches in Washington's Lafayette Park and New York's Central Park.

When Hitler instituted his "final solution" of the "Jewish question"—the gas chambers and ovens of the concentration camps—

some of my relatives were among the victims. I was profoundly conscious of the need for a place of refuge, not only for Jews but for others of all faiths and nationalities whom Hitler had marked for destruction. Regrettably, refugees had few places to go; the democracies found many excuses for not opening their doors.

Said after visiting Europe in 1938; reprinted in Kolatch, p. 38

"The Nazi terrors had brought many Johnny-come-latelies into the Zionist fold."

EMANUEL CELLER (1888–1981) was a long-time congressman from Brooklyn, New York. He was an activist for immigration reform and fought the restrictive policies of the 1920s that kept many eastern European Jews out of the United States. He became a champion of Zionism and successfully helped move the American government to a more pro-Zionist position. Here he's commenting on the involvement of American Jews in Zionist activities before the Second World War.

The Nazi terrors had brought many Johnny-come-latelies into the Zionist fold. I suppose I could be counted among those. The reasons were of compelling force. No country would take the Jews.... There were Jews already in Palestine who since before the turn of the century were draining the marshes, reviving the tired, wasted soil, building for the day of statehood.

Reprinted in Kolatch, p. 83

> "One can be an internationalist without being indifferent to the members of one's tribe. The Zionist cause is very close to my heart."

ALBERT EINSTEIN (1879–1955) was one of the greatest Jews in history—a man whose life work in physics would ultimately transform the human way of understanding the universe. While he was not a religious Jew, over the course of his life (and through his confrontation with growing German anti-Semitism), he would come to embrace Zionism, though he was often critical of it as a movement. He was one of the forces behind the creation of the Hebrew University in 1925, and was offered the presidency of Israel after the death of its first president, Chaim Weizmann.

One can be an internationalist without being indifferent to the members of one's tribe. The Zionist cause is very close to my heart.... I am glad that there should be a little patch of earth on which our kindred brethren are not considered aliens.

From a letter to Paul Epstein, October 5, 1919

I consider this the greatest day of my life. Before, I have always found something to regret in the Jewish soul, and that is the forgetfulness of its own people. Today, I have been made happy by the sight of the Jewish people learning to recognize themselves and to make themselves recognized as a force in the world.

From his travel diary, regarding his visit to Palestine, 1922

Should we be unable to find a way to honest cooperation and honest pacts with the Arabs, then we have learned nothing during our 2,000 years of suffering.

From a letter to Chaim Weizmann, 1929

We may regret that we have to use methods that are repulsive and stupid to us, but to bring about better conditions in the international sphere, we must first of all maintain our experience by all means at our disposal.

> From a communication with a Jewish group in Uruguay, May 4, 1948

My heart says yes, but my reason says no.

> Response to the frequent question of whether
> he would someday live in Israel

I am the more distressed over these circumstances because my relationship with the Jewish people became my strongest human tie once I achieved complete clarity about our precarious position among the nations of the world.

> From his rejection of the presidency of Israel in a communication
> with Abba Eban, November 18, 1952

"When Jews in the United States say 'the centrality of Israel' they mean ... that in the very act of worrying about Israel, Diaspora existence acquires verve and meaning."

Perhaps the best way to describe **Arthur Hertzberg** (1921–2006) is as a brilliant gadfly. In a remarkably illustrious career, he combined the roles of congregational rabbi, scholar, educator, and Jewish communal leader—and he did so rarely without controversy. He served as president of both the American Jewish Policy Foundation and the American Jewish Congress, vice president of the World Jewish Congress, and a leading representative of world Jewry in Catholic–Jewish dialogue.

Our situation is not like everyone else's. Israel is a state which is treated by the rest of the world as different, and we treat that state as different, and we are treated by it as different because the involvement by Jews, each in the other, and the various parts of the Jewish people, each in the other, is of a unique quality. Remember, every lie has in it just the necessary element of truth which carries it. The big anti-Zionist lie, the attack on Zionism, is carried by a truth which we like to deny for public relations purposes, the truth that the Jews really are singular. There is no other country with an 80 percent irridenta which has a United Jewish Appeal and you and me around to worry about it twenty-four hours a day.

Zionism was created to make an end of the Diaspora. As a matter of fact it has both acted to preserve it and to sharpen the angularities of its relationship with the rest of the world. Zionism said, "We will now regularize and normalize you." What it has succeeded in doing by its very political and military successes is to produce an odd kind of revocation of the unique self-definitions and the unique energies of the Jewish people. Therefore, one can talk about national liberation movements until one is blue in the face. Our propaganda may convince college freshmen but it won't convince others. Zionism is not really the national liberation movement of the Jewish people in any sense in which other national liberation movements recognize it. A national liberation is the liberation movement of someone from a foreign oppressor; it isn't the liberation movement of one thousand Jews from Milwaukee proudly wearing Koach buttons on a visit to the territory in which they're not living but in whose liberation the movement of a people which feels itself socially, culturally, spiritually, and religiously at odds with its environment and nonetheless uses its involvement in Zion in maintaining that peculiar identity.

I've often said that the Israel–Diaspora relationship is a paradox. Israel uses the Diaspora and looks to it as the ultimate source of its survivalist energies. Aliyah, not merely money, is the essential demand. The Diaspora looks to Israel and says that its involvement in Israel is what is going to make it survive. When Israel affirms the centrality of Israel, it really means that all Jewish organizations should devote their primary energies to the preservation of the state. When Jews in the United States say "the centrality of Israel" they mean something quite different; they mean that in the very act of worrying about Israel, Diaspora existence acquires verve and meaning. Now these are peculiar, unique, sui generis relationships which come out of a peculiar and unique history about which you can't easily sloganeer. Our problem is that we've been sloganeering with the things which come readily to hand, and the slogans no longer work because the world knows that the Jews are not really like everybody else. The world knows something which the thunderers of classic Zionism as well as the thunderers of classic assimilationism both denied. The Jews are not going to "normalize" themselves in the near future, either as a nation or as individuals within the world.

That being so, the problem today is not how you explain that Zionism is not racism. Everybody knows that Zionism is not racism. The problem is how you explain honestly this unique set of relationships in the world which are the ties among world Jewry. Oddly enough, the anti-Semites are ahead of us. Khrushchev, in the early 1960s, was saying that the trouble with Russian Jews was that they were a bunch of "cosmopolitans." We said the Russian Jews were wonderful citizens of Russia, good Communists, only let them have a few Yiddish schools and let them go to synagogue without harassment. Khrushchev knew something that we weren't yet admitting; he knew that the Jews of Russia wanted out, at least the "Jewish Jews" of Russia did. We say today that these Jews of Russia are really citizens of Israel or of the Jewish world, and that they are precisely what Khrushchev said they were in the 1960s. They are involved by their Jewish identity, in ways in which no other sub-ethnic group in the Soviet Union is involved, with people outside the Soviet Union. We are not going to answer the anti-Semites or the anti-Zionists until we are willing to put on the line not the rhetoric with which we delude ourselves very often as well as others, but the rhetoric of truth—and that is that we are different.

From Arthur Hertzberg, *Being Jewish in America: The Modern Experience* (New York: Schocken Books, 1979), pp. 242–244

"Jews are people who hold hands around the world."

MORRIS ABRAM (1918–2000) was one of the most dynamic American Jewish leaders of our time. Born in Georgia, he served as vice chair of the U.S. Commission on Civil Rights, held several positions in the United Nations, and may have served in more presidential administrations than any other person—those of Kennedy, Johnson, Carter, Reagan, and George H. W. Bush. In the Jewish world, he was president of the American Jewish Committee and chairman of the National Conference on Soviet Jewry, as well as chairman of the Conference of Presidents of Major American Jewish Organizations.

When the Six-Day War erupted, on June 5, 1967, I, as president of the American Jewish Committee, called on liberal Christian church allies to join together in support of Israel at a giant rally in Lafayette Park across from the White House. I expected an outpouring from these churches with whom we had been linked on so many fronts. After all, Nasser had challenged not only Israel, but also the United Nations and internationally recognized maritime laws.

By the time the rally was mounted in Washington, Israel had destroyed the Egyptian Air Force; David of the Middle East had half-slaughtered the Arab Goliath. The underdog had triumphed, and many of our Christian allies vanished. Yet, Israel's cause was not less valid on the fourth day of the war than on the first. I could not believe it, but the "advanced" religious leaders of the Protestant establishment began turning their backs on Israel and Jewish Americans, whose history and fates were intertwined with the survivors of Hitler's gas ovens.

In the thirteen years since, with notable exceptions, so-called liberal church organizations have made common cause with Arab, African, and other Third World nations which conduct campaigns of vilification of Israel, even siding against fellow Christians in Lebanon who are defended by Israeli arms.

The portents of this shift have reverberated within American political and social life with enormous consequences still not fully grasped and certainly not resolved.

But June 1967, the date Nasser ordered the UN observers out of the Sinai and marched on Israel, marks the beginning of the revival of a fearful collective unconscious in world Jewry. On the day after the attack there appeared in the halls of the American Jewish Committee Americans of Jewish ancestry so totally assimilated as to have changed the actual pronunciation of their names, haunted now by the specter of history and the common fate of Jews. I recall, for example, how Admiral Lewis Strauss (pronounced by him Straws) appeared at the Committee's headquarters and offered his services. My former wife Jane was strikingly perceptive, when she observed: "Jews are people who hold hands around the world."

From Morris B. Abram, *The Day Is Short* (New York: Harcourt Brace Jovanovich, 1982), pp. 149–150

"The Six-Day War united the members of the generation that witnessed the founding of the state with those of a new generation."

DANIEL J. ELAZAR (1934–1999) was one of the foremost political scientists of our time. As founder and president of the Jerusalem Center for Public Affairs, he contributed greatly to seeking solutions to the problems of Israel and world Jewry. He had particular expertise in Jewish community organization, the Jewish political tradition, and Israel's government and politics.

June 1967 marked a watershed in contemporary Jewish affairs. The Six-Day War united the members of the generation that witnessed the founding of the state with those of a new generation, one that grew up accepting the existence of Israel as a matter of fact, only to encounter suddenly the harsh possibility of its destruction, making both generations deeply aware of the shared fate of all Jews, and the way that fate is now bound up with the political entity that is the State of Israel.

From an article in *American Jewish Yearbook*, 1969

"Out of this land [Israel] once came a great message to the world: justice, freedom and human dignity."

MAX M. FISHER (1908–2005) was a prominent industrialist, philanthropist, and Jewish community leader: Over the course of his lifetime he led and reorganized every major Jewish organization in the United States. At a time when American Jewish political loyalties tended toward the Democratic Party, Fisher was a member of the Republican National Committee and enjoyed a particularly close relationship with President Richard M. Nixon.

Out of this land [Israel] once came a great message to the world: justice, freedom and human dignity. And we Jews choose to believe that out of this land will yet come another such message. To be given a chance to make our contribution to that goal, to be able to do our part by re-establishing our people, to build for the peace that will surely come, to have a small share in creating that Israel…. All this is a privilege beyond price.

From a 1971 speech to the Jewish Agency

"Historically the Zionists turned out to be right."

LILLIAN HELLMAN (1905–1984) was a prominent American playwright and the author of such classics as *The Children's Hour*, *The Little Foxes*, and a memoir, *Pentimento*. She is perhaps most famous from the movie *Julia*, which portrayed her life during Nazism. While she was never known either for her Zionism or her strong connection to the Jewish people, in this passage she (begrudgingly?) gives Zionism a certain amount of credit.

Historically the Zionists turned out to be right. What are they saying? That Europe is doomed for the Jews. Liberal democracy won't save us. The Socialists won't save us. And the Communist revolutionaries won't save us. Whatever else may be wrong with Zionists, on that fundamental insight they were absolutely right.

From Carl E. Rollyson, *Lillian Hellman: Her Legend and Her Legacy*
(New York: St. Martin's Press, 1988), p. 488

"Hope it's symbolical."

HARPO MARX (1888–1964) was the silent member of the comedic Marx Brothers. It was sweetly ironic, then, that he was the only one of the (identifiably Jewish) Marx brothers who was known to have made any comments on Israel. He wrote this in May 1963 in a letter to former president Harry S Truman, along with a photo of himself in the Harry S Truman Forest in Israel.

There were several reasons for taking this photo—mostly my great pride in there being such a place [as the Truman Forest] and such a man as you. My reason for sending it is simpler—I thought you might not know how tall and strong the trees have grown. Hope it's symbolical [*sic*].

"When I go to Israel every stone and every tree is a reminder of hard labor and glory, of prophets and psalmists, of loyalty and holiness. The Jews go to Israel not only for physical security for themselves and their children; they go to Israel for renewal, for the experience of resurrection.... Israel enables us to bear the agony of Auschwitz without radical despair, to sense a ray of God's radiance in the jungles of history."

ABRAHAM JOSHUA HESCHEL (1907–1972) was one of the most profound definers of Judaism in the contemporary period. Theologian, educator, poet, author, activist—there was virtually no corner of the Jewish world that he left untouched. Heschel's major concern in his theology was the sanctifying of time rather than space, and this accounts for his comparatively few statements on the place of Israel—both land and State—in Jewish thought. The major exception was *Israel: An Echo of Eternity*, which he wrote after visiting Israel in the wake of the Six Day War.

1945 ... A new conception: The world is a slaughter-house. Hope is obscene. It is sinful to remain sane.

Six million lives gone. Wherever we dwell, we live in a graveyard. Only one way out, the way to the inferno.

1945 ... Is this what is left of us: chimneys in the extermination camps?

What shall come after the holocaust: nights of despair, no dawn, never, but shrieks in perpetuity? Anguish forever, no relief, life is gall, history a scourge? Has the world lost its soul? Have civilization and humanity nothing in common?

Has Auschwitz annihilated our future as well?

Three out of four Jews in Europe—dead. Two out of five of us anywhere in the world—dead. Will the spirit of those who survived be reduced to ashes? The Allied armies which freed the concentration camps came upon tens of thousands of emaciated bodies, skeletons, dry bones. "Son of man, can these bones live?" Judaism was reduced to dry bones, faith in God was on trial. Will this people, crushed, battered, crippled, decimated, impaled, find strength to survive?

What should have been our answer to Auschwitz? Should this people, called to be a witness to the God of mercy and compassion, persist in its witness and cling to Job's words: "Even if He slay me yet will I trust in Him" (Job 13:15), or should this people follow the advice of Job's wife, "Curse God and die!" (Job 2:9), immerse itself into the anonymity of a hundred nations all over the world, and disappear once and for all?

Our people's faith in God at this moment in history did not falter. At this moment in history Isaac was indeed sacrificed, his blood shed. We all died in Auschwitz, yet our faith survived. We knew that to repudiate God would be to continue the holocaust.

We have once lived in a civilized world, rich in trust and expectation. Then we all died, were condemned to dwell in hell. Now we are living in hell. Our present life is our after-life.

We did not blaspheme, we built. Our people did not sally forth in flight from God. On the contrary, at that moment in history we saw the beginning of a new awakening, the emergence of a new concern for a Living God theology. Escape from Judaism giving place increasingly to a new attachment, to a rediscovery of our legacy.

How would the world have looked at the Jewish people if the survivors of the concentration camps had gone the path of complete assimilation? Flight from God? From Judaism?

What would be the face of Western history today if the end of twentieth-century Jewish life would have been Bergen-Belsen, Dachau, Auschwitz? The State of Israel is not an atonement. It would be blasphemy to regard it as a compensation. However, the existence of Israel reborn makes life less unendurable. It is a slight hinderer of hindrances to believing in God.

We are tired of expulsions, of pogroms, we have had enough of extermination camps. We are tired of apologizing for our existence. If I should go to Poland or Germany, every stone, every tree would remind me of contempt, hatred, murder, of children killed, of mothers burned alive, of human beings asphyxiated.

When I go to Israel every stone and every tree is a reminder of hard labor and glory, of prophets and psalmists, of loyalty and holiness. The Jews go to Israel not only for physical security for themselves and their children; they go to Israel for renewal, for the experience of resurrection.

Is the State of Israel God's humble answer to Auschwitz? A sign of God's repentance for men's crime of Auschwitz? No act is as holy as the act of saving human life. The Holy Land, having offered a haven to more than two million Jews—many of whom would not have been alive had they remained in Poland, Russia, Germany, and other countries—has attained a new sanctity.

So many lives of people whose bodies were injured and whose souls were crushed found a new life and a new sprit in the land. The State of Israel, as it were, sought to respond to the prophet's exhortation: "Strengthen the weak hands, and make firm the feeble knees" (Isaiah 35:3).

In 1937, the period of Nazi persecution and expulsion of the Jews from Germany, I concluded a book about Don Isaac Abravanel, who lived during the time of the expulsion of the Jews from Spain in 1492, with the following words:

> The Jews, who played a leading role in the politics, economics and social affairs of their country left (had to leave) their Spanish homeland. The conquest of the New World was achieved without them. Had they remained on the Iberian peninsula they would surely have participated in the deeds of the Conquistadores. When the latter came to Haiti they found 1,1000,000 inhabitants; twenty years later only 1,000 remained.

In 1492 the Jews, who were desperate, had no inkling what an act of grace was involved in their misery. Driven out of Spain, they had no part in the atrocities soon to be carried out in the New World.

And yet, there is no answer to Auschwitz.... To try to answer is to commit a supreme blasphemy. Israel enables us to bear the agony of Auschwitz without radical despair, to sense a ray of God's radiance in the jungles of history.

> From Abraham Joshua Heschel, *Israel: An Echo of Eternity* (New York: Farrar, Straus and Giroux, 1969), pp. 111–115

"The treatment of non-Orthodox Judaism in Israel is an issue which should properly be the subject of world-wide Jewish dissent."

JOACHIM PRINZ (1902–1988) was one of the foremost rabbis and Jewish communal leaders in American Jewish history. Born in Germany, he was an outspoken foe of Nazism and was often arrested by the Gestapo. No less a personage than Adolph Eichmann spied on his last meeting with his congregation before departing for the United States in 1937. Later, Prinz was a leading activist in the civil rights movement and was the speaker at the August 1963 March on Washington who preceded Martin Luther King, Jr., and his immortal "I Have a Dream" speech. In this passage, he comments on the treatment of non-Orthodox religious leaders in Israel.

When I converted David Ben Gurion's daughter-in-law to Judaism in the city of London in 1946, the conversion was not recognized by the Chief Rabbis of Israel, and she had to be re-converted. Yet I am a fully ordained "rabbi in Israel." When my granddaughter, who lives in a kibbutz in Israel, was to be married in that kibbutz, I was not permitted to perform the ceremony. The treatment of non-Orthodox Judaism in Israel is an issue which should properly be the subject of world-wide Jewish dissent.

> From *Moment* magazine, December 1976

"Jewish self-haters, without taking the trouble to look into Zionist history, subscribe to the most outrageous statements."

MARIE SYRKIN (1899–1989) was one of the great Zionist commentators of her time. She was a writer, translator, educator, poet, and Zionist activist as well as the first to teach Holocaust literature at an American university. In this interview in *Moment* magazine, she reflects on her long career in Jewish life and letters, and was commenting on the rise of a leftist Jewish position that was increasingly critical of Israel.

I don't want to be on record as agreeing that emotionally I want Israel to extend from the Nile to the Euphrates. I don't share that emotion. I see no point in rehashing the whole argument about the rights of the Palestinians and the rights of the Jews and how the Palestinians were abused and deliberately developed as a *casus belli* (a reason for war) by the Arab states. Certainly today one has to take account of the realities of the situation. I quite agree that the demographic character of the West Bank would make its incorporation into Israel a great folly, a great injustice to Israel quite as much as to the Arabs. As so many of us say, that would totally destroy the democratic and the Jewish character of the Jewish state, so I totally oppose it.

But that doesn't mean I subscribe to every accusation the Palestinians make. And Jewish self-haters, without taking the trouble to look into Zionist history, subscribe to the most outrageous statements. I think that this willful ignorance and the readiness to accept the worst interpretation—the Jews were aggressors from the first moment, they kicked out all the Arabs, etc. etc.—the acceptance of the libels, the readiness to perceive the rights of every group except one's own, which is characteristic of a great many Jews, is a form of Jewish self-hatred.

From an interview in *Moment* magazine, September 1983

"The establishment of the State of Israel, in a political sense, was an almost supernatural occurrence."

JOSEPH BAER SOLOVEITCHIK (1903–1993) enjoyed an almost uncontested status as the preeminent philosopher of modern Orthodoxy. For his students, and for the public in general, he was known simply as "The Rav." Rabbi Soloveitchik taught for more than a generation at Yeshiva University in New York, but published relatively little during his lifetime. His most definitive statement on Israel and Zionism is his essay "Kol Dodi Dofeik" ("Listen! The voice of my Beloved knocks"—from Song of Songs 5:2). The *dodi* (beloved) of Song of Songs is God, and the emergence of the Jewish state is nothing less than the Beloved knocking on the door of history. "Kol Dodi Dofeik" was originally delivered as a sermon in commemoration of Yom Ha'atzmaut, Israel Independence Day, in 1956.

First, the knock of opportunity was heard in the political arena. No one can deny that from the standpoint of international relations, the establishment of the State of Israel, in a political sense, was an almost supernatural occurrence....

Second, the knocking of the Beloved could be heard on the battlefield. The small Israeli Defense Forces defeated the mighty armies of the Arab countries. The miracle of "the many in the hands of the few" took place before our very eyes.

Third, the Beloved began to knock as well on the door of the theological tent, and it may very well be that this is the strongest knock of all.... All the claims of Christian theologians that God deprived the Jewish people of its rights in the land of Israel, and that all the biblical promises regarding Zion and Jerusalem refer, in an allegorical sense, to Christianity and the Christian Church, have been publicly refuted by the establishment of the State of Israel and have been exposed as falsehoods, lacking all validity.

Fourth, the Beloved is knocking in the hearts of the perplexed and assimilated youths. The era of self-concealment (*hastarat panim*) at the beginning of the 1940s resulted in great confusion among the Jewish masses and, in particular, among the Jewish youth.... Buried, hidden thoughts and paradoxical reflections emerge from the depths of the souls of even the most avowed assimilationists. And once a Jew begins to think and contemplate, once his sleep is disturbed—who knows where his thoughts will take him, what form of expression his doubts and queries will assume?

The fifth knock of the Beloved is perhaps the most important of all. For the first time in the history of our exile, divine providence has surprised our enemies with the sensational discovery that Jewish blood is not free for the taking, is not *hefker* [free for the taking]!

The sixth knock, which we must not ignore, was heard when the gates of the land were opened. A Jew who flees from a hostile country now knows that he can find a secure refuge in the land of his ancestors.... Now that the era of divine self-concealment (*hester panim*) is over, Jews who have been uprooted from their homes can find lodging in the Holy Land.

"We believe that the eternal covenant established at Sinai ordained a unique religious purpose for *Am Yisrael. Medinat Yisrael*, the Jewish State, is therefore unlike all other states. Its obligation is to strive towards the attainment of the Jewish people's highest moral ideals to be a *mamlechet kohanim* (a kingdom of priests), a *goy kadosh* (a holy people), and *l'or goyim* (a light unto the nations)."

The Reform movement in the United States has had a long history of struggle with the implications of Zionism. Therefore, the **Reform Judaism &**

Zionism: A Centenary Platform, which was adopted by the Central Conference of American Rabbis at its annual convention in 1997, proved to be the most comprehensive articulation of the Reform movement's unquestioned and unfading commitment to Israel—a commitment that includes the building of a strong and meaningful movement for progressive Judaism in Israel itself.

PREAMBLE:

In recognition of the centenary of the first World Zionist Congress (August 29, 1897), the Central Conference of American Rabbis hereby issues its first platform dedicated exclusively to the relationship between Reform Judaism and Zionism.

In 1885 the framers of the Pittsburgh Platform of Reform Judaism declared that they no longer expected Jews to return to a national homeland in Palestine. The Platform's authors proclaimed: "We consider ourselves no longer a nation, but a religious community, and, therefore, expect neither a return to Palestine ... nor the restoration of any of the laws concerning the Jewish state."

By 1937 the CCAR had reversed its stand on Jewish peoplehood, and declared in its "Columbus Platform" that "Judaism is the soul of which Israel [the people] is the body." The document further states: "We affirm the obligation of all Jewry to aid in its [Palestine's] up-building as a Jewish homeland by endeavoring to make it not only a haven of refuge for the oppressed but also a center of Jewish culture and spiritual life." This affirmation of Jewish peoplehood was accompanied by a reaffirmation of Reform Judaism's universal message: "We regard it as our historic task to cooperate with all men in the establishment of the kingdom of God, of universal brotherhood, justice, truth and peace on earth. This is our Messianic goal."

The CCAR returned again to the question of Zionism in 1976, asserting in its "Centenary Perspective": "We are bound to ... the newly reborn State of Israel by innumerable religious and ethnic ties.... We have both a stake and a responsibility in building the State of Israel, assuring its security and defining its Jewish character." The "Centenary Perspective" also affirmed the legitimacy of the Diaspora and the historic universalism of Reform Judaism: "The State of Israel and the Diaspora, in fruitful dialogue, can show how a people transcends nationalism even as it affirms it, thereby setting an example for humanity, which remains largely concerned with dangerously parochial goals." Here again, the CCAR embraced Zionism as a means of fulfilling its universal vision and its opposition to narrow nationalism.

A century after Theodor Herzl called for the creation of a modern Jewish state and nearly fifty years since the State of Israel joined the family of modern nations, the fundamental issues addressed in the previous CCAR pronouncements continue to challenge us, making this a fitting time to re-examine and redefine the ideological and spiritual bonds that connect *Am Yisrael* [the People of Israel] to *Eretz Yisrael* [the Land of Israel] and to *Medinat Yisrael* [the State of Israel]. The CCAR affirms through this Platform those principles which will guide Reform Judaism into the 21st century.

I. Judaism: A Religion and a People

The restoration of *Am Yisrael* to its ancestral homeland after nearly two thousand years of statelessness and powerlessness represents an historic triumph of the Jewish people, providing a physical refuge, the possibility of religious and cultural renewal on its own soil, and the realization of God's promise to Abraham: "to your offspring I assign this land." From that distant moment until today, the intense love between Am Yisrael and Eretz Yisrael has not subsided.

We believe that the eternal covenant established at Sinai ordained a unique religious purpose for *Am Yisrael*. *Medinat Yisrael*, the Jewish State, is therefore unlike all other states. Its obligation is to strive towards the attainment of the Jewish people's highest moral ideals to be a *mamlechet kohanim* [a kingdom of priests], a *goy kadosh* [a holy people], and *l'or goyim* [a light unto the nations].

II. From Degradation to Sovereignty

During two millennia of dispersion and persecution, *Am Yisrael* never abandoned hope for the rebirth of a national home in Eretz Yisrael. The *Shoah* [Holocaust] intensified our resolve to affirm life and pursue the Zionist dream of a return to Eretz Yisrael. Even as we mourned for the loss of one-third of our people, we witnessed the miraculous rebirth of *Medinat Yisrael*, the Jewish people's supreme creation in our age.

Centuries of Jewish persecution, culminating in the *Shoah*, demonstrated the risks of powerlessness. We, therefore, affirm *Am Yisrael*'s reassertion of national sovereignty, but we urge that it be used to create the kind of society in which full civil, human, and religious rights exist for all its citizens. Ultimately, *Medinat Yisrael* will be judged not on its military might but on its character.

While we view *Eretz Yisrael* as sacred, the sanctity of Jewish life takes precedence over the sanctity of Jewish land.

III. Our Relationship to the State of Israel

Even as *Medinat Yisrael* serves uniquely as the spiritual and cultural focal point of world Jewry, Israeli and Diaspora Jewry are inter-dependent, responsible for one another, and partners in the shaping of Jewish destiny. Each *kehilla* [Jewish community], though autonomous and self-regulating, shares responsibility for the fate of Jews everywhere. By deepening the social, spiritual, and intellectual relationship among the *kehillot* worldwide, we can revitalize Judaism both in Israel and the Diaspora.

IV. Our Obligations to Israel

To help promote the security of *Medinat Yisrael* and ensure the welfare of its citizens, we pledge continued political support and financial assistance.

Recognizing that knowledge of Hebrew is indispensable both in the study of Judaism and in fostering solidarity between Israeli and Diaspora Jews, we commit ourselves to intensifying Hebrew instruction in all Reform institutions. Hebrew, the language of our sacred texts and prayers, is a symbol of the revitalization of *Am Yisrael*.

To enhance appreciation of Jewish peoplehood and promote a deeper understanding of Israel, we resolve to implement educational programs and religious practices that reflect and reinforce the bond between Reform Judaism and Zionism.

To deepen awareness of Israel and strengthen Jewish identity, we call upon all Reform Jews, adults and youths, to study
in, and make regular visits to, Israel.

While affirming the authenticity and necessity of a creative
and vibrant Diaspora Jewry, we encourage *aliyah* [immigra-
tion] to Israel in pursuance of the precept of *yishuv Eretz
Yisrael* [settling the Land of Israel]. While Jews can live Torah-
centered lives in the Diaspora, only in *Medinat Yisrael* do they
bear the primary responsibility for the governance of society,
and thus may realize the full potential of their individual and
communal religious strivings.

Confident that Reform Judaism's synthesis of tradition and
modernity and its historic commitment to *tikkun olam* [repair-
ing the world] can make a unique and positive contribution to
the Jewish state, we resolve to intensify our efforts to inform
and educate Israelis about the values of Reform Judaism. We
call upon Reform Jews everywhere to dedicate their energies
and resources to the strengthening of an indigenous Progressive
Judaism in *Medinat Yisrael*.

V. Israel's Obligations to the Diaspora

Medinat Yisrael exists not only for the benefit of its citizens
but also to defend the physical security and spiritual integrity of
the Jewish people. Realizing that Am Yisrael consists of a coalition of different, sometimes conflicting, religious interpretations, the Jewish people will be best served when *Medinat
Yisrael* is constituted as a pluralistic, democratic society.
Therefore we seek a Jewish state in which no religious interpretation of Judaism takes legal precedence over another.

VI. Redemption

We believe that the renewal and perpetuation of Jewish
national life in Eretz Yisrael is a necessary condition for the
realization of the physical and spiritual redemption of the
Jewish people and of all humanity. While that day of redemption remains but a distant yearning, we express the fervent hope
that *Medinat Yisrael*, living in peace with its neighbors, will
hasten the redemption of Am Yisrael, and the fulfillment of our

messianic dream of universal peace under the sovereignty of God.

The achievements of modern Zionism in the creation of the State of Israel, in reviving the Hebrew language, in absorbing millions of immigrants, in transforming desolate wastes into blooming forests and fields, in generating a thriving new economy and society, are an unparalleled triumph of the Jewish spirit.

We stand firm in our love of Zion. We resolve to work for the day when waves of Jewish pride and confidence will infuse every Jewish heart, in fulfillment of the promise: When God restores the fortunes of Zion we shall be like dreamers. Our mouths will fill with laughter and our tongues with songs of joy. Then shall they say among the nations God has done great things for them.

Glossary

aliyah: "Ascent" to the Land of Israel as a new immigrant (*oleh, olim*). "To make aliyah" is to move to Israel. In the historical sense, aliyah refers to a particular wave of immigration to Israel (First Aliyah, Second Aliyah).

Am Yisrael: The people of Israel.

baal teshuvah: "One who returns." A previously unobservant Jew who becomes observant.

Eretz Yisrael: The Land of Israel.

galut, golah: Exile (or, in its Greek form, Diaspora)—any geographic place that is outside the Land of Israel. In the ideological sense, it means the spiritual and/or psychological sense of living in exile.

haftarah: A reading from the prophetic books of the Bible.

Haggadah, *haggadot* (pl.): Text used at the Passover seder that tells the story of the Exodus.

halakhah: Traditional Jewish law.

halutzim: "Pioneers," or the pioneering generation in Israel

haredi, haredim: "Those who tremble." Ultra-Orthodox Jews.

Hasidism, Hasid: "Pious." The mystical stream of Judaism, characterized by its great fervor in worship.

Havdalah: Ceremony that concludes Shabbat.

huppah: Jewish wedding canopy, representing the home the married couple will make together.

Kaddish: A public declaration of praise for God; traditionally, a prayer said in memory of the dead.

kibbutz, kibbutzim: A collective settlement in Israel, operating along socialist principles of ownership and production.

Kabbalat Shabbat: Service for welcoming the Sabbath on Friday evening.

Knesset: The Parliament of the state of Israel.

Kotel: Also known as the *kotel ha-maaravi*, the Western Wall (the term "Wailing Wall" is considered obsolete). The retaining wall of the Temple Mount in Jerusalem—the only remnant of the Second Temple.

maskil: "An enlightened one," the nineteenth-century term for an eastern European Jew who embraced the *Haskalah* (Jewish Enlightenment) in literature and thought.

Medinat Yisrael: The State of Israel.

midrash, *midrashim* (pl.): Classical rabbinic biblical interpretation.

minyan: Prayer group of ten adult Jews.

olim: Immigrants to Israel.

parasha: The weekly Torah portion.

payis: The side curls worn by Ultra-Orthodox Jews as a fulfillment of the biblical mitzvah to refrain from shaving the side of one's head.

sabra: A Jew born in the Land of Israel. (Also a particular species of cactus found in the Land of Israel.)

Sh'ma: Proclamation at the center of Jewish worship.

Shoah: The Holocaust

siddur: Prayer book.

sofer: A scribe who writes Torah scrolls, tefillin, *ketubot* (Jewish wedding documents), and the like.

tallit: Prayer shawl.

Tanach: The Hebrew Bible, including the Torah, the Prophets, and Writings tefillin: The phylacteries worn on the arm and head, containing biblical passages.

tikkun olam: Repair of the world.

Tzahal: The Israeli armed forces, also known as the IDF (Israel Defense Forces).

tzitzit: Specially knotted fringes on the four corners of the tallit.

yekke: A (more or less) affectionate term for a German Jew.

Yishuv: "Settlement," referring to the body of Jewish residents in Palestine before the creation of the State of Israel in 1948.

Suggestions for Further Reading and Sources of Current Information

Newspapers, Magazines, and Websites:

Azure: Ideas for the Jewish Nation (www.azure.org.il)
  A journal that deals extensively with Jewish political ideas and social philosophy, particularly as they affect Israel.

FORWARD (www.forward.com)
  America's foremost weekly newspaper on Jewish events, culture, and ideas. There is always something in it about Israel.

Ha-Aretz (www.haaretz.com)
  The English-language version of one of Israel's most important daily newspapers.

The Jerusalem Post (www.jpost.com)
  Israel's daily English-language newspaper.

The Jerusalem Report
  The *Newsweek* of the Jewish people.

Moment (www.momentmag.com)
  One of American Jewry's foremost Jewish magazines, with news and opinion pieces about Israel.

Jewish Telegraph Agency (JTA) (www.jta.org)
  The constantly-updating news source about the Jewish world.

New Republic (www.tnr.com)
  One of America's most influential journals. It always contains articles and op-eds on Israel.

Books:

Bard, Mitchell Geoffrey. *Myths and Facts: A Guide to the Arab-Israel Conflict.* New York: American-Israeli Cooperative Enterprise, 2002.

Burstein, Chaya. *A Kid's Catalog of Israel.* Philadelphia: Jewish Publication Society of America, 1998.

Dershowitz, Alan. *The Case for Israel*. New York: Wiley, 2004.

———. *The Case for Peace: How the Arab-Israeli Conflict Can be Resolved*. New York: Wiley, 2005.

———. *What Israel Means to Me: By 80 Prominent Writers, Performers, Scholars, Politicians, and Journalists*. New York: Wiley, 2006.

Gold, Dore. *The Fight for Jerusalem: Radical Islam, the West, and the Future of the Holy City*. Washington, D.C.: Regnery Publishing Company, 2007.

Gordis, Daniel. *If a Place Can Make You Cry: Dispatches from an Anxious State*. New York: Crown, 2002.

———. *Coming Together, Coming Apart: A Memoir of Heartbreak and Promise in Israel*. New York: Wiley, 2006.

Hazony, Yoram. *The Jewish State: The Struggle for Israel's Soul*. New York: Basic Books, 2001.

Hertzberg, Arthur. *The Zionist Idea: A Historical Analysis and Reader*. Philadelphia: Jewish Publication Society of America, 1997.

Hoffman, Lawrence A. *Israel—A Spiritual Travel Guide: A Companion for the Modern Jewish Pilgrim*. Woodstock, VT: Jewish Lights Publishing, 2005.

Korn, Eugene. *The Jewish Connection to Israel, the Promised Land: A Brief Introduction for Christians*. Woodstock, VT: Jewish Lights Publishing, 2007.

Laqueur, Walter. *A History of Zionism: From the French Revolution to the Establishment of the State of Israel*. New York: Schocken, 2003.

Lewis, Bernard. *Semites and Anti-Semites: An Inquiry into Conflict and Prejudice*. New York: W.W. Norton and Company, 1999.

Lozowick, Yaacov. *Right to Exist: A Moral Defense of Israel's Wars*. New York: Anchor, 2004.

Lyons, Len. *The Ethiopian Jews of Israel: Personal Stories of Life in the Promised Land* Woodstock, VT: Jewish Lights Publishing, 2007.

Oren, Michael. *Six Days of War: June 1967 and the Making of the Modern Middle East*. New York: Presidio Press, 2003.

———. *Power, Faith, and Fantasy: America in the Middle East: 1776 to the Present*. New York: W.W. Norton, 2007.

Peters, Joan. *From Time Immemorial: The Origins of the Arab-Jewish Conflict over Palestine*. Chicago: JKAP Publications, 2001.

Sachar, Howard M. *A History of Israel: From the Rise of Zionism to Our Time*. New York: Knopf, 1996.

Segev, Tom. *One Palestine, Complete: Jews and Arabs Under the British Mandate*. New York: Owl Books, 2001.

Sofer, Barbara. *Kids Love Israel, Israel Loves Kids: A Travel Guide for Families*. Minneapolis: Kar-Ben Publishing, 1995.

Index of Contributors

Credits

"Israel is redefining the meaning of Jewish peoplehood not only be being the latest and, in some measure, most exciting chapter..." © 2007 Steven Bayme

"My ties to Israel are thus both real and ideologically messy...." © 2007 Elliot N. Dorff

"Nothing short of frigid temperature can raise goose bumps like the words sung in 'Hatikvah'..." © 2007 Aaron Press Taylor

"Only in a Jewish state do we have the political sovereignty and judicial autonomy that we need to be the *or la-goyim,* a light to the nations..." © 2007 Avraham Weiss

"My dream for Israel is for it to retain its lofty place as a source of ongoing inspiration..." © 2007 Stanley P. Gold

"It is utopian Zion, this Israel is a dream we pursue, a garden in space and time..." © 2007 Goldie Milgram

"My Zionism might be different from my grandfather's Zionism, but it is predicated upon the same fundamental understanding..." © 2007 Ariel Beery

"Our people has yet to demonstrate that we have the capacity to translate prophetic imperatives into the governing norms..." © 2007 Stanley M. Davids

"I wonder how many of the next generation are walking away from serious engagement with Israel..." © 2007 Steven M. Cohen

"As a passionate lover of Israel and its people, I feel compelled to opt for a vision of peace and security..." © 2007 Moshe Waldoks

"As we celebrate Israel's reality and reflect on its past, we should remind ourselves that we are still at the threshold..." © 2007 David M. Gordis

"I bought myself a T-shirt. It was green with blue lettering...." © 2007 Robert B. Barr

"So I, as a Bible scholar, have a lofty dream of Israel as aiming for something awesome and having a mission to make that awesome goal a reality..." © 2007 Richard Elliott Friedman

"The time has arrived for a democratic Israel to stand fully upright...." © 2007 Rosanne Miller Selfon

"Israel is the arena in which our politics and ethics are tested..." © 2007 Elliot Ratzman

"The *mikveh* is ultimately about renewal and rebirth...." © 2007 Niles Elliot Goldstein

"I believe that the Israel I love should be and *must* be an Israel of justice for all its citizens..." © 2007 Peter Edelman

"The vision: make the world a better place through the creation of a model society in the State of Israel..." © 2007 Dan Ehrenkrantz

"I came to Judaism in an unfolding process of recognition...." © 2007 Laurie L. Patton

"For me, Israel exists simultaneously in its heroic past, its precarious present, and it visionary future..." © 2007 Robert Wexler

"I don't believe in chosen peoples and promised lands. I don't think God plays favorites or deals in real estate...." © 2007 Rami M. Shapiro

Richard James Horatio Gotthiel, Louis D. Brandeis, and Solomon Schechter excerpts reprinted from *The Zionist Idea: A Historical Analysis and Reader* © 1996 by Arthur Hertzberg, published by The Jewish Publication Society, with permission of the publisher.

Felix Frankfurter excerpt from *The Diaries of Felix Frankfurter* by Joseph P. Lash. Copyright © 1975 by Joseph P. Lash. Used by permission of W. W. Norton & Company, Inc.

Milton Steinberg excerpts from "Israel and the Nations" in *Basic Judaism,* copyright 1947 by Milton Steinberg and renewed 1974 by David Joel Steinberg and Jonathan Steinberg, reprinted by permission of Harcourt, Inc.

Stephen S. Wise, letter to Fanny Mayer Korn, reprinted from *Stephen S. Wise: Servant of the People* © 1969 by Carl Hermann Voss, published by The Jewish Publication Society, with the permission of the publisher.

Morris Abram excerpt from *Day Is Short, The-An Autobiography,* copyright © 1982 by Morris B. Abram, reprinted by permission of Harcourt, Inc.

Additional Sources:

Stephen S. Wise, letter to John Haynes Holmes, reprinted in Stephen Samuel Wise, *The Personal Letters of Stephen Wise* (Boston, MA: Beacon Press, 1956), p. 271.

Albert Einstein quotes reprinted in Walter Isaacson, *Einstein: His Life and Universe* (New York: Simon & Schuster, 2007).

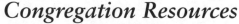

Congregation Resources

The Art of Public Prayer, 2nd Edition: Not for Clergy Only *By Lawrence A. Hoffman*
6 x 9, 272 pp, Quality PB, 978-1-893361-06-5 **$19.99** *(A SkyLight Paths book)*

Becoming a Congregation of Learners: Learning as a Key to Revitalizing
Congregational Life *By Isa Aron, PhD; Foreword by Rabbi Lawrence A. Hoffman*
6 x 9, 304 pp, Quality PB, 978-1-58023-089-6 **$19.95**

Finding a Spiritual Home: How a New Generation of Jews Can Transform the
American Synagogue *By Rabbi Sidney Schwarz*
6 x 9, 352 pp, Quality PB, 978-1-58023-185-5 **$19.95**

Jewish Pastoral Care, 2nd Edition: A Practical Handbook from Traditional &
Contemporary Sources *Edited by Rabbi Dayle A. Friedman*
6 x 9, 528 pp, HC, 978-1-58023-221-0 **$40.00**

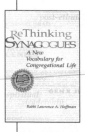

Jewish Spiritual Direction: An Innovative Guide from Traditional and Contemporary
Sources *Edited by Rabbi Howard A. Addison and Barbara Eve Breitman*
6 x 9, 368 pp, HC, 978-1-58023-230-2 **$30.00**

The Self-Renewing Congregation: Organizational Strategies for Revitalizing
Congregational Life *By Isa Aron, PhD; Foreword by Dr. Ron Wolfson*
6 x 9, 304 pp, Quality PB, 978-1-58023-166-4 **$19.95**

Spiritual Community: The Power to Restore Hope, Commitment and Joy
By Rabbi David A. Teutsch, PhD 5½ x 8½, 144 pp, HC, 978-1-58023-270-8 **$19.99**

The Spirituality of Welcoming: How to Transform Your Congregation into a
Sacred Community *By Dr. Ron Wolfson* 6 x 9, 224 pp, Quality PB, 978-1-58023-244-9 **$19.99**

Rethinking Synagogues: A New Vocabulary for Congregational Life
By Rabbi Lawrence A. Hoffman 6 x 9, 240 pp, Quality PB, 978-1-58023-248-7 **$19.99**

Children's Books

What You Will See Inside a Synagogue
By Rabbi Lawrence A. Hoffman and Dr. Ron Wolfson; Full-color photos by Bill Aron
A colorful, fun-to-read introduction that explains the ways and whys of Jewish
worship and religious life.
8½ x 10½, 32 pp, Full-color photos, HC, 978-1-59473-012-2 **$17.99** *For ages 6 & up* *(A SkyLight Paths book)*

The Kids' Fun Book of Jewish Time
By Emily Sper 9 x 7½, 24 pp, Full-color illus., HC, 978-1-58023-311-8 **$16.99**

In God's Hands
By Lawrence Kushner and Gary Schmidt 9 x 12, 32 pp, HC, 978-1-58023-224-1 **$16.99**

Because Nothing Looks Like God
By Lawrence and Karen Kushner
Introduces children to the possibilities of spiritual life.
11 x 8½, 32 pp, Full-color illus., HC, 978-1-58023-092-6 **$16.95** *For ages 4 & up*

Also Available: **Because Nothing Looks Like God Teacher's Guide**
8½ x 11, 22 pp, PB, 978-1-58023-140-4 **$6.95** *For ages 5–8*

Board Book Companions to *Because Nothing Looks Like God*
5 x 5, 24 pp, Full-color illus., SkyLight Paths Board Books *For ages 0–4*

What Does God Look Like? 978-1-893361-23-2 **$7.99**

How Does God Make Things Happen? 978-1-893361-24-9 **$7.95**

Where Is God? 978-1-893361-17-1 **$7.99**

The Book of Miracles: A Young Person's Guide to Jewish Spiritual Awareness
By Lawrence Kushner. All-new illustrations by the author
6 x 9, 96 pp, 2-color illus., HC, 978-1-879045-78-1 **$16.95** *For ages 9 and up*

In Our Image: God's First Creatures
By Nancy Sohn Swartz 9 x 12, 32 pp, Full-color illus., HC, 978-1-879045-99-6 **$16.95** *For ages 4 & up*

Also Available as a Board Book: **How Did the Animals Help God?**
5 x 5, 24 pp, Board, Full-color illus., 978-1-59473-044-3 **$7.99** *For ages 0–4* *(A SkyLight Paths book)*

What Makes Someone a Jew?
By Lauren Seidman
Reflects the changing face of American Judaism.
10 x 8½, 32 pp, Full-color photos, Quality PB Original, 978-1-58023-321-7 **$8.99** *For ages 3–6*

Children's Books
by Sandy Eisenberg Sasso

Adam & Eve's First Sunset: God's New Day
Engaging new story explores fear and hope, faith and gratitude in ways that will delight kids and adults—inspiring us to bless each of God's days and nights.
9 x 12, 32 pp, Full-color illus., HC, 978-1-58023-177-0 **$17.95** *For ages 4 & up*

Also Available as a Board Book: **Adam and Eve's New Day**
5 x 5, 24 pp, Full-color illus., Board, 978-1-59473-205-8 **$7.99** *For ages 0–4 (A SkyLight Paths book)*

But God Remembered
Stories of Women from Creation to the Promised Land
Four different stories of women—Lillith, Serach, Bityah, and the Daughters of Z—teach us important values through their faith and actions.
9 x 12, 32 pp, Full-color illus., HC, 978-1-879045-43-9 **$16.95** *For ages 8 & up*

Cain & Abel: Finding the Fruits of Peace
Shows children that we have the power to deal with anger in positive ways. Provides questions for kids and adults to explore together.
9 x 12, 32 pp, Full-color illus., HC, 978-1-58023-123-7 **$16.95** *For ages 5 & up*

God in Between
If you wanted to find God, where would you look? This magical, mythical tale teaches that God can be found where we are: within all of us and the relationships between us.
9 x 12, 32 pp, Full-color illus., HC, 978-1-879045-86-6 **$16.95** *For ages 4 & up*

God's Paintbrush: Special 10th Anniversary Edition
Wonderfully interactive, invites children of all faiths and backgrounds to encounter God through moments in their own lives. Provides questions adult and child can explore together.
11 x 8½, 32 pp, Full-color illus., HC, 978-1-58023-195-4 **$17.95** *For ages 4 & up*

Also Available: **God's Paintbrush Teacher's Guide**
8½ x 11, 32 pp, PB, 978-1-879045-57-6 **$8.95**

God's Paintbrush Celebration Kit
A Spiritual Activity Kit for Teachers and Students of All Faiths, All Backgrounds
Additional activity sheets available:
8-Student Activity Sheet Pack (40 sheets/5 sessions), 978-1-58023-058-2 **$19.95**
Single-Student Activity Sheet Pack (5 sessions), 978-1-58023-059-9 **$3.95**

In God's Name
Like an ancient myth in its poetic text and vibrant illustrations, this award-winning modern fable about the search for God's name celebrates the diversity and, at the same time, the unity of all people.
9 x 12, 32 pp, Full-color illus., HC, 978-1-879045-26-2 **$16.99** *For ages 4 & up*

Also Available as a Board Book: **What Is God's Name?**
5 x 5, 24 pp, Board, Full-color illus., 978-1-893361-10-2 **$7.99** *For ages 0–4 (A SkyLight Paths book)*

Also Available: **In God's Name video and study guide**
Computer animation, original music, and children's voices. 18 min. **$29.99**

Also Available in Spanish: **El nombre de Dios**
9 x 12, 32 pp, Full-color illus., HC, 978-1-893361-63-8 **$16.95** *(A SkyLight Paths book)*

Noah's Wife: The Story of Naamah
When God tells Noah to bring the animals of the world onto the ark, God also calls on Naamah, Noah's wife, to save each plant on Earth. Based on an ancient text.
9 x 12, 32 pp, Full-color illus., HC, 978-1-58023-134-3 **$16.95** *For ages 4 & up*

Also Available as a Board Book: **Naamah, Noah's Wife**
5 x 5, 24 pp, Full-color illus., Board, 978-1-893361-56-0 **$7.95** *For ages 0–4 (A SkyLight Paths book)*

For Heaven's Sake: Finding God in Unexpected Places
9 x 12, 32 pp, Full-color illus., HC, 978-1-58023-054-4 **$16.95** *For ages 4 & up*

God Said Amen: Finding the Answers to Our Prayers
9 x 12, 32 pp, Full-color illus., HC, 978-1-58023-080-3 **$16.95** *For ages 4 & up*

Current Events/History

The Story of the Jews: A 4,000-Year Adventure—A Graphic History Book
Written & illustrated by Stan Mack
Witty, illustrated narrative of all the major happenings from biblical times to the twenty-first century. 6 x 9, 288 pp, illus., Quality PB, 978-1-58023-155-8 **$16.95**

Hannah Senesh: Her Life and Diary, the First Complete Edition
By Hannah Senesh; Foreword by Marge Piercy; Preface by Eitan Senesh
6 x 9, 352 pp, HC, 978-1-58023-212-8 **$24.99**

The Jewish Prophet: Visionary Words from Moses and Miriam to Henrietta Szold and A. J. Heschel *By Rabbi Dr. Michael J. Shire*
6½ x 8½, 128 pp, 123 full-color illus., HC, 978-1-58023-168-8
Special gift price **$14.95**

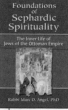

Foundations of Sephardic Spirituality: The Inner Life of Jews of the Ottoman Empire
By Rabbi Marc D. Angel, PhD 6 x 9, 224 pp, HC, 978-1-58023-243-2 **$24.99**

Judaism and Justice: The Jewish Passion to Repair the World
By Rabbi Sidney Schwarz
6 x 9, 250 pp, HC, 978-1-58023-312-5 **$24.99**

Ecology

Ecology & the Jewish Spirit: Where Nature & the Sacred Meet
Edited by Ellen Bernstein 6 x 9, 288 pp, Quality PB, 978-1-58023-082-7 **$16.95**

Torah of the Earth: Exploring 4,000 Years of Ecology in Jewish Thought
Vol. 1: Biblical Israel: One Land, One People; Rabbinic Judaism: One People, Many Lands
Vol. 2: Zionism: One Land, Two Peoples; Eco-Judaism: One Earth, Many Peoples
Edited by Arthur Waskow
Vol. 1: 6 x 9, 272 pp, Quality PB, 978-1-58023-086-5 **$19.95**
Vol. 2: 6 x 9, 336 pp, Quality PB, 978-1-58023-087-2 **$19.95**

The Way Into Judaism and the Environment
By Jeremy Benstein 6 x 9, 224 pp, HC, 978-1-58023-268-5 **$24.99**

Grief/Healing

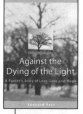

Against the Dying of the Light: A Parent's Story of Love, Loss and Hope
By Leonard Fein
5½ x 8½, 176 pp, Quality PB, 978-1-58023-197-8 **$15.99**

Grief in Our Seasons: A Mourner's Kaddish Companion *By Rabbi Kerry M. Olitzky*
4½ x 6½, 448 pp, Quality PB, 978-1-879045-55-2 **$15.95**

Healing of Soul, Healing of Body: Spiritual Leaders Unfold the Strength & Solace in Psalms *Edited by Rabbi Simkha Y. Weintraub, CSW*
6 x 9, 128 pp, 2-color illus. text, Quality PB, 978-1-879045-31-6 **$14.99**

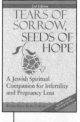

Jewish Paths toward Healing and Wholeness: A Personal Guide to Dealing with
Suffering *By Rabbi Kerry M. Olitzky; Foreword by Debbie Friedman.*
6 x 9, 192 pp, Quality PB, 978-1-58023-068-1 **$15.95**

Mourning & Mitzvah, 2nd Edition: A Guided Journal for Walking the Mourner's
Path through Grief to Healing *By Anne Brener, LCSW*
7½ x 9, 304 pp, Quality PB, 978-1-58023-113-8 **$19.99**

The Perfect Stranger's Guide to Funerals and Grieving Practices
A Guide to Etiquette in Other People's Religious Ceremonies *Edited by Stuart M. Matlins*
6 x 9, 240 pp, Quality PB, 978-1-893361-20-1 **$16.95** *(A SkyLight Paths book)*

Tears of Sorrow, Seeds of Hope, 2nd Edition: A Jewish Spiritual Companion for
Infertility and Pregnancy Loss *By Rabbi Nina Beth Cardin*
6 x 9, 208 pp, Quality PB, 978-1-58023-233-3 **$18.99**

A Time to Mourn, A Time to Comfort, 2nd Edition: A Guide to Jewish
Bereavement *By Dr. Ron Wolfson*
7 x 9, 384 pp, Quality PB, 978-1-58023-253-1 **$19.99**

When a Grandparent Dies: A Kid's Own Remembering Workbook for Dealing
with Shiva and the Year Beyond *By Nechama Liss-Levinson, PhD*
8 x 10, 48 pp, 2-color text, HC, 978-1-879045-44-6 **$15.95** *For ages 7–13*

Spirituality

The Adventures of Rabbi Harvey: A Graphic Novel of Jewish Wisdom and Wit in the Wild West *By Steve Sheinkin*
Jewish and American folktales combine in this witty and original graphic novel collection. Creatively retold and set on the western frontier of the 1870s.
6 x 9, 144 pp, Full-color illus., Quality PB, 978-1-58023-310-1 **$16.99**
Also Available: **The Adventures of Rabbi Harvey Teacher's Guide**
8½ x 11, 32 pp, PB, 978-1-58023-326-2 **$8.99**

Ethics of the Sages: *Pirke Avot*—Annotated & Explained
Translation and Annotation by Rabbi Rami Shapiro
5½ x 8½, 192 pp, Quality PB, 978-1-59473-207-2 **$16.99** *(A SkyLight Paths book)*

A Book of Life: Embracing Judaism as a Spiritual Practice
By Michael Strassfeld 6 x 9, 528 pp, Quality PB, 978-1-58023-247-0 **$19.99**

Meaning and Mitzvah: Daily Practices for Reclaiming Judaism through Prayer, God, Torah, Hebrew, Mitzvot and Peoplehood *By Rabbi Goldie Milgram*
7 x 9, 336 pp, Quality PB, 978-1-58023-256-2 **$19.99**

The Soul of the Story: Meetings with Remarkable People
By Rabbi David Zeller 6 x 9, 288 pp, HC, 978-1-58023-272-2 **$21.99**

Aleph-Bet Yoga: Embodying the Hebrew Letters for Physical and Spiritual Well-Being
By Steven A. Rapp. Foreword by Tamar Frankiel, PhD and Judy Greenfeld. Preface by Hart Lazer.
7 x 10, 128 pp, b/w photos, Quality PB, Layflat binding, 978-1-58023-162-6 **$16.95**

Entering the Temple of Dreams: Jewish Prayers, Movements, and Meditations for the End of the Day *By Tamar Frankiel, PhD, and Judy Greenfeld*
7 x 10, 192 pp, illus., Quality PB, 978-1-58023-079-7 **$16.95**

Does the Soul Survive? A Jewish Journey to Belief in Afterlife, Past Lives & Living with Purpose *By Rabbi Elie Kaplan Spitz; Foreword by Brian L. Weiss, MD*
6 x 9, 288 pp, Quality PB, 978-1-58023-165-7 **$16.99**

First Steps to a New Jewish Spirit: Reb Zalman's Guide to Recapturing the Intimacy & Ecstasy in Your Relationship with God *By Rabbi Zalman M. Schachter-Shalomi with Donald Gropman* 6 x 9, 144 pp, Quality PB, 978-1-58023-182-4 **$16.95**

God in Our Relationships: Spirituality between People from the Teachings of Martin Buber *By Rabbi Dennis S. Ross* 5½ x 8½, 160 pp, Quality PB, 978-1-58023-147-3 **$16.95**

Judaism, Physics and God: Searching for Sacred Metaphors in a Post-Einstein World
By Rabbi David W. Nelson 6 x 9, 368 pp, Quality PB, inc. reader's discussion guide, 978-1-58023-306-4 **$18.99**;
HC, 352 pp, 978-1-58023-252-4 **$24.99**

The Jewish Lights Spirituality Handbook: A Guide to Understanding, Exploring & Living a Spiritual Life *Edited by Stuart M. Matlins*
What exactly is "Jewish" about spirituality? How do I make it a part of my life? Fifty of today's foremost spiritual leaders share their ideas and experience with us.
6 x 9, 456 pp, Quality PB, 978-1-58023-093-3 **$19.99**

Bringing the Psalms to Life: How to Understand and Use the Book of Psalms
By Daniel F. Polish 6 x 9, 208 pp, Quality PB, 978-1-58023-157-2 **$16.95**;
HC, 978-1-58023-077-3 **$21.95**

God & the Big Bang: Discovering Harmony between Science & Spirituality
By Daniel C. Matt 6 x 9, 216 pp, Quality PB, 978-1-879045-89-7 **$16.99**

Minding the Temple of the Soul: Balancing Body, Mind, and Spirit through Traditional Jewish Prayer, Movement, and Meditation *By Tamar Frankiel, PhD, and Judy Greenfeld*
7 x 10, 184 pp, illus., Quality PB, 978-1-879045-64-4 **$16.95**
Audiotape of the Blessings and Meditations: 60 min. **$9.95**
Videotape of the Movements and Meditations: 46 min. **$20.00**

One God Clapping: The Spiritual Path of a Zen Rabbi *By Alan Lew with Sherril Jaffe*
5½ x 8½, 336 pp, Quality PB, 978-1-58023-115-2 **$16.95**

There Is No Messiah ... and You're It: The Stunning Transformation of Judaism's Most Provocative Idea *By Rabbi Robert N. Levine, DD*
6 x 9, 192 pp, Quality PB, 978-1-58023-255-5 **$16.99**

These Are the Words: A Vocabulary of Jewish Spiritual Life
By Arthur Green 6 x 9, 304 pp, Quality PB, 978-1-58023-107-7 **$18.95**

Meditation

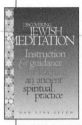

The Handbook of Jewish Meditation Practices
A Guide for Enriching the Sabbath and Other Days of Your Life
By Rabbi David A. Cooper Easy-to-learn meditation techniques.
6 x 9, 208 pp, Quality PB, 978-1-58023-102-2 **$16.95**

Discovering Jewish Meditation: Instruction & Guidance for Learning an Ancient
Spiritual Practice *By Nan Fink Gefen*
6 x 9, 208 pp, Quality PB, 978-1-58023-067-4 **$16.95**

A Heart of Stillness: A Complete Guide to Learning the Art of Meditation
By David A. Cooper 5½ x 8½, 272 pp, Quality PB, 978-1-893361-03-4 **$16.95** *(A SkyLight Paths book)*

Meditation from the Heart of Judaism: Today's Teachers Share Their
Practices, Techniques, and Faith *Edited by Avram Davis*
6 x 9, 256 pp, Quality PB, 978-1-58023-049-0 **$16.95**

Silence, Simplicity & Solitude: A Complete Guide to Spiritual Retreat at Home
By David A. Cooper 5½ x 8½, 336 pp, Quality PB, 978-1-893361-04-1 **$16.95**
(A SkyLight Paths book)

The Way of Flame: A Guide to the Forgotten Mystical Tradition of Jewish
Meditation *By Avram Davis* 4½ x 8, 176 pp, Quality PB, 978-1-58023-060-5 **$15.95**

Ritual/Sacred Practice/Journaling

The Jewish Dream Book: The Key to Opening the Inner Meaning of
Your Dreams *By Vanessa L. Ochs with Elizabeth Ochs; Full-color illus. by Kristina Swarner*
Instructions for how modern people can perform ancient Jewish dream practices
and dream interpretations drawn from the Jewish wisdom tradition.
8 x 8, 128 pp, Full-color illus., Deluxe PB w/flaps, 978-1-58023-132-9 **$16.95**

The Jewish Journaling Book: How to Use Jewish Tradition to Write
Your Life & Explore Your Soul *By Janet Ruth Falon*
Details the history of Jewish journaling throughout biblical and modern times, and
teaches specific journaling techniques to help you create and maintain a vital journal,
from a Jewish perspective. 8 x 8, 304 pp, Deluxe PB w/flaps, 978-1-58023-203-6 **$18.99**

The Book of Jewish Sacred Practices: CLAL's Guide to Everyday & Holiday
Rituals & Blessings *Edited by Rabbi Irwin Kula and Vanessa L. Ochs, PhD*
6 x 9, 368 pp, Quality PB, 978-1-58023-152-7 **$18.95**

Jewish Ritual: A Brief Introduction for Christians
By Rabbi Kerry M. Olitzky and Rabbi Daniel Judson
5½ x 8½, 144 pp, Quality PB, 978-1-58023-210-4 **$14.99**

The Rituals & Practices of a Jewish Life: A Handbook for Personal Spiritual
Renewal *Edited by Rabbi Kerry M. Olitzky and Rabbi Daniel Judson*
6 x 9, 272 pp, illus., Quality PB, 978-1-58023-169-5 **$18.95**

The Sacred Art of Lovingkindness: Preparing to Practice
By Rabbi Rami Shapiro 5½ x 8½, 176 pp, Quality PB, 978-1-59473-151-8 **$16.99**
(A SkyLight Paths book)

Science Fiction/Mystery & Detective Fiction

Mystery Midrash: An Anthology of Jewish Mystery & Detective Fiction
Edited by Lawrence W. Raphael; Preface by Joel Siegel
6 x 9, 304 pp, Quality PB, 978-1-58023-055-1 **$16.95**

Criminal Kabbalah: An Intriguing Anthology of Jewish Mystery & Detective Fiction
Edited by Lawrence W. Raphael; Foreword by Laurie R. King
6 x 9, 256 pp, Quality PB, 978-1-58023-109-1 **$16.95**

Wandering Stars: An Anthology of Jewish Fantasy & Science Fiction
Edited by Jack Dann; Introduction by Isaac Asimov
6 x 9, 272 pp, Quality PB, 978-1-58023-005-6 **$16.95**

More Wandering Stars: An Anthology of Outstanding Stories of Jewish Fantasy and
Science Fiction *Edited by Jack Dann; Introduction by Isaac Asimov*
6 x 9, 192 pp, Quality PB, 978-1-58023-063-6 **$16.95**

Inspiration

God's To-Do List: 103 Ways to Be an Angel and Do God's Work on Earth
By Dr. Ron Wolfson 6 x 9, 150 pp, Quality PB, 978-1-58023-301-9 **$15.99**

God in All Moments: Mystical & Practical Spiritual Wisdom from Hasidic Masters
Edited and translated by Or N. Rose with Ebn D. Leader
5½ x 8½, 192 pp, Quality PB, 978-1-58023-186-2 **$16.95**

Our Dance with God: Finding Prayer, Perspective and Meaning in the Stories of Our
Lives *By Karyn D. Kedar* 6 x 9, 176 pp, Quality PB, 978-1-58023-202-9 **$16.99**

Also Available: **The Dance of the Dolphin** (HC edition of *Our Dance with God*)
6 x 9, 176 pp, HC, 978-1-58023-154-1 **$19.95**

The Empty Chair: Finding Hope and Joy—Timeless Wisdom from a Hasidic Master,
Rebbe Nachman of Breslov *Adapted by Moshe Mykoff and the Breslov Research Institute*
4 x 6, 128 pp, 2-color text, Deluxe PB w/flaps, 978-1-879045-67-5 **$9.95**

The Gentle Weapon: Prayers for Everyday and Not-So-Everyday Moments—
Timeless Wisdom from the Teachings of the Hasidic Master, Rebbe Nachman of Breslov
Adapted by Moshe Mykoff and S. C. Mizrahi, together with the Breslov Research Institute
4 x 6, 144 pp, 2-color text, Deluxe PB w/flaps, 978-1-58023-022-3 **$9.99**

God Whispers: Stories of the Soul, Lessons of the Heart *By Karyn D. Kedar*
6 x 9, 176 pp, Quality PB, 978-1-58023-088-9 **$15.95**

An Orphan in History: One Man's Triumphant Search for His Jewish Roots
By Paul Cowan; Afterword by Rachel Cowan. 6 x 9, 288 pp, Quality PB, 978-1-58023-135-0 **$16.95**

Restful Reflections: Nighttime Inspiration to Calm the Soul, Based on Jewish Wisdom
By Rabbi Kerry M. Olitzky & Rabbi Lori Forman 4½ x 6½, 448 pp, Quality PB, 978-1-58023-091-9 **$15.95**

Sacred Intentions: Daily Inspiration to Strengthen the Spirit, Based on Jewish Wisdom
By Rabbi Kerry M. Olitzky and Rabbi Lori Forman 4½ x 6½, 448 pp, Quality PB, 978-1-58023-061-2 **$15.95**

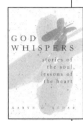
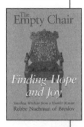

Kabbalah/Mysticism/Enneagram

Awakening to Kabbalah: The Guiding Light of Spiritual Fulfillment
By Rav Michael Laitman, PhD 6 x 9, 192 pp, HC, 978-1-58023-264-7 **$21.99**

Seek My Face: A Jewish Mystical Theology *By Arthur Green*
6 x 9, 304 pp, Quality PB, 978-1-58023-130-5 **$19.95**

Zohar: Annotated & Explained
Translation and annotation by Daniel C. Matt; Foreword by Andrew Harvey
5½ x 8½, 176 pp, Quality PB, 978-1-893361-51-5 **$15.99** *(A SkyLight Paths book)*

Cast in God's Image: Discover Your Personality Type Using the Enneagram and Kabbalah
By Rabbi Howard A. Addison
7 x 9, 176 pp, Quality PB, Layflat binding, 20+ journaling exercises, 978-1-58023-124-4 **$16.95**

Ehyeh: A Kabbalah for Tomorrow
By Arthur Green 6 x 9, 224 pp, Quality PB, 978-1-58023-213-5 **$16.99**

The Enneagram and Kabbalah, 2nd Edition: Reading Your Soul
By Rabbi Howard A. Addison 6 x 9, 192 pp, Quality PB, 978-1-58023-229-6 **$16.99**

Finding Joy: A Practical Spiritual Guide to Happiness *By Dannel I. Schwartz with Mark Hass*
6 x 9, 192 pp, Quality PB, 978-1-58023-009-4 **$14.95**

The Flame of the Heart: Prayers of a Chasidic Mystic *By Reb Noson of Breslov. Translated by*
Duvid Sears with the Breslov Research Institute 5 x 7¼, 160 pp, Quality PB, 978-1-58023-246-3 **$15.99**

The Gift of Kabbalah: Discovering the Secrets of Heaven, Renewing Your Life on Earth
By Tamar Frankiel, PhD 6 x 9, 256 pp, Quality PB, 978-1-58023-141-1 **$16.95;**
HC, 978-1-58023-108-4 **$21.95**

Kabbalah: A Brief Introduction for Christians
By Tamar Frankiel, PhD 5½ x 8½, 208 pp, Quality PB, 978-1-58023-303-3 **$16.99**

The Lost Princess and Other Kabbalistic Tales of Rebbe Nachman of Breslov
The Seven Beggars and Other Kabbalistic Tales of Rebbe Nachman of Breslov
Translated by Rabbi Aryeh Kaplan; Preface by Rabbi Chaim Kramer
Lost Princess: 6 x 9, 400 pp, Quality PB, 978-1-58023-217-3 **$18.99**
Seven Beggars: 6 x 9, 192 pp, Quality PB, 978-1-58023-250-0 **$16.99**

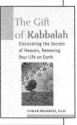

See also *The Way Into Jewish Mystical Tradition* in Spirituality / Lawrence Kushner

Spirituality/Lawrence Kushner

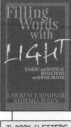

Filling Words with Light: Hasidic and Mystical Reflections on Jewish Prayer
By Lawrence Kushner and Nehemia Polen
5½ x 8½, 176 pp, HC, 978-1-58023-216-6 **$21.99**

The Book of Letters: A Mystical Hebrew Alphabet
Popular HC Edition, 6 x 9, 80 pp, 2-color text, 978-1-879045-00-2 **$24.95**
Collector's Limited Edition, 9 x 12, 80 pp, gold foil embossed pages, w/limited edition silkscreened print, 978-1-879045-04-0 **$349.00**

The Book of Miracles: A Young Person's Guide to Jewish Spiritual Awareness
6 x 9, 96 pp, 2-color illus., HC, 978-1-879045-78-1 **$16.95** *For ages 9 and up*

The Book of Words: Talking Spiritual Life, Living Spiritual Talk
6 x 9, 160 pp, Quality PB, 978-1-58023-020-9 **$16.95**

Eyes Remade for Wonder: A Lawrence Kushner Reader *Introduction by Thomas Moore*
6 x 9, 240 pp, Quality PB, 978-1-58023-042-1 **$18.95**

God Was in This Place & I, i Did Not Know: Finding Self, Spirituality and Ultimate Meaning 6 x 9, 192 pp, Quality PB, 978-1-879045-33-0 **$16.95**

Honey from the Rock: An Introduction to Jewish Mysticism
6 x 9, 176 pp, Quality PB, 978-1-58023-073-5 **$16.95**

Invisible Lines of Connection: Sacred Stories of the Ordinary
5½ x 8½, 160 pp, Quality PB, 978-1-879045-98-9 **$15.95**

Jewish Spirituality—A Brief Introduction for Christians
5½ x 8½, 112 pp, Quality PB, 978-1-58023-150-3 **$12.95**

The River of Light: Jewish Mystical Awareness
6 x 9, 192 pp, Quality PB, 978-1-58023-096-4 **$16.95**

The Way Into Jewish Mystical Tradition
6 x 9, 224 pp, Quality PB, 978-1-58023-200-5 **$18.99**; HC, 978-1-58023-029-2 **$21.95**

Spirituality/Prayer

Pray Tell: A Hadassah Guide to Jewish Prayer
By Rabbi Jules Harlow, with contributions from many others
8½ x 11, 400 pp, Quality PB, 978-1-58023-163-3 **$29.95**

Witnesses to the One: The Spiritual History of the *Sh'ma* By Rabbi Joseph B. Meszler;
Foreword by Rabbi Elyse Goldstein 6 x 9, 176 pp, HC, 978-1-58023-309-5 **$19.99**

My People's Prayer Book Series

Traditional Prayers, Modern Commentaries *Edited by Rabbi Lawrence A. Hoffman*
Provides diverse and exciting commentary to the traditional liturgy, helping modern men and women find new wisdom in Jewish prayer, and bring liturgy into their lives. Each book includes Hebrew text, modern translation, and commentaries from all perspectives of the Jewish world.

Vol. 1—The *Sh'ma* and Its Blessings
7 x 10, 168 pp, HC, 978-1-879045-79-8 **$24.99**
Vol. 2—The *Amidah*
7 x 10, 240 pp, HC, 978-1-879045-80-4 **$24.95**
Vol. 3—*P'sukei D'zimrah* (Morning Psalms)
7 x 10, 240 pp, HC, 978-1-879045-81-1 **$24.95**
Vol. 4—*Seder K'riat Hatorah* (The Torah Service)
7 x 10, 264 pp, HC, 978-1-879045-82-8 **$23.95**
Vol. 5—*Birkhot Hashachar* (Morning Blessings)
7 x 10, 240 pp, HC, 978-1-879045-83-5 **$24.95**
Vol. 6—*Tachanun* and Concluding Prayers
7 x 10, 240 pp, HC, 978-1-879045-84-2 **$24.95**
Vol. 7—Shabbat at Home
7 x 10, 240 pp, HC, 978-1-879045-85-9 **$24.95**
Vol. 8—*Kabbalat Shabbat* (Welcoming Shabbat in the Synagogue)
7 x 10, 240 pp, HC, 978-1-58023-121-3 **$24.99**
Vol. 9—Welcoming the Night: *Minchah* and *Ma'ariv* (Afternoon and Evening Prayer) 7 x 10, 272 pp, HC, 978-1-58023-262-3 **$24.99**
Vol. 10—Shabbat Morning: *Shacharit* and *Musaf* (Morning and Additional Services) 7 x 10, 240 pp, HC, 978-1-58023-240-1 **$24.99**

Spirituality/Women's Interest

The Quotable Jewish Woman: Wisdom, Inspiration & Humor from the Mind & Heart
Edited and compiled by Elaine Bernstein Partnow
6 x 9, 496 pp, Quality PB, 978-1-58023-236-4 **$19.99**; HC, 978-1-58023-193-0 **$29.99**

The Knitting Way: A Guide to Spiritual Self-Discovery *By Linda Skolnick and Janice MacDaniels* 7 x 9, 240 pp, Quality PB, 978-1-59473-079-5 **$16.99** *(A SkyLight Paths book)*

The Quilting Path: A Guide to Spiritual Self-Discovery through Fabric, Thread and Kabbalah
By Louise Silk 7 x 9, 192 pp, Quality PB, 978-1-59473-206-5 **$16.99** *(A SkyLight Paths book)*

The Divine Feminine in Biblical Wisdom Literature: Selections Annotated &
Explained *Translated and Annotated by Rabbi Rami Shapiro*
5½ x 8½, 240 pp, Quality PB, 978-1-59473-109-9 **$16.99** *(A SkyLight Paths book)*

Lifecycles, Vol. 1: Jewish Women on Life Passages & Personal Milestones
Edited and with Introductions by Rabbi Debra Orenstein
6 x 9, 480 pp, Quality PB, 978-1-58023-018-6 **$19.95**

Lifecycles, Vol. 2: Jewish Women on Biblical Themes in Contemporary Life
Edited and with Introductions by Rabbi Debra Orenstein and Rabbi Jane Rachel Litman
6 x 9, 464 pp, Quality PB, 978-1-58023-019-3 **$19.95**

Moonbeams: A Hadassah Rosh Hodesh Guide *Edited by Carol Diament, PhD*
8½ x 11, 240 pp, Quality PB, 978-1-58023-099-5 **$20.00**

ReVisions: Seeing Torah through a Feminist Lens *By Rabbi Elyse Goldstein*
5½ x 8½, 224 pp, Quality PB, 978-1-58023-117-6 **$16.95**

The Women's Haftarah Commentary: New Insights from Women Rabbis on the
54 Weekly Haftarah Portions, the 5 Megillot & Special Shabbatot
Edited by Rabbi Elyse Goldstein 6 x 9, 560 pp, HC, 978-1-58023-133-6 **$39.99**

The Women's Torah Commentary: New Insights from Women Rabbis on the 54
Weekly Torah Portions *Edited by Rabbi Elyse Goldstein*
6 x 9, 496 pp, HC, 978-1-58023-076-6 **$34.95**

The Year Mom Got Religion: One Woman's Midlife Journey into Judaism
By Lee Meyerhoff Hendler 6 x 9, 208 pp, Quality PB, 978-1-58023-070-4 **$15.95**

See Holidays for *The Women's Passover Companion: Women's Reflections on the Festival of Freedom* and *The Women's Seder Sourcebook: Rituals & Readings for Use at the Passover Seder.* Also see Bar/Bat Mitzvah for *The JGirl's Guide: The Young Jewish Woman's Handbook for Coming of Age.*

Travel

Israel—A Spiritual Travel Guide, 2nd Edition
A Companion for the Modern Jewish Pilgrim
By Rabbi Lawrence A. Hoffman 4¾ x 10, 256 pp, Quality PB, illus., 978-1-58023-261-6 **$18.99**
Also Available: **The Israel Mission Leader's Guide** 978-1-58023-085-8 **$4.95**

12-Step

100 Blessings Every Day: Daily Twelve Step Recovery Affirmations, Exercises for
Personal Growth & Renewal Reflecting Seasons of the Jewish Year
By Rabbi Kerry M. Olitzky; Foreword by Rabbi Neil Gillman
4½ x 6½, 432 pp, Quality PB, 978-1-879045-30-9 **$15.99**

Recovery from Codependence: A Jewish Twelve Steps Guide to Healing Your Soul
By Rabbi Kerry M. Olitzky 6 x 9, 160 pp, Quality PB, 978-1-879045-32-3 **$13.95**

Renewed Each Day: Daily Twelve Step Recovery Meditations Based on the Bible
By Rabbi Kerry M. Olitzky and Aaron Z.
Vol. 1—Genesis & Exodus: 6 x 9, 224 pp, Quality PB, 978-1-879045-12-5 **$14.95**
Vol. 2—Leviticus, Numbers & Deuteronomy: 6 x 9, 280 pp, Quality PB, 978-1-879045-13-2 **$18.99**

Twelve Jewish Steps to Recovery: A Personal Guide to Turning from Alcoholism &
Other Addictions—Drugs, Food, Gambling, Sex ...
By Rabbi Kerry M. Olitzky and Stuart A. Copans, MD; Preface by Abraham J. Twerski, MD
6 x 9, 144 pp, Quality PB, 978-1-879045-09-5 **$14.95**

Holidays/Holy Days

Rosh Hashanah Readings: Inspiration, Information and Contemplation
Yom Kippur Readings: Inspiration, Information and Contemplation
Edited by Rabbi Dov Peretz Elkins with Section Introductions from Arthur Green's These Are the Words
An extraordinary collection of readings, prayers and insights that enable the modern worshiper to enter into the spirit of the High Holy Days in a personal and powerful way, permitting the meaning of the Jewish New Year to enter the heart.
RHR: 6 x 9, 400 pp, HC, 978-1-58023-239-5 **$24.99**
YKR: 6 x 9, 368 pp, HC, 978-1-58023-271-5 **$24.99**

Jewish Holidays: A Brief Introduction for Christians
By Rabbi Kerry M. Olitzky and Rabbi Daniel Judson
5½ x 8½, 144 pp, Quality PB, 978-1-58023-302-6 **$16.99**

Leading the Passover Journey: The Seder's Meaning Revealed, the Haggadah's Story Retold *By Rabbi Nathan Laufer*
Uncovers the hidden meaning of the Seder's rituals and customs.
6 x 9, 224 pp, HC, 978-1-58023-211-1 **$24.99**

Reclaiming Judaism as a Spiritual Practice: Holy Days and Shabbat
By Rabbi Goldie Milgram
7 x 9, 272 pp, Quality PB, 978-1-58023-205-0 **$19.99**

7th Heaven: Celebrating Shabbat with Rebbe Nachman of Breslov
By Moshe Mykoff with the Breslov Research Institute
5⅛ x 8¼, 224 pp, Deluxe PB w/flaps, 978-1-58023-175-6 **$18.95**

The Women's Passover Companion: Women's Reflections on the Festival of Freedom *Edited by Rabbi Sharon Cohen Anisfeld, Tara Mohr, and Catherine Spector*
Groundbreaking. A provocative conversation about women's relationships to Passover as well as the roots and meanings of women's seders.
6 x 9, 352 pp, Quality PB, 978-1-58023-231-9 **$19.99**

The Women's Seder Sourcebook: Rituals & Readings for Use at the Passover Seder *Edited by Rabbi Sharon Cohen Anisfeld, Tara Mohr, and Catherine Spector*
Gathers the voices of more than one hundred women in readings, personal and creative reflections, commentaries, blessings, and ritual suggestions that can be incorporated into your Passover celebration.
6 x 9, 384 pp, Quality PB, 978-1-58023-232-6 **$19.99**

Creating Lively Passover Seders: A Sourcebook of Engaging Tales, Texts & Activities
By David Arnow, PhD 7 x 9, 416 pp, Quality PB, 978-1-58023-184-8 **$24.99**

Hanukkah, 2nd Edition: The Family Guide to Spiritual Celebration
By Dr. Ron Wolfson. Edited by Joel Lurie Grishaver.
7 x 9, 240 pp, illus., Quality PB, 978-1-58023-122-0 **$18.95**

The Jewish Family Fun Book: Holiday Projects, Everyday Activities, and Travel Ideas with Jewish Themes *By Danielle Dardashti and Roni Sarig. Illus. by Avi Katz.*
6 x 9, 288 pp, 70+ b/w illus. & diagrams, Quality PB, 978-1-58023-171-8 **$18.95**

The Jewish Gardening Cookbook: Growing Plants & Cooking for Holidays & Festivals *By Michael Brown* 6 x 9, 224 pp, 30+ b/w illus., Quality PB, 978-1-58023-116-9 **$16.95**

The Jewish Lights Book of Fun Classroom Activities: Simple and Seasonal Projects for Teachers and Students *By Danielle Dardashti and Roni Sarig*
6 x 9, 240 pp, Quality PB, 978-1-58023-206-7 **$19.99**

Passover, 2nd Edition: The Family Guide to Spiritual Celebration
By Dr. Ron Wolfson with Joel Lurie Grishaver 7 x 9, 352 pp, Quality PB, 978-1-58023-174-9 **$19.95**

Shabbat, 2nd Edition: The Family Guide to Preparing for and Celebrating the Sabbath
By Dr. Ron Wolfson 7 x 9, 320 pp, illus., Quality PB, 978-1-58023-164-0 **$19.99**

Sharing Blessings: Children's Stories for Exploring the Spirit of the Jewish Holidays
By Rahel Musleah and Rabbi Michael Klayman
8½ x 11, 64 pp, Full-color illus., HC, 978-1-879045-71-2 **$18.95** *For ages 6 & up*

Life Cycle
Marriage / Parenting / Family / Aging

Jewish Fathers: A Legacy of Love
Photographs by Lloyd Wolf. Essays by Paula Wolfson. Foreword by Rabbi Harold Kushner.
Honors the role of contemporary Jewish fathers in America. Each father tells in his own words what it means to be a parent and Jewish, and what he learned from his own father. Insightful photos.
10¾ x 9⅞, 144 pp with 100+ duotone photos, HC, 978-1-58023-204-3 **$30.00**

The New Jewish Baby Album: Creating and Celebrating the Beginning of a Spiritual Life—A Jewish Lights Companion
By the Editors at Jewish Lights. Foreword by Anita Diamant. Preface by Rabbi Sandy Eisenberg Sasso.
A spiritual keepsake that will be treasured for generations. More than just a memory book, *shows you how—and why it's important*—to create a Jewish home and a Jewish life. 8 x 10, 64 pp, Deluxe Padded HC, Full-color illus., 978-1-58023-138-1 **$19.95**

The Jewish Pregnancy Book: A Resource for the Soul, Body & Mind during Pregnancy, Birth & the First Three Months
By Sandy Falk, MD, and Rabbi Daniel Judson, with Steven A. Rapp
Includes medical information, prayers and rituals for each stage of pregnancy, from a liberal Jewish perspective. 7 x 10, 208 pp, Quality PB, b/w photos, 978-1-58023-178-7 **$16.95**

Celebrating Your New Jewish Daughter: Creating Jewish Ways to Welcome Baby Girls into the Covenant—New and Traditional Ceremonies *By Debra Nussbaum Cohen; Foreword by Rabbi Sandy Eisenberg Sasso* 6 x 9, 272 pp, Quality PB, 978-1-58023-090-2 **$18.95**

The New Jewish Baby Book, 2nd Edition: Names, Ceremonies & Customs—A Guide for Today's Families *By Anita Diamant* 6 x 9, 336 pp, Quality PB, 978-1-58023-251-7 **$19.99**

Parenting As a Spiritual Journey: Deepening Ordinary and Extraordinary Events into Sacred Occasions *By Rabbi Nancy Fuchs-Kreimer*
6 x 9, 224 pp, Quality PB, 978-1-58023-016-2 **$16.95**

Parenting Jewish Teens: A Guide for the Perplexed
By Joanne Doades 6 x 9, 200 pp, Quality PB, 978-1-58023-305-7 **$16.99**

Judaism for Two: A Spiritual Guide for Strengthening and Celebrating Your Loving Relationship *By Rabbi Nancy Fuchs-Kreimer and Rabbi Nancy H. Wiener; Foreword by Rabbi Elliot N. Dorff* Addresses the ways Jewish teachings can enhance and strengthen committed relationships. 6 x 9, 224 pp, Quality PB, 978-1-58023-254-8 **$16.99**

Embracing the Covenant: Converts to Judaism Talk About Why & How
By Rabbi Allan Berkowitz and Patti Moskovitz 6 x 9, 192 pp, Quality PB, 978-1-879045-50-7 **$16.95**

The Guide to Jewish Interfaith Family Life: An InterfaithFamily.com Handbook
Edited by Ronnie Friedland and Edmund Case 6 x 9, 384 pp, Quality PB, 978-1-58023-153-4 **$18.95**

Introducing My Faith and My Community
The Jewish Outreach Institute Guide for the Christian in a Jewish Interfaith Relationship
By Rabbi Kerry M. Olitzky 6 x 9, 176 pp, Quality PB, 978-1-58023-192-3 **$16.99**

Making a Successful Jewish Interfaith Marriage: The Jewish Outreach Institute Guide to Opportunities, Challenges and Resources *By Rabbi Kerry M. Olitzky with Joan Peterson Littman*
6 x 9, 176 pp, Quality PB, 978-1-58023-170-1 **$16.95**

The Creative Jewish Wedding Book: A Hands-On Guide to New & Old Traditions, Ceremonies & Celebrations *By Gabrielle Kaplan-Mayer*
9 x 9, 288 pp, b/w photos, Quality PB, 978-1-58023-194-7 **$19.99**

Divorce Is a Mitzvah: A Practical Guide to Finding Wholeness and Holiness When Your Marriage Dies *By Rabbi Perry Netter; Afterword by Rabbi Laura Geller.*
6 x 9, 224 pp, Quality PB, 978-1-58023-172-5 **$16.95**

A Heart of Wisdom: Making the Jewish Journey from Midlife through the Elder Years
Edited by Susan Berrin; Foreword by Harold Kushner
6 x 9, 384 pp, Quality PB, 978-1-58023-051-3 **$18.95**

So That Your Values Live On: Ethical Wills and How to Prepare Them
Edited by Jack Riemer and Nathaniel Stampfer
6 x 9, 272 pp, Quality PB, 978-1-879045-34-7 **$18.99**

Theology/Philosophy/The Way Into... Series

The Way Into... series offers an accessible and highly usable "guided tour" of the Jewish faith, people, history and beliefs—in total, an introduction to Judaism that will enable you to understand and interact with the sacred texts of the Jewish tradition. Each volume is written by a leading contemporary scholar and teacher, and explores one key aspect of Judaism. *The Way Into...* series enables all readers to achieve a real sense of Jewish cultural literacy through guided study.

The Way Into Encountering God in Judaism
By Neil Gillman
For everyone who wants to understand how Jews have encountered God throughout history and today.
6 x 9, 240 pp, Quality PB, 978-1-58023-199-2 **$18.99**; HC, 978-1-58023-025-4 **$21.95**

Also Available: **The Jewish Approach to God:** A Brief Introduction for Christians
By Neil Gillman
5½ x 8¼, 192 pp, Quality PB, 978-1-58023-190-9 **$16.95**

The Way Into Jewish Mystical Tradition
By Lawrence Kushner
Allows readers to interact directly with the sacred mystical text of the Jewish tradition. An accessible introduction to the concepts of Jewish mysticism, their religious and spiritual significance and how they relate to life today.
6 x 9, 224 pp, Quality PB, 978-1-58023-200-5 **$18.99**; HC, 978-1-58023-029-2 **$21.95**

The Way Into Jewish Prayer
By Lawrence A. Hoffman
Opens the door to 3,000 years of Jewish prayer, making available all anyone needs to feel at home in the Jewish way of communicating with God.
6 x 9, 208 pp, Quality PB, 978-1-58023-201-2 **$18.99**

The Way Into Judaism and the Environment
By Jeremy Benstein
Explores the ways in which Judaism contributes to contemporary social-environmental issues, the extent to which Judaism is part of the problem and how it can be part of the solution.
6 x 9, 288 pp, HC, 978-1-58023-268-5 **$24.99**

The Way Into *Tikkun Olam* (Repairing the World)
By Elliot N. Dorff
An accessible introduction to the Jewish concept of the individual's responsibility to care for others and repair the world.
6 x 9, 320 pp, HC, 978-1-58023-269-2 **$24.99**

The Way Into Torah
By Norman J. Cohen
Helps guide in the exploration of the origins and development of Torah, explains why it should be studied and how to do it.
6 x 9, 176 pp, Quality PB, 978-1-58023-198-5 **$16.99**; HC, 978-1-58023-028-5 **$21.95**

The Way Into the Varieties of Jewishness
By Sylvia Barack Fishman, PhD
Explores the religious and historical understanding of what it has meant to be Jewish from ancient times to the present controversy over "Who is a Jew?"
6 x 9, 288 pp, HC, 978-1-58023-030-8 **$24.99**

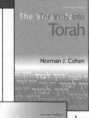